PROPHECY AND KINGSHIP IN ADOMNÁN'S 'LIFE OF SAINT COLUMBA'

Prophecy and kingship in Adomnán's 'Life of Saint Columba'

Michael J. Enright

FOUR COURTS PRESS

Typeset in 10.5 pt on 12.5 pt Ehrhardt by
Carrigboy Typesetting Services for
FOUR COURTS PRESS LTD
7 Malpas Street, Dublin 8, Ireland
www.fourcourtspress.ie
and in North America for
FOUR COURTS PRESS
c/o ISBS, 920 NE 58th Avenue, Suite 300, Portland, OR 97213.

A catalogue record for this title is available
from the British Library.

ISBN 978–1–84682–382–4

SPECIAL ACKNOWLEDGMENT

Publication of this book has been aided by a grant from the Office for
Research of the Thomas Harriot College of Arts and Sciences of
East Carolina University, USA.

Printed in England
by CPI Antony Rowe, Chippenham, Wilts.

Contents

Introduction

Written near the end of the seventh century and perhaps into the first few years of the eighth, the *Vita sancti Columbae* is one of the four surviving saints' Lives of the period after those of Brigit and Patrick.[1] It is a precious witness to a purpose, an outlook and a community's practice for a time when reliable information is at a premium. Its author, Adomnán, was ideally placed to be a biographer of Columba. He was a kinsman of the saint of Cenél Conaill of Donegal, was the ninth abbot of Columba's Iona confederation, an accomplished writer and scholar praised by Bede who remarks that 'he was a good and wise man with an excellent knowledge of the scriptures' (HE V 15), and an ecclesiastical statesman respected in royal courts in Ireland, Dál Riata, Pictland and Northumbria. He belonged to a descent group that had ruled Cenél Conaill since the late sixth century; seven of his relatives had been over-kings of the Northern Uí Néill. He may have been well versed in law as well as scripture for he was the architect of the *Cáin Adomnáin*, the 'Law of the Innocents', that aimed to protect woman, children and clerics from violence. It was promulgated at the Synod of Birr in 697; its ninety-one guarantors represented every notable power group in Ireland and northern Britain. Adomnán had also himself negotiated to free Irish captives during a diplomatic visit to Northumbria whose new ruler was his former pupil. Aside from the Life of Columba, Adomnán also wrote *De locis sanctis* on the important sites of the holy land, and perhaps a brief penitential text that goes under the name *Canones Adomnani*.

He was born in 627/8 near Raphoe in Co. Donegal but it is not known when he entered the religious life although one may guess that it was at a major Columban house like Durrow.[2] He may have gone to Iona at an early age – he would have been in his mid-thirties in 664 when the Synod of Whitby in Northumbria sought to enforce the Roman dating of Easter – and would thus have witnessed the gradual decline of Iona's influence in the following decades. Becoming abbot in 679 after the death of his predecessor Failbe, the years of his abbacy were strenuous and one can sympathize with his plaint in *De locis sanctis*

1 I am counting Tirechán's material as a *vita*. In general, see Kim McCone, 'An introduction to early Irish saints' lives', *Maynooth Review*, 11 (1984), 26–59; Máire Herbert, 'Latin and vernacular hagiography of Ireland from the origins to the sixteenth century', *Histoire internationale de la litérature hagiographique latine et vernaculaire en Occident des origins à 1550*, 3 (2001), 329–60. 2 Brian Lacey, 'Adomnán and Donegal' in Jonathan M. Wooding et al. (eds), *Adomnán of Iona: theologian, lawmaker, peacemaker* (Dublin, 2010), pp 20–36.

that he had written it although 'daily beset by laborious and almost insupportable ecclesiastical business from every quarter'.[3] Following Bede, it was in 688 that he assented to 'Roman' observances and afterwards sought to persuade other Columban houses to follow his example. This cannot have been easy to do, but it is clear that he would have been absorbed in other work as well since the necessary years of negotiations and coalition-building that led to his Law of the Innocents must have begun in the early 690s at the latest. It was an astonishing accomplishment and a sterling witness to his great skill in powers of persuasion. Adomnán died in 704 and Iona seems to have entered a period of dissention and internal conflict, probably related both to the Easter question and to the politics of Ireland, Dál Riata and Pictland. Adomnán is counted among the saints of the Irish church. A Life, *Betha Adamnáin*, was written between 961 and 964 but it is of value only for the society of that period.[4]

Adomnán's hero was Columba and into his *vita* he poured all the love and admiration that one might bestow on an elder brother who had made good. Aside from some poetry and annalistic references, it is the main source of our knowledge but is partly based on other hagiographical models like the lives of Anthony, Martin and Benedict. Some materials from an earlier collection of miracle stories about Columba by Cumméne Ailbe (abbot from 657 to 669) may have been borrowed by Adomnán but, if so, they were reworked in the interest of his own portrait and purpose. By Adomnán's time, a world of story about Columba already existed. As Richard Sharpe points out, Adomnán relates no fewer than ten times how information from the saint's time was passed to him.[5]

Columba died in 597 aged about seventy-six and that would place his birth *c*.521. His name in Irish may have been Cremthann or Crimthann so that Columba, 'dove', is a monastic and symbolic name as, indeed, it is described in the *vita*.[6] His family probably aimed at a religious life for their son as he was fostered with a priest named Cruithnechán, studied as a deacon with Gemmán in Leinster and still later with the famous 'bishop Vinniau'.[7] These are spare details but they encompass most of what Adomnán wants us to know about his subject's life until his middle age. All of his emphasis is on Columba's life after the age of about forty-two when he left Ireland for the Scottish coast. Circumstantial evidence connects this departure with scandal and ecclesiastical censure after the saint had played a role in the defeat of Diarmait mac Cerbaill of the Southern Uí Néill through an alliance that included two of Columba's kinsmen. With twelve companions, including an uncle and two cousins, Columba sailed for the territory of Dál Riata, which had previously been

3 Denis Meehan (ed.), *Adamnán's De Locis Sanctis* (Dublin, 1958), pp 120–1.   4 Máire Herbert and Pádraig Ó Riain (eds), *Betha Adamnain: the Irish life of Adamnán* (London, 1988).   5 Richard Sharpe, *Adomnán of Iona: Life of St Columba* (London, 1995), p. 56.   6 Alan O. Anderson and Marjorie O. Anderson (eds), *Adomnán's Life of Columba* (London, 1961), p. 67; Pádraig Ó Riain, *A dictionary of Irish saints* (Dublin, 2011), p. 211.   7 On the latter figure, see Ó Riain, *Dictionary*, pp

colonized by Irish settlers and whose ruler probably maintained political links with Cenél Conaill and other northern Irish powers. Little in this narrative about notables seems incidental. Unlike the historically powerless and impecunious Patrick of the previous century, Columba's life (and that of the ninth abbot) was played out at the very top of the insular status pyramid. That has important implications for an understanding of Adomnán's text, since sophistication in the craft of ruling was familiar territory; the persons who practiced it were known. Adomnán is expertly versed in the kind of politics that he describes. His dealings with the princes and ecclesiastical potentates are intimate and are keyed to the needs of governance in church and state. Columba would almost certainly have engaged in some missionary work, however, not only because he was a convinced Christian probably attentive to the message of going to and teaching the nations, but because the building of missions in the early Middle Ages was inextricably meshed with the building of advantageous political relations.[8] Both purposes could ably be served by advancing Iona as a refuge for nobles in exile, for example, and it seems to have become known for doing so. It was there that a roughly 13-year-old Oswald of Northumbria (603/4–42) and his six brothers and followers took refuge before, apparently, spending the next seventeen years in Ireland, and it was surely there that Oswald began to learn the fluent Irish of his later years.[9] This would lead to political alliance and to the Iona-led conversion of Northumbria over the next generation.

Aside from a brief introduction to the careers of Adomnán and Columba, one further bit of explanation is important for understanding the pages that follow. That is the topic of biblical typology.[10] Adomnán employs it repeatedly because, as will become apparent, the biblical text and especially the Old Testament (OT), is his unimpeachable standard for the establishment of true, that is God-willed, politico-religious legitimacy. Typology is one of the common forms of biblical exegesis. It maintains the view that God placed anticipations of Christ and his revelation in the laws, prophets, people and events of the Old Testament. This principle is probably best expressed in the popular saying that 'In the Old Testament the New Testament is concealed; in the New Testament the Old Testament is revealed'. Moses or Adam or Melchizedek may thus be seen as types for which Christ is the antitype; the 'sacrifice of Isaac' can be seen as foreshadowing the sacrifice of Christ on the cross or, as Paul said in I Cor. 10,

321–4. 8 Arnold Angenendt, *Kaiserherrschaft und Königstaufe* (Berlin, 1984), pp 91–259, passim. 9 H. Moisl, 'The Bernician royal dynasty and the Irish in the seventh century', *Peritia*, 2 (1983), 103–26. 10 J. Danielou, *From shadows to reality: studies in the biblical typology of the fathers* (London, 1960); Henri de Lubac, *Exégèse médiéval: les quatre sens de l'écriture* I, II (Paris, 1959); Frances M. Young, *Biblical exegesis and the formation of Christian culture* (Cambridge, 1997); Erich Auerbach, 'Figura' in Auerbach, *Scenes from the drama of European literature* (New York, 1959), pp 11–79; *Mimesis: the representation of reality in western literature* (Princeton, NJ, 2003), pp 73–6; Northrop Frye, *The great code: the Bible and literature* (New York, 1982), pp 78–138; A.C. Charity, *Events and their afterlife: the dialectics of Christian typology in the Bible and Dante* (Cambridge, 1987).

many things that the Jews did under Moses 'were done in a figure of us'. The Latin term *figura* is used to translate the Greek *typos*, hence typology.[11] This means of exegesis was profoundly important. It meant (as opposed to heretical interpretations of the second century), for example, that the entire Bible was holy scripture and not just the parts concerned with Christ and his apostles. All Hebrew scripture was thus actually a kind of prophecy that created a link between the total phenomena of one period and that of another. As Erich Auerbach wrote, 'figural interpretation establishes a connection between two events or persons, the first of which signifies not only itself but also the second, while the second encompasses or fulfils the first'.[12] People and events are thus joined in a providential stream that can always lead to other kinds of contemporary or future fulfilments. God forsees all ends and directs them to eternally chosen purposes. That includes, of course, post-biblical events as well. Typology is thus a specialized form of repetition that conforms to divine will. To recognize this moving stream, however, to identify the constituent details of meaningful relations that exist within it, requires an extraordinary degree of spiritual training or, alternatively, an extraordinary gift of divine grace that enables apprehension of God's system of cosmic order. Such trained or gifted persons become prophets, God's sentrys along the stream. The connections that they endorse or perceive to be coming can be pointed out to others so that their mystic vision can teach to palpable results.

This perception of the history, laws and notable personages of the Hebrews had a powerful transformative effect on the early medieval North. Insular peoples like the Irish (or the Angles of Northumbria) could now interpret their own cultures and institutions as continuously guided features of God's providence in a universal scheme of salvation that was simultaneously a moral view of multiple linkages to the biblical past.[13] Because, moreover, Irish culture was one that already possessed learned orders trained in prophetic techniques and ritual, it may be suggested that these native orders would have been especially drawn to the prophets of the Old Testament and to a regard for the influence that they had enjoyed. The spread of Christianity would then have been markedly advanced by this coincidence of comparably esteemed institutional behaviours, which would have encouraged a particular veneration for those biblical books touching on or devoted to the prophets. Prophecy would have become an ever more highly revered phenomenon. Adomnán's *vita* may well contain evidence indicative of such an outlook and past.

The present work seeks to better understand Adomnán's portrait of Columba, and to modify scholarly views concerned with it. It argues that Adomnán meant to depict his hero as a prophet from the womb who then trained his followers in

11 Auerbach, 'Figura', pp 49–60. 12 Ibid., p. 53. 13 Raymond Kottje, *Studien zum Eifluss des Alten Testaments auf Recht und Liturgie des frühen Mittelalters (6–8. Jahrhunderts)* (Bonn, 1970); D. Ó Corráin, L. Breatnach and A. Breen, 'The laws of the Irish', *Peritia*, 3 (1984), 382–438.

prophetic skill in the same way that Samuel, Elijah and Elisha trained theirs. He constantly drew on biblical precedents that he took to be a model for both monastic and secular life. In particular, Adomnán sought to reform insular kingship along the lines of prophet–king–people relationships found in the Old Testament. The study thus concentrates on those parts of the Life that focus on prophecy, kingship and, to a limited extent, Adomnán's view of his predecessor as a prophetic champion of God's holy warfare. Chapter one looks to early biblical prophetic practice and to the phenomenon of the prophetic call, which, it is maintained, is followed in the *vita* where Columba becomes the prophet called and commissioned by God to anoint rulers and to oversee their governance. Chapter two examines *some* aspects of Adomnán's motives for writing, suggests that a quarrel with Armagh's claim to primacy played a significant role, and compares Adomnán's Life of Columba with Muirchú's Life of Patrick as a means of clarifying the issues and identifying the strategies involved. It also looks to a sequence of chapters covering what is, arguably, prophetic training, and identifies some Old Testament figures that may have further inspired Adomnán. Chapter three interprets Adomnán's memorable statement that Columba is God's chosen battle champion and finds its conceptual source not in any work or link relating to Constantine's victory at the Milvian Bridge, as is often supposed, but rather in the biblical concept of holy war against Israel's enemies. This finding is then related to other features of Adomnán's thinking concerning Northumbria and to his socio–political rationale for writing.

An earlier version of chapter one appeared in *Peritia*, 21 (2010) and I should like to thank the editor, Donnchadh Ó Corráin, and publisher, Brepols, for permission to use that material. Thanks also to East Carolina University for a small grant that defrayed the costs of publication. I am grateful to Michael Potterton, editor at Four Courts Press, who accepted the book and capably oversaw its publication thereafter; also to my former students Ryan Goodman, Luke Simonds and Peter Coffman who laboured heavily at producing a readable typescript. This book is dedicated to my daughter Anne-Kristin, to my son Edward, and to the memory of my grandfather, Patrick Kenneally.

CHAPTER ONE

Prophets and princes on isles of ocean: Adomnán's 'call' for an Old Testament-style regime

In discussing *Vita Columbae* (*VC*), scholars sometimes refer to the saint as a prophet. The time is now ripe to focus more precisely on that condition, a matter neglected even by those who have written about the *vita* at some length.[1] Yet even a cursory examination of the text reveals it to be of singular importance to Adomnán. If one may set aside the brief remarks of his first preface, in which he explains that he is writing at the entreaties of the brethren, and in which he offers his own version of the *sermo rusticus*, the theme of mystic foreknowledge is already the topic of the opening remarks of the second preface where he interprets the name of his hero. It is a name, he says, that is the same as that of the prophet Jonah, which, in three different languages – Hebrew, Greek and Latin – means 'dove'. Only divine providence can have bestowed such a name on the holy man. It signifies the descent of the Holy Spirit and is rightfully borne by the founder because of his dove-like innocence and because he 'offered in himself a dwelling for the Holy Spirit'. As a 'bright light in the last days of the world', Columba was himself an object of prophecy. From his boyhood, he devoted himself to religion and 'to the study of wisdom'. 'Brilliant in intellect and great in counsel', he lived a tireless life of enduring sacrifice in which he was loving to all. His face showed 'a holy gladness because his heart was full of the joy of the Holy Spirit'. And so we learn that *nomen est omen*, that Columba was enriched with this prophetic spirit by God's gift 'from the days of his infancy'. A citation from Proverbs is said to be appropriate: 'a good name is rather to be chosen than great riches'.

It is still not enough. In the middle of this same preface, Adomnán declares that this divine gift will provide the ordering principle for his work. Columba's life will be told first in terms of 'prophetic revelations', the second book will be of 'divine miracles worked through him' and the third will concern 'angelic apparitions and certain phenomena of heavenly light seen above the man of

---

1 In this work, I have used the Latin text of Anderson and Anderson (eds), *Adomnán's Life of Columba* [hereafter *VC*] and the translation of Sharpe, *Adomnán*. The Bible version is the Vulgate: B. Fischer I. Gribomont, H.F.D. Sparks, W. Thiele, Robert Weber, H.I. Frede and Roger Gryson (eds), *Biblia sacra iuxta vulgatam versionem* (Stuttgart, 1994); the English translation is the Douay-Rheims-Challoner version reset by Baronius Press (London, 2005). In a few cases, I have silently changed vulgate biblical names to those now more familiar.

6

God'. One might expect then that the first part of VC would deal with prophecies and the other two with signs and works of other kinds. Even for the second book, however, that is not the case, for a high proportion of those miracles also draw on the saint's prophetic capacity, a fact later noted by Adomnán himself, who heads Book II with the statement that it contains miracles of power 'which are often also prophetically foreknown' and who adds, still later, at the beginning of Book III, that the miracles of power 'were often accompanied by the grace of prophecy'. Nor, indeed, despite the fact that Book III is ostensibly about 'visions of angels' and 'manifestations of heavenly light', is that section greatly different. The angels often appear to act as the heralds or messengers of divine knowledge passed on to the holy man, while at least part of the significance of the play of heavenly lights around him is to stress the extraordinary quality of the oracular gift of the Holy Spirit operating within him.[2] There is a deeply held belief at work here to the effect that certain kinds of knowledge generate or are accompanied by both light and heat and such is already indicated by the second preface, where our 'son of promise' is to be a 'bright light in the last days' and where the reference to 'certain phenomena of heavenly light seen above the man of God' are naturally associated with the descent of the fire and light-bringing Holy Spirit otherwise often viewed metaphorically as a dove who bestows gifts of speech and mystic powers. A similar kind of linkage is made in the programmatic chapter one of Book I, where a frequent heavenly light that shines over the holy man is coupled by reference to his company with angels 'shining with light' and the 'revelations of the Holy Spirit', which enabled him to see the souls of the just carried heavenwards. Most such allusions mention light alone but several refer to fire as well. In short, contrary to expectations, much of Book III also emphasizes the signs and symbols that accompany mystic prophecy.[3] The book appears to aim towards a culmination of Adomnán's statements on the subject, since it highlights the most spectacular of all prophetic displays, a continuous visitation of the saint by the Holy Spirit, which lasted for three exhaustingly pyrotechnical days and nights (III 18). This 'incomparable abundance' of the grace of the Holy Spirit enabled him to know secrets hidden since the world began and revealed to him all that was difficult in the holy scriptures.[4] How could he not be a prophet?

2 On these topics, see James Bruce, *Prophecy, miracle, angels and heavenly light? The eschatology, pneumatology and missiology of Adomnán's Life of Columba* (Eugene, OR, 2004). 3 Fire and light are constantly linked to mysticism itself. See, for example, William James, *The varieties of religious experience* (London, 1904; 2nd ed. Cambridge, MA, 1985), originally delivered as the Gifford Lectures on Natural Religion at Edinburgh University in 1901 and 1902. Lectures X to XVIII provide many examples. So does the classic work by Evelyn Underhill first published in 1911: *Mysticism: the nature and development of spiritual consciousness* (Oxford, 2005). Chapter IV, 'The illumination of the self', is helpful. 4 On receiving hidden knowledge through inspiration of the Holy Spirit, see the perceptive article by Jennifer O'Reilly, 'The wisdom of the scribe and the fear of the Lord in the Life of Columba' in Dauvit Broun and Thomas Owen Clancy (eds), *Spes Scotorum: hope of Scots. Saint Columba, Iona and Scotland* (Edinburgh, 1999), pp 159–215.

Adomnán is so earnestly concerned about the saint's wondrous ability to know things in places near, far and in the future that he is moved to explain the gift in several different chapters of the work. Let us mention two of them. Near the beginning of I 1, Adomnán states that 'as a young man', Columba began to enjoy 'the spirit of prophecy, to predict the future and to tell those with him about things happening elsewhere. He could see what was done afar off, because he was there in the spirit though not in the body. For as St Paul says, "He that is joined unto the Lord is one spirit"'. Adomnán depicts Columba as being pressed by the brethren about this and makes the holy man reply that 'by divine grace he had several times experienced a miraculous enlarging of the grasp of the mind so that he seemed to look at the whole world caught in one ray of sunlight'. Later (I 43), this theme is broached again. Columba on Iona is described as groaning in sorrow because two men of royal lineage have just died in Ireland of mutually inflicted wounds. 'A week from today', he declares, someone will come from Ireland with news of the incident. What we actually find here is not straight-forward prophecy but rather, as often in *VC*, something like a clairvoyant mixture in which prophecy *strictu sensu* may be only one element in a flow of mystic experiences. All such events are apparently subsumable under the rubric of a 'spirit of prophecy'. Columba is now questioned by another soldier of Christ, Luigbe moccu Blai, as to how his prophetic revelations actually work: 'How are they revealed to you? By sight or hearing or in some way men know not?' The saint replies that it is a delicate subject about which he may not speak except under a promise of silence because it is a 'most secret mystery'. Once given, he tells Luigbe that

> There are some people – few indeed – to whom the grace of God has given the power to see brightly and most dearly, with a mental grasp miraculously enlarged, at one and the same time as if lit by a single sunbeam, even the entire orbit of the whole earth and the sea and sky around it.

As he had in I 1, Adomnán turns to St Paul to explain his oblique response about 'some people'. Columba speaks in that way in order not to seem boastful, a device for maintaining humility used by Paul when describing his own visions of the spirit. But these references to Paul are partly a red herring since Adomnán has actually lifted Columba's answers from St Benedict's explanation of a similar condition to the deacon Servandus in Gregory the Great's *Dialogues*, II 35 and IV 8.[5] Quite interestingly, Gregory had also cited St Paul's statement, *qui autem adheret Domino unus spiritus est*, in an earlier dialogue (II 16), itself also a response to a questioner as in *VC*. While there are differences in the ways the material is employed, Adomnán is considerably indebted to Gregory for aspects of his treatment of the theme.

5 Umberto Moricco (ed.), *Gregorii Magni Dialogi libri IV* (Rome, 1924), pp 128–31, 240.

8

Should one then announce the discovery that Adomnán is a Johnny-one-note? That the only arrow in his quiver trails a pennon labelled 'spirit of prophecy'? Surely not. Adomnán does have other things to say. One may insist, however, that his repetitive displays of the saint's prophetic ability in a variety of contexts are the loudest note of his song from beginning to end. On the day of his death, in the final chapter of VC, Columba is still teaching and predicting the future for his monks. And Adomnán returns to the whole matter again in his final summary so that it is clear that for him it is the topic that closes the circle that began with Jonah and the name of 'dove' that signifies the presence of the mystical holy spirit. That being the case, why are we not blessed with a series of studies on Adomnán and prophecy? Here I can only guess. Strange as it may seem, the importance of the 'spirit of prophecy' has not hitherto been properly recognized. Its incessant variations have perhaps become something like the background noise that one filters out in order to concentrate on the 'real' meaning of the text or the 'real' work at hand. It is part of Adomnán's mental baggage that does not require explanation because it is a hagiographic commonplace. There is no 'hook' to hang it on so that it may stand out as an issue or a problem for readers, no 'hook' that is a focus of interest such as those examining ordinations of rulers or the reasons for a cluster-of-princes section in the book (see sections I and IV).

In my opinion, prophecy as Adomnán understood it is the real focus of his work; it is the key to a true appreciation of his portrait of his hero. The best way to approach this crux is to turn to a series of chapters, a neglected cluster of linked messages as I see them, in which Adomnán most carefully (if also overly subtly) sets out his interpretation of the divine origin and significance of the saint's power and his deepest conviction about Columba's importance for Ireland and Britain; it is a statement about what he as a hagiographer was seeking to achieve by his concentration on Columba as a prophet in VC. The chapters to be examined and interpreted are 1–5 of Book III, which starts with a dream of Columba's mother before his birth and ends, not incidentally, with Áedán mac Gabráin's anointing in III 5.[6] In between are III 2 on a ray of light seen over the holy boy; III 3 on St Brendan's witness of angels accompanying the saint as he

6 Beyond seeking a name for Columba's mother, few scholars have paid much attention to VC III 1. This seriously underestimates its importance. In each of the former two books, Adomnán sees the first chapter as providing a guide for interpretation. Hence, I 1 introduces or further introduces crucial themes such as revelation by the Holy Spirit, battle-championship, royal ordination and the saint's spirit of prophecy. In II 1, Adomnán is more explicit: he has Columba change water into wine as his first miracle and compares it to Christ's first proof of power. He goes on to state that he wishes the comparison to 'shine like a lantern at the entrance of this book'. This idea of a lantern at the entrance to a book is a notable interpretive key and should also be applied to III 1. A recent exception to the lack of commentary on this chapter is Bruce, *Prophecy, miracles, angels*, pp 133–5, where, however, he misunderstands it because he associates the mantle with mission and pilgrimage rather than with a signalling of the authority of the future prophet and its extent. In my opinion, his association of the mantle with the royal power of God in the kingdom of God to come is a case of overtheologizing Adomnán's more practical mid-level concept. However, there are many elements in Bruce's study that are quite illuminating and his book is valuable.

9

crosses a plain; and III 4 on St Uinniau's description of an angel as Columba's companion. Along the way, because it provides an important aid towards evaluating Adomnán's motivations, I shall return to a discussion of the reasons for Diarmait mac Cerbaill's appearance and prominence in the text. It will be argued that all five of these chapters have been designed to demonstrate that Columba is the equal (at least!) of the great Old Testament (OT) prophets, that his works were divinely predestined because he too had been divinely 'called' and 'sent' as they had been, and hence OT texts on the prophets have a particular relevance to his career. In the final analysis, Columba had been sent by God as the teaching patron of kings and the authoritative guide of their governance in all the nations of Ireland and Britain. His successor abbots, it is implied, participate in this, and act according to God's will when they, like Adomnán, seek to carry out this same heavenly mandate. The fruit of Columba's prophetic guidance is then shown through analysis of a medley of themes appearing in a series of chapters in Book I 7–15 dealing with battles and princes that are calculated to answer the question: what can Columba do for kings? Adomnán viewed both groups of chapters in books III and I as related and wished them to be interpreted accordingly. Finally, I shall also argue that motifs from the two groups mentioned reinforce the argument that Adomnán aimed at furthering a thorough reformation of kingship that, in both Ireland and North Britain, should include an Ionan oversight over anointed kings and their peoples. He probably aimed at replicating an OT regime of the judge/prophet who super-vised the behaviour of rulers. He had been specifically 'called' by God to do so.

How Columba became an Old Testament prophet

Because so many allusions must be made to III 1, it seems most convenient to print it as a whole.

> An angel of the Lord appeared in a dream to St Columba's mother one night after his conception but before his birth. He seemed to stand beside her and to give her a robe of marvellous beauty, decorated with what looked like the colours of every flower. After a little time, he asked for it back and took it from her hands. Then he raised the robe and spread it out, letting go of it on the empty air. She was disappointed that it was taken away from her and spoke to the man of holy appearance: 'Why do you take away from me so quickly this delightful mantle?' she said. 'Because', he answered, 'this is a cloak of such glorious honour that you will no longer be able to keep it with you'. Then the woman saw the robe moving further and further from her as if in flight, growing greater and greater so that it seemed to be broader than the plains and to exceed in measure the mountains and the forests. Then she heard a voice which said: 'Woman, do not be distressed, for you shall bear to the man to whom you are joined in marriage a son of such flower that he shall be reckoned as one of the prophets. He is destined by God to lead innumerable souls to the heavenly kingdom'. As she heard these words, his mother woke up.

To the sophisticated reader of *VC* who first approaches this chapter, it may appear to be a fairly familiar, even a routine display of medieval Irish hagiographic motifs. A dream visitation of the saint's mother will not surprise; neither will the cloak, which he might think to associate with the royal mantle in the king's chariot at Tara as depicted in *De Shíl Chonairi Móir*, for that, too, could change in size.[7] A glance at material in the immediately following chapters would tend to confirm that impression, since a recording of angelic apparitions is hardly the stuff of novelty in Lives of the saints. It would appear reasonable to conclude that there is little new or useful here for a deeper analysis but that it simply demonstrates the holiness of the saint and the degree of God's special regard for him. From one perspective, this appreciation is faultless, for we do indeed witness an almost mundane assembly of miraculous motifs. Contrary to what scholars appear to have accepted, however, it is not a generalized sanctity, even one of a high order, that is being justified. Rather, as I will maintain, these passages point to something of an emphatically specialized nature, a set of coded statements reinforced with illustrative material, designed to demonstrate that Columba is God's specially created prophet to the Irish, Britons, English and Picts – the equal of revered scriptural figures like Jeremiah, Isaiah, Elisha, Samuel and Paul[8] – who was divinely commissioned to bring these nations to Christianity within the Iona fold. Columba was thus not only the equal of Patrick, who, in Armagh's view, had evangelized much of Ireland;[9] he was his superior, since his standing with God was higher and since his missionary field was correspondingly larger.

At first glance, this proposition might well appear to overburden the interpretive capacity of the evidence. That is only true until one takes the initial decisive step towards decipherment by realizing that these first five narratives of Book III are vignettes designed to suit an OT genre in which Adomnán's stories find their home; it is known to biblical scholars as the 'call of the prophet'.[10] That vision is central to Adomnán's entire conception of his protagonist, since it is a

---

7 Lucius Gwynn (ed. and trans.), 'De Shíl Chonairi Móir', *Ériu*, 6 (1912), 130–43. 8 See especially *VC* II 32. 9 Charles Doherty, 'The cult of St Patrick and the politics of Armagh in the seventh century' in Jean-Michel Picard (ed.), *Ireland and northern France, AD600–850* (Dublin, 1991), pp 53–93; Richard Sharpe, 'St Patrick and the see of Armagh', *Cambridge Medieval Celtic Studies*, 4 (1982), 33–59; Liam de Paor, 'The aggrandizement of Armagh' in T. Desmond Williams (ed.), *Historical Studies*, 8 (Dublin, 1968), pp 95–110; Richard Sharpe, 'Armagh and Rome in the seventh century' in Próinséas Ní Chatháin and Michael Richter (eds), *Irland und Europa. die Kirche im Frühmittelalter* (Stuttgart, 1984), pp 58–73. 10 In a very large literature, I have found the following to be most helpful: Norman C. Habel, 'The form and significance of the call narrative', *Zeitschrift für die Alttestamentliche Wissenschaft*, 77 (1965), 297–323; David E. Aune, *Prophecy in early Chrisitianity and the ancient Mediterranean world* (Grand Rapids, MI, 1983), pp 16–23, 81–103; R.R. Wilson, *Prophecy and society in ancient Israel* (Philadelphia, PA, 1980); Rolf Knierim, 'The vocation of Isaiah', *Vetus Testamentum*, 18 (1968), 47–68; Klaus Baltzer, 'Considerations regarding the office and calling of the prophet', *Harvard Theological Review*, 61 (1968), 567–81; Walter Zimmerli, *Ezekiel I: a commentary on the book of the prophet Ezekiel* (Philadelphia, PA, 1979), pp 9–147; B. Peckham, *History and prophecy: the development of late Judean literary traditions* (New York, 1993).

perfect match for the anecdotal and structural elements of VC, both of which are geared to express the scheme of a divinely bestowed supreme prophetic awareness. The argument that Adomnán is here adapting a specific OT theme, however, also requires that we learn something about its operation in the Bible, and of the many prophets involved in its development. In that way, through an extended analysis of 'call narratives' (which find their closest echo in VC III 1 and III 5),[11] one can eventually show both the origin and relevance of the themes that Adomnán chooses to deploy in his five-chapter sequence. The first chapter contains significant clues but one main focus lies in the motif of Columba as a prophet from the womb, and another in the significance of the robe or mantle as the indicator of his 'glorious honour'. These are important pointers to the use of a biblical code, which takes us back to the world of the OT. This is Adomnán's intellectual home, and to understand him we must first understand it. A fairly extensive discussion of the figure of the OT prophet is thereby required before the present argument can be fully developed.

Ancient Israel of the pre-monarchic and monarchic periods knew of many hundreds of prophets at any given time. Some were members of apparently large roving brotherhoods or craft-guilds who transmitted their techniques of mantic ecstasy from leader to disciple or from father to son.[12] Samuel, for example, the first of the so-called greater prophets after Moses and Joshua, appears to have presided over one of those brotherhoods.[13] Some others were court prophets, like Nathan to King David, and many scores of such figures were attached to and made their living at the temple, and at various shrines like Shiloh, Bethel, Gilgal or Shechem. Still others, like Elijah and Elisha, were renowned visionary outsiders who might, however, as their reputations grew, become the leaders of bands of ecstatic devotees of their own.[14] Serious confrontations and quarrels between prophets and their followers may have been fairly frequent. Nor was Yahweh unwilling to take part or to deliberately infuse some of them with a false 'spirit of prophecy'. When King Ahab asked his prophets whether or not they approved of a projected war against Syria, they happily answered that he would be prosperous and victorious (3 Reges 22:10–12). Such inquiries before battle were common (see also Ez 21:21–23). One of the prophets made a helmet with horns of iron and declared that with these the king would gore Syria until he destroyed it. When forced to do so, however, Micaiah ben Imlah, an outsider and critic of the government, contradicted his court colleagues and issued a prediction of defeat and desolation. Beaten and imprisoned for it, he later proved

---

11 See especially Habel, Aune, Knierim and Zimmerli in the preceding note.   12 J. Lindblom, *Prophecy in ancient Israel* (Philadelphia, PA, 1962), pp 65–108.   13 Ibid., pp 83–95; Murray Newman, 'The prophetic call of Samuel' in Bernhard W. Anderson (ed.), *Israel's prophetic heritage: essays in honor of James Muilenburg* (New York, 1962), pp 86–97.   14 Robert P. Carroll, 'The Elijah–Elisha sagas: some remarks on prophetic succession in ancient Israel', *Vetus Testamentum*, 19 (1969), 400–15; Ben Witherington, *Jesus the seer: the progress of prophecy* (Peabody, MA, 1999), pp 81–103.

right. It was not because his colleagues were not genuine prophets or had spoken against the will and spirit of Yahweh; it was rather that Yahweh wished Ahab's defeat and had placed a 'lying spirit' in the mouth of all the king's prognosticators in order to deceive them (3 Reges 22:19–23).[15]

Like the drumming shamans of northern Europe or the dervish brotherhoods of the Middle East (see also 1 Reges 10:5), comparisons with both are very frequent among OT scholars,[16] the prophets of Israel and Judah appear to have induced their prophetic trances with music and dancing. Hebrew prophets were viewed as practitioners of a craft to be learned, with its own hierarchy of apprentices and masters, and in many ways do not seem much different from the groups of chanting and prophesying *filid* of early medieval Ireland. There is a loose consensus among experts, however, that the ecstatic bands became less prominent over time so that one no longer finds reliable reference to them in Isaiah and Jeremiah; they are conspicuous, on the other hand, in stories about Samuel, Elijah and Elisha.[17] Perhaps it should be added that some prophets may have occupied special niches. According to the standard work on OT theology by Gerhard von Rad, 'there is also reason to believe that prophets of a certain kind had an important role assigned them in warfare – it was they who gave the command to attack'. Warnings to neighbouring peoples about Israel's waging of war 'was a matter for the prophets'.[18] Interestingly, whereas the idea of women as priests was quite inconceivable, the idea of women as prophets was not.

The greater prophets, whether from court, temple or the peripheral areas, were all 'called' by God to their tasks. The certainty of having received this call was 'one of the most characteristic features of the prophetic consciousness'. And it was this reception of a divine mandate that established the legitimacy and authority of the message declared.[19] A prophet like Jeremiah was in constant conflict with false prophets and he knows they are false because the Lord tells him so: 'I sent them not, neither have I commanded them, nor have I spoken to them: they prophesy unto you a lying vision ...' (Jer 14:14). These men have not been 'sent' and it is their commissioning by God that is indispensable. The OT provides examples of such commissioning, which can include both speech and narrative elements (see, for example, Jer 1:4–10; Moses in Ex 3:1–12; Gideon in Jdg 6:11–17; Isaiah in Is 6:1–13; Ezekiel in Ez 1:1–3:11; Deutero-Isaiah in Is

---

15 One thinks of the Greek muses of holy Helicon who breathed a sacred voice into Hesiod's mouth with which to celebrate things to come, while also declaring 'we know how to say many false things that seem like truthful sayings, but we know also how to speak the truth when we wish to'. Richard Lattimore (trans.), *Hesiod* (Ann Arbor, MI, 1959), p. 124, ll 27–8. 16 Lindblom, *Prophecy*, pp 47–65; R.R. Wilson, 'Prophecy and ecstasy', *Journal of Biblical Literature*, 98 (1979), 321–37; Sigmund Mowinckel, *The spirit and the word: prophecy and tradition in ancient Israel* (Minneapolis, MN, 2002), pp 89–99. 17 Lindblom, *Prophecy*, pp 69–71; James G. Williams, 'The prophetic "Father": a brief explanation of the term "Sons of the Prophets"', *Journal of Biblical Literature*, 85 (1966), 344–8; Witherington, *Jesus the seer*, pp 94–7. 18 Gerhard von Rad, *Old Testament theology: the theology of Israel's prophetic tradition* (2 vols, New York, 1965), II, p. 52 (a translation of *Theologie des alten Testaments* (Munich, 1960)). 19 Ibid., pp 50–79.

40:1–11). Such 'call narratives' are also found in apocalyptic literature and in the New Testament (NT). They validate the prophet and make him a legitimate spokesman for Yahweh; the call 'implies a consecration and a preparation for the coming prophetic work' so that the person is made a herald and mouthpiece for Yahweh.[20] These prophets might wear a special dress, be marked with a sign on their foreheads, act as oracles for questioners, be miracle workers, knowers of secrets and bring good or bad fortune.[21] They were frequently involved in politics where they could act as advisors, plotters, exhorters, warners or even overthrowers of kings. As in the VC, a 'spirit of prophecy' lies at the core of all of these acts and qualities.

The 'calls' might occur in different ways and although formulas have been worked out by scholars, there is considerable disagreement.[22] A fairly simple and straightforward example is the call of Amos, who was an unlettered herdsman told by the chief priest of Bethel, Amaziah, to prophesy no more in Bethel because 'it is the king's sanctuary, and it is the house of the kingdom' that Amos was rebelling against. Amos replies that he is neither a prophet nor the son of a prophet, meaning perhaps that he is not a prophet by training or education. Rather he was chosen to be a prophet out of the blue, simply dragooned and set to work: 'And the Lord took me when I followed the flock, and the Lord said to me: "Go prophesy to my people Israel"' (Am 7:13–15). A more elaborate call narrative is that of Gideon (Jdg 6:11–17). An angel of the Lord came and sat under an oak tree and then appeared to Gideon, who was threshing wheat by a wine press: 'the Lord is with thee, O most valiant of men'. Here, as in other cases, angels may appear to prophets bearing a divine message or simply be present in order to aid them in their tasks. In this case, the context is the oppression of the Midianites who have defeated Israel. Gideon is not a bit overawed by the divine messenger. If the Lord is with us, he questions, then why has he given us over to the hands of Midian? The Lord now looked upon him and said: 'Go in this thy strength', and thou shalt deliver Israel: 'know that I have sent thee'. The commission has been delivered but, as frequently happens, the prophet is reluctant to accept and is ready to argue or object: 'wherewith shall I deliver Israel? Behold my family is the meanest in Manassas and I am the least in my father's house'. Yahweh reassures him, stating that he will smite the Midianites as one man for 'I will be with thee'. And so, after several miracles as signs of support and encouragement, including a miraculous sacrificial fire and a fleece made dry and wet, Gideon goes forth to battle as a prophet. Notice that here is the source of an important crux mentioned in 1 Reges. Samuel is reluctant to make a king for Israel, and so is Yahweh, because hitherto the prophet alone

20 Lindblom, *Prophecy*, p. 192; James F. Ross, 'The prophet as Yahweh's messenger' in Anderson (ed.), *Israel's prophetic heritage*, pp 98–107; von Rad, *Old Testament theology*, II, pp 36–9. 21 Lindblom, *Prophecy*, pp 65–95. 22 Ibid., pp 182–97; von Rad, *Old Testament theology*, II, pp 50–70; Baltzer, 'Calling of the prophet'; Aune, *Prophecy*, pp 88–101.

functioned as military leader or battle marshal. Note, too, the objection of the designated leader as being the least of his tribe, which also recalls Saul's puzzlement at being selected for kingship. Gideon will also go on to lead a very small force against a large army (Jdg 7:2–8), which recalls the Oswald miracle of VC I 1. It is in such comparisons, as we shall see, that one finds the sources for Adomnán's concept of the prophet who can at the same time be seen as a battle champion capable of granting victory to kings.[23] That peculiar combination is not Irish but derives from the examples of Gideon and Samuel. As we shall see, it is the call-of-the-prophet narratives followed by the major deeds of the prophet that provide the central inspiration for much of Adomnán's picture of Columba.

The call narratives of Isaiah and Ezekiel can help us to understand the deep sense of miraculous occasion with which Adomnán seeks to invest VC III 1 and, later, III 5. His apparent rhetorical grandiosity is actually caused by an intense feeling of biblical occasion and comparison and not by any hagiographer's desire to exaggerate. Isaiah had a remarkably long career as a prophet from about 740BC and perhaps into the seventh century.[24] His call, his inaugural vision, occurs in Is 6: 'in the year that king Ozias died, I saw the Lord sitting upon a throne'. Around him were angels, seraphim with multiple wings, and his train, his robe or mantle, filled the temple. Isaiah was shocked and frightened at having looked upon the Lord 'because I am a man of unclean lips'.

> And one of the seraphim flew to me, and in his hand was a live coal, which he had taken with the tongs off the altar. And he touched my mouth, and said: Behold this hath touched thy lips, and thy iniquities shall be taken away, and thy sin shall be cleansed.

Fire is the element that cleanses and purifies. The prophet Malachi declares that Yahweh 'is like a refining fire' and he 'shall sit refining and cleansing the silver, and he shall purify the sons of Levi, and he shall refine them as gold. And as silver' (Mal 3:2–3). If Yahweh's actions are like those of a smith, so are those of his prophets. He makes Jeremiah an assayer, for example, a 'trier' in the Douay-Rheims version, who will test their behaviour for purity of content.

> I have set thee for a strong trier among my people: and thou shalt know and prove their way. All these princes go out of the way, they walk deceitfully, *they are* brass and iron: they are all corrupted. The bellows have failed, the lead is consumed in the fire, the founder hath melted in vain: for their wicked deeds are not consumed. Call them reprobate silver, for the Lord hath rejected them. (Jer 6:27–30)

---

23 Michael Enright, *Iona, Tara and Soissons: the origin of the royal anointing ritual* (Berlin, 1985), pp 59–60; Michael Enright, 'Royal succession and abbatial prerogative in Adomnán's *Vita Columba*', *Peritia*, 4 (1985), 83–103 at 100–1; Sharpe, *Adomnán*, p. 250, n. 37.   24 von Rad, *Old Testament theology*, II, pp 147–75; Peter D. Quinn-Miscall, *Reading Isaiah: poetry and vision* (Louisville, KY, 2001), pp 23–6; John Goldingay, *Isaiah* (Peabody, MA, 2001), pp 1–31.

It is possible to speak of this 'mettle detection' as an 'office' as does von Rad: 'This office of assayer, which Jeremiah believed had been entrusted to him, and which all the prophets from Amos to Malachi each in his own way regarded as theirs also, demanded sustained vigilance in passing judgment upon men and circumstances'.[25] If Columba is a prophet, for example, then he has a special right to test the people and has received a commission to assay princes. From the OT's point of view, his task is like that of a smith whose bellows may not fail and whose founding must be constant. A prophet must also act as a watchman (Jer 6:17; Ez 3:17) who is sent. In the divine council that Isaiah witnessed, he heard the voice of the Lord saying: 'Whom shall I send? And who shall go for us?' And he answered: 'Lo, here am I, send me'.

Ezekiel, too, heard a voice.[26] The 'word of the Lord' came to him in a cloud of fire and Yahweh declared that he would send him to the children of Israel, to a rebellious people. They have provoked Yahweh to anger 'and thou shalt speak my words to them'. Yahweh now speaks of a scroll, a *liber* in the Vulgate:

> Open thy mouth and eat what I give thee. And I looked, and behold, a hand was sent to me, wherein was a book rolled up: and he spread it before me, and it was written within and without: and there were written in it lamentations and canticles, and woe. And he said to me: Son of man, eat all that thou shalt find: eat this book, and go speak to the children of Israel. And I opened my mouth and he caused me to eat that book: And he said to me: Son of man, thy belly shall eat, and thy bowels shall be filled with this book, which I give thee. And I did eat it: and it was sweet as honey in my mouth. (Ez 2:7–9, 3:1–3)

Ezekiel is to receive in his heart and say exactly 'all the words that I speak to thee', and that is perhaps one reason for the emphasis on Yahweh's giving of a book to his prophet (or of his angel doing so in *VC* III 5). He is to be a herald who carries within him the precise message of the king so that variations do not occur in transmission (another prophet, the lesser known Zechariah [5:1] will actually see a flying scroll). But because all the house of Israel have a hard forehead and an obstinate heart:

> Behold I have made thy face stronger than their faces: and thy forehead harder than their foreheads. I have made thy face like an adamant and like flint. (Ez 3:7–8)

It is only when reading such call narratives that one begins to realize why Adomnán finds his dream of Columba's mother so important, why he chooses it as the opening chapter of Book III. He accepts the biblical view that prophets must be 'called' and 'sent' by God, and what we have here is a foreshadowing of Columba's own call that is yet to come. It is not easy to outdo a scorching of the

---

25 von Rad, *Old Testament theology*, II, pp 74, 203.   26 Ibid., pp 220–37; Zimmerli, *Ezekiel*, pp 68–74; Margaret S. Odell, 'You are what you eat: Ezekiel and the scroll', *Journal of Biblical Literature*,

prophet's lips, a volume to be devoured, or a forehead like flint, but such miraculous occurrences in the Bible do indicate that Columba's advent must be similarly signaled with mystery and symbol. We must be clear, however. VC III 1 is not actually a call narrative – that occurs in VC III 5. Instead, it is meant to recall and prompt us about the scriptural call genre itself, so that we may keep it in mind as an interpretative key as we traverse the next three chapters leading up to III 5. The sequence as a whole tells us about the making of a prophet and, as we shall see, Adomnán had his own reasons for constructing it that way. There is more to say about all of this but, for now, let us look to two other call narratives that appear to have had an especially noteworthy significance for Adomnán. After a citation of these, followed by reference to some aspects of the glorious mantle motif, we shall then be in a position to more fully appreciate the origins of Adomnán's plan for his prophet of Iona.

Along with the call of Samuel, which is decisive in establishing the nature of Columba's relations with kings and their sons, the 'calls' of Jeremiah and Deutero-Isaiah appear important for Adomnán's fashioning of Columba's behaviour. Jeremiah ($c.640–c.580$BC) belonged to a powerful priestly family and was wealthy enough to buy land when he wished, and to hire a secretary who expected a lucrative salary (45:1–5; 51:59). He is a reluctant prophet who counsels submission to Babylon and to Nebuchadnezzar II, and who advises the captives in Babylon to live as best they can by settling down and raising families in exile.[27] In contrast, practically nothing is known about Second Isaiah beyond the probabilities that he lived in Babylon and flourished around the 530s.[28] He, too, is known as 'Isaiah' because his lessons explore and extend many of those examined by his eighth-century namesake, and his words were appended at some unknown point to those of the earlier figure. He possesses the greatest poetic talent of all the prophets. Unlike modern scholars, Adomnán would not have distinguished one Isaiah from the other and would have interpreted all their prophecies as stemming from one. In view of Adomnán's emphasis in III 1, on Columba as a prophet chosen before birth, it is crucial to observe that both Jeremiah and Second Isaiah – and these two alone – are described as the prophets chosen by Yahweh 'from the womb'. That suggests one element of their significance to Adomnán, but other characteristics figure also.

The Book of Jeremiah describes the turbulent life of a great, tormented and cantankerous visionary. His call narrative begins in 1:4:

117 (1998), 229–48. **27** von Rad, *Old Testament theology*, II, pp 191–219; Lindblom, *Prophecy*, pp 189–97. **28** von Rad, *Old Testament theology*, II, pp 238–62. The Book of Isaiah is very complex and reflects at least three different periods: $c.739–687$BC, 540–535 and 515–500. These correspond to the traditional scholarly divisions of the text at Isaiah 1–39, 40–55 and 56–66, and in turn to the names Isaiah (of Jerusalem), Second or Deutero-Isaiah and Third or Trito-Isaiah. A useful brief introduction to the prophets is John F.A. Sawyer, *Prophecy and the prophets of the Old Testament* (Oxford,1987). For the medieval and modern traditions, the best introduction is Niels Christian Hvidt, *Christian prophecy: the post-biblical tradition* (Oxford, 2007) (with a foreword by Joseph

> And the word of the Lord came to me, saying: Before I formed thee in the bowels of thy mother, I knew thee: and before thou comest forth out of the womb, I sanctified thee, and made thee a prophet unto the nations.

He was quite literally born to be a prophet, and was opposed to this vocation from the first moment that he heard of it. 'And I said: Ah, ah, ah, Lord God: behold, I cannot speak, for I am a child'. Jeremiah described himself as a 'child' here or a 'boy', *quia puer ego sum* in the Vulgate. He is thus comparable to Samuel, who is also a boy when he is called (1 Reges 3). But Yahweh will not be crossed in his selection of servants.

> And the Lord said to me: Say not: I am a child: for thou shalt go to all that I shall send thee: and whatsoever I shall command thee, thou shalt speak. Be not afraid at their presence: for I am with thee to deliver thee, saith the Lord. And the Lord put forth his hand, and touched my mouth: and the Lord said to me: Behold I have given my words in thy mouth. Lo, I have set thee this day over the nations, and over kingdoms, to root up, and to pull down, and to waste, and to destroy, and to build, and to plant. (1:4-10)

If Jeremiah reluctantly accepts all this, and always seeks to obey the Lord, he is never far from resentment and rage, since Yahweh forces him to predict the destruction of Jerusalem and its temple; it makes him into a laughing-stock and a victim of persecution. Indeed, he is placed in the stocks in Jerusalem and his relatives seek to harm him. He is the 'assayer' of his people directed to separate the dross from the pure metal, but it is he who is burnt with the fire. 'Cursed be the day wherein I was born: let not the day in which my mother bore me be blessed' (20:14). Yahweh has wronged him and it is Yahweh's fault! The prophet rises to upbraid his God: 'Thou hast deceived me, O Lord, and I am deceived; thou hast been stronger than I, and thou hast prevailed. I am become a laughing stock all the day, all scoff at me' (20:7). Although he tries to speak no longer in God's name, he is scorched inwardly when he seeks to stop: 'Then I said; I will not make mention of him, nor speak any more in his name: and there came in my heart as a burning fire, shut up in my bones, and I was wearied, not being able to bear it' (20:9). It is interesting that Jeremiah interprets his prophetic compulsion to be like a burning fire in his bones rather than a word or force from outside that seeks to control him. It is an anguish that breaks his will, and his suffering is lifelong. In the end, as far as we know it, he is carried off into Egypt so that he lacks the consolation of the large company of Jewish exiles in Babylon.

But what does it mean to be appointed 'a prophet unto the nations'?[29] Jeremiah is a prophet to Judah, but his brief includes an interpretation of its

Cardinal Ratzinger). **29** See, for example, Witherington, *Jesus the seer*, pp 132–3. Clearer perhaps is Goldingay, *Isaiah*, pp 19–20, where he shows that the nations are Yahweh's agents in bringing disaster to Judah, in delivering and restoring Judah, and finally in coming to Yahweh and in

behaviour within the sphere of international relations. He turns with a will to predictions of wasting and destroying – against Egyptians, Philistines, Moabites, Ammonites, Edomites, Syrians, Arabs, Elamites and Babylonians, over a half dozen chapters (25; 46–51). Yahweh's sword will rage against the nations. Scholars like von Rad have seen these oracles as a renewal of the theme of Israel's 'sacred warfare' (an area in which Samuel was a master), which recalls the way in which the prophets had once actually spoken when Israel – or rather, Yahweh – went into battle against the foe.[30] Jeremiah is to root up, pull down, waste, destroy, build and plant! Because Israel has forsaken Yahweh and given herself to Baal, the covenant is broken and trouble will come from the north. Jeremiah has a vision of a boiling cauldron that is tilted from north to south so that a flow of evil tracks towards Judah (1:13–14). Hearing God's holy words, Jeremiah becomes 'as a drunken man' (23:9) and this motif is taken up in other chapters. Yahweh shall remove all mirth from the bridegroom and his bride and the nations shall drink of desolation.

> For thus saith the Lord of hosts the God of Israel: Take the cup of wine of this fury at my hand: and thou shalt make all the nations to drink thereof, unto which I shall send thee. And they shall drink and be troubled ... And I took the cup at the hand of the Lord, and I presented it to all the nations to drink of it to which the Lord sent me. (25:15–18)

Jeremiah then serves the drink to the kings and princes of Judah as well as the dozens of other kings throughout the Middle East. Yahweh tells them to drink, be drunk and vomit: 'And if they refuse to take the cup at thy hand to drink, thou shalt say to them: Thus saith the Lord of hosts: Drinking you shall drink'.

As dubious as it might seem to a modern critic unaware of the range of connections, a good case can be made for the proposition of an Irish reader pondering Jeremiah in the seventh century AD and reaching the conclusion that the ancient Hebrews had much in common with established aspects of Irish culture. The universal God had manifestly created similar conditions. In Jeremiah's chapters, we find reference to a warlike king-god whose wife is the land but who may choose to consort with another god, to a boiling cauldron that tilts and pours out abstraction, thus recalling the doctrine of the Irish 'Cauldron of poesy', and to a figure who prophesies while distributing drink to kings, and who thereby exhibits characteristics quite similar to those of the prophetess in *Baile Cuind* also of the seventh century.[31] Even aside from Christian doctrine,

experiencing his worship. What God has done for Judah is to be proclaimed to all.   **30** von Rad, *Old Testament theology*, II, p. 52; Knierim, 'Vocation of Isaiah', 66. He refers to the early tradition of Holy War in which Yahweh would ascend to Zion in an expedition to protect it and to Is 31: 4–5, where the Lord will be as a lion or young lion growling over his prey. Such conceptions were still alive in the eighth century long after the time of Samuel.   **31** P.L. Henry, 'The cauldron of poesy', *Studia Celtica*, 14/15 (1979/80), 114–28; Liam Breatnach, 'The cauldron of poesy', *Ériu*, 32 (1981),

then, Adomnán would have reason to think of linking OT prophecy with native poetic theory and particularly with native kingship theory. It is not the differences that would have impressed the abbot, a theologian saturated with biblical learning, but rather the similarities, all of which would encourage the idea of describing Columba as a prophet acting within an OT mould, one who was perfectly suited to replace the inaugurating smith of the Tara myths.[32]

Isaiah, which includes Second Isaiah writing in the time of the Persian king Cyrus $c.539$BC, is the most complex of the prophetic books. There are thus a number of different messages and emphases. Three of these strike one as most relevant for present purposes. First is the repetition of the idea of the prophet being called from the womb. At first this is addressed to Jacob/Israel: 'Thus saith the Lord that made and formed thee, thy helper from the womb: Fear not, O my servant Jacob, and thou most righteous whom I have chosen' (44:2). In 49:1–6, however, it appears to be spoken by the prophet himself:

> Give ear ye islands, and hearken, ye peoples from afar (*audite insulae et adtendite populi de longe*). The Lord hath called me from the womb, from the bowels of my mother he hath been mindful of my name (*de ventre matris meae recordatus est nominis mei*). And he hath made my mouth like a sharp sword: in the shadow of his hand he hath protected me, and hath made me as a chosen arrow: in his quiver he hath hidden me. And he said to me: Thou are my servant Israel, for in thee will I glory ... and now saith the Lord that formed me from the womb to be his servant, that I may bring back Jacob unto him, and Israel will not be gathered together: and I am glorified in the eyes of the Lord, and my God is made my strength. And he said: it is a small thing that thou shouldst be my servant to raise up the tribes of Jacob, and to convert the dregs of Israel. Behold, I have given thee to be the light of the Gentiles, that thou mayst be my salvation even to the farthest part of the earth.

We thus see that two of the most celebrated of biblical prophets had been chosen by God before birth. They were thereby divinely selected and made holy in a particularly portentous way and for an especially important task, even while 'hidden' in God's quiver. Adomnán has deliberately woven this motif of the divine imprinting of a prophet into the birth narrative of his own saintly relative. Columba can then fit or fulfil the statements made at the beginning of the second preface of *VC*, where he is compared to the prophet Jonah and where the divine symbolism of his dove-like name has been highlighted just as the biblical prophet remarks that God 'hath been mindful of my name'. Because of the emphasis on Columba's mother in *VC* III 1, however, it is not unlikely that Adomnán also wants us to think of the Annunciation, of the angel's appearance to the Blessed Virgin Mary. As we saw in the case of Gideon, an angel may well be the bearer of

45–93; Gerard Murphy, 'On the dates of two sources used in Thurneysen's *Heldensage*', *Ériu*, 16 (1952), 145–51. Clearer in *Baile in Scáil*.   **32** I have argued that a smith or druid-smith would have been the inaugurator of Tara rulers in Michael Enright, *The Sutton Hoo sceptre and the roots of Celtic*

a prophetic call, although the emphasis on dreams (rather than visions) is actually more characteristic of the later prophets and of post-exilic religiosity than it is of Isaiah and Jeremiah. As we shall see, however, Adomnán is probably more impressed by the story of Anna, the mother of the prophet Samuel.

Notice also the intriguing coincidence of these prophetic declarations being combined with a command that the 'islands' and peoples from afar should hearken to them. Might not Adomnán have thought of his own archipelago and his own 'island soldiers' as he would term them? One of the perennial problems of the Book of Isaiah for modern biblical scholars is the difficulty, indeed the practical impossibility, of determining exactly who the speaker in the text is and who is being spoken to, whether Israel, Judah, Babylon, the prophet himself or various personifications.[33] The citation from 49:1–6, for example, is one of the famous 'servant songs', which, as von Rad states, 'we cannot fully understand'.[34] It is usually taken to refer to the prophet, however. We are thereby confronted with linked references to a prophet from the womb whose name is significant to God and who is to be a light to the gentiles of the farthest part of the earth. We are indeed brought back to the themes of the VC. The materials of VC III 1 and the Second Preface of the VC can now be seen to be related through a common inspirational source. The prophecy of Mochta,[35] Patrick's disciple, in the Second Preface is thus far more significant than it appears at first glance: 'a son will be born whose name Columba will become famous through all the provinces of the ocean's islands, and he will be a bright light in the last days of the world'. Islands, light and a prenatally formed prophet are all common features in Isaiah and VC. It is thus plausible to suppose that Adomnán has drawn on Isaiah to provide a most splendid justification for Columba's career on his islands of the Hebrides and beyond. According to this construction, Cúl Dreimne's bloody field, by which Adomnán dates Columba's decision to 'first set sail from Ireland to be a pilgrim', is at most a hint but not a catalyst for the saint's decision to undertake a missionary journey to the gentiles. God had actually chosen the prophet Columba for this task from his mother's womb. The 'islands' or 'the provinces of the ocean's islands', as Adomnán has Mochta enlarge the concept, are not just the coastal outliers of Scotland; they include Man, Ireland and Britain, a claim decidedly contrary to those made by supporters of Armagh. It is now of greater interest to note that Columba's 'fame' and 'bright light' over those is predicted

---

kingship theory (Dublin, 2006). **33** Goldingay, *Isaiah*, pp 236–50. **34** von Rad, *Old Testament theology*, II, p. 250. **35** Richard Sharpe, 'Saint Mauchteus, *discipulus Patricii*' in A. Bammesberger and A. Wollmann (eds), *Britain, 400–620: language and history* (Heidelberg, 1990), pp 85–93; Sharpe, *Adomnán*, pp 244–5. The theme of preaching through the provinces of the ocean's islands also resonates with the wondrous flowery mantle or robe of VC III in Is 61, where the prophet states that the spirit of the Lord is upon him and hath sent him to preach. He is joyful because 'he hath clothed me with the garments of salvation: and with the robe of justice he hath covered me. ... For as the earth bringeth forth her bud, and as the garden causeth her seed to shoot forth: so shall the Lord God make justice to spring forth, and praise before all the nations' (Is 61:10–11).

by no less a figure than a disciple of Patrick's friendly to the future *paruchia Columbae*, which God grants him the grace to discern. This is the sole mention of Patrick in *VC*, who is thereby indirectly co-opted to provide a judgment entirely at variance with the aggressive spirit of the *Book of the Angel* or of Tirechán or Muirchú. It suggests that Adomnán has taken the tack of appealing to the spirit of Patrick against the *superbia* of his followers. While clearly making a claim to wide power, he has phrased it in a remarkably gentle manner. Unfortunately, it is impossible to tell whether Mochta's eirenic words about a narrow separation between monasteries refer only to those of his own foundation or to all those monasteries following Patrick. If the latter, it is a delicate reminder of Columba's influence with a hint of willingness to compromise, but such is by no means certain. What is clear is that Adomnán's manipulation of certain biblical texts and their echoes in the *VC* is calculated; our knowledge of the links with these texts affects all of this material and places it in a different light.

Lest these peculiar 'island' references be undervalued, it is necessary to point out that Second Isaiah contains frequent additional allusions with significant nuances that affect an interpretation. In 42:1–10, for example, the 'servant' who appears to be the prophet is told by Yahweh:

> Behold my servant, I will uphold him ... I have given my spirit upon him, he shall bring forth judgment to the Gentiles ... He shall not be sad, nor troublesome till he set judgment in the earth: and the islands shall wait for his law ... I the Lord have called thee in justice, and taken thee by the hand, and preserved thee. And I have given thee for a covenant of the people, for a light of the Gentiles: That thou mightest open the eyes of the blind, and bring forth the prisoner out of prison. ... Sing ye to the Lord a new song, his praise is from the ends of the earth: you that go down to the sea, and all that are therein: ye islands, and ye inhabitants of them.

These verses arouse interest because of Iona's reputation as a place of refuge for endangered princes, and may also have recalled to Adomnán his own successful efforts at prisoner release and law-making, both ecclesiastical and profane. It is potentially useful ammunition. This passage also sounds much like a preamble to 49:1–6 cited above, although that lacks the stress on judgment and law. 49:7 goes on to declare of this servant from the womb that kings and princes will 'rise up' to adore him, while 49:23 finds him worthy beyond all rulers:

> And kings shall be thy nursing fathers, and queens thy nurses: they shall worship thee with their face toward the earth, and they shall lick up the dust of thy feet.

Jeremiah's message was not much different in terms of the prophet's power: 'Lo, I have set thee this day over the nations, and over kingdoms, to root up and to pull down, and to waste, and to destroy, and to build, and to plant' (1:10).

22

How should one regard those comparisons? The danger of reading too much into such texts is always present, perhaps especially because of the ambiguity surrounding addressees in Second Isaiah. Over the last century and half, scholars have held a variety of different views on the question but even the germ of these modern concerns is unlikely to have entered the mind of a seventh-century abbot-theologian. He would have been struck, rather, by the importance of the authoritative 'call' in the Bible, by the presence of the uterine motif in two major prophets, by prophetic references to islands, with hearkening peoples waiting for the prophet's law. Other explorations will validate this intertextual approach, but it is perhaps now convenient to offer some further confirmatory evidence that substantiates the hypothesis of Adomnán's intense interest in and borrowing from Isaiah. This evidence to be examined is especially noteworthy because it can serve a dual purpose in our investigation: on the one hand it authenticates Adomnán's usage of a concept of prophecy in Isaiah, while on the other offering a route towards solving a long-disputed kingship theme concerning Diarmait mac Cerbaill.

Babylon's dominance lasted less than a century. And when Cyrus the Great of the Persians entered Babylon in 539BC, the exiled Jews seem to have been wildly enthusiastic at his coming. Not only does Cyrus allow the exiles to return to Judah, he returns the Jerusalem Temple treasure looted by Nebuchadnezzar.[36] His successors will support the rebuilding of the Temple with state funds. In the Book of Ezra, we are told that Yahweh himself inspires Cyrus:

> the Lord stirred up the spirit of Cyrus, king of the Persians: and he made a proclamation throughout all his kingdom, and in writing also, saying: thus saith Cyrus king of the Persians: the Lord, the God of heaven hath given to me all the Kingdoms of the earth, and he hath charged me to build him a house in Jerusalem, which is in Judea. Who is there among you of all his people? His God be with him. Let him go up to Jerusalem, which is in Judea, and build the house of the Lord the God of Israel: he is the god that is in Jerusalem. (1 Esr 1–3)

The Persian policy of religious and linguistic toleration is a boon for the Jews. Second Isaiah is overjoyed as he proclaims the end of the exile:

> Be comforted, be comforted, my people saith your God. Speak ye to the heart of Jerusalem, and call to her: for her evil is come to an end, her iniquity is forgiven: she hath received of the hand of the Lord double for all her sins. (Is 40:1–2)

According to Isaiah, the Lord says to Cyrus: 'thou art my shepherd, and thou shalt perform all my pleasure'. This surprising line is taken dramatically further:

---

36 See, for example, J. Alberto Soggin, *A history of ancient Israel* (Philadelphia, PA, 1984), pp 261–6; J. Maxwell Miller and John H. Hayes, *A history of ancient Israel and Judah* (Philadelphia, PA, 1986), pp 440–50; Richard J. Mouw, *When the kings come marching in: Isaiah and the New Jerusalem*

Thus saith the Lord to my anointed Cyrus (*haec dicit Dominus christo meo Cyro*), whose right hand I have taken hold of, to subdue nations before his face, and to turn the backs of kings, and to open the doors before him, and the gates shall not be shut. I will go before thee, and will humble the great ones of the earth: I will break in pieces the gates of brass, and will burst the bars of iron. And I will give thee hidden treasures, and the concealed riches of secret places: that thou mayest know that I am the Lord who call thee by thy name, the God of Israel. For the sake of my servant Jacob, and Israel my elect, I have even called thee by thy name: I have a made a likeness of thee, and thou hast not known me. I am the Lord and there is none else: there is no god beside me: I girded thee, and thou hast not known me. (45:1–5)

This is an amazing passage, one of the most unexpected in the OT. A non-Jewish alien conqueror is prophetically acclaimed as Yahweh's 'shepherd', his chosen king, who is divinely inspired, who is called by name, whose hand is held by God who goes before him. Cyrus has become a redeeming 'master of the nations' who accomplishes the will of Yahweh and he is an anointed king, an anointed emperor in fact, despite his exclusion from the line of David and despite his paganism.

Why Adomnán links paganism, empire, royal unction and sacral death
in VC *I 36*

Consider now the conundrum of Diarmait mac Cerbaill (544–65) in Irish historiography in the light of this biblical exaltation of a pagan king.[37] Although historically rather unsuccessful in the field, Diarmait seems to have been revered as an ancestor figure and quickly became the enduring focus of contemporary and long-term saga. He was the last pagan high-king of Tara and legend holds that the site was cursed by saints and abandoned after his reign. The *feis Temro*, the ritual marriage feast of Tara by which the ruler wedded or re-wedded his kingdom, was last celebrated by him in 558/60. Although he and Columba were cousins, they had become enemies by 561 at the latest since it was in that year that the Battle of Cúl Dreimne (or Drebene) was fought in Sligo, where Diarmait was defeated by a coalition of forces led by Áed mac Ainmirech of Cenél Conaill (also a cousin of Columba). AU reports that Diarmait fought with the aid of a 'druidic fence' – it is not known what that is – but the battle was won *per orationes Coluim Cille*. AU estimates that three thousand men died in the battle and some critics at least blamed Columba for their deaths. That too became a matter of

(Grand Rapids, MI, 2002). 37 Francis John Byrne, *Irish kings and high-kings* (London, 1973; 2nd ed. Dublin, 2001), pp 87–112; Máire Herbert, *Iona, Kells and Derry* (Oxford, 1988), pp 27–9; D.A. Binchy, 'The Fair of Tailtiu and the Feast of Tara', *Ériu*, 18 (1958), 113–38; Edel Bhreathnach, '*Níell cáich úa Néill nasctar géill*: the political context of *Baile Chuinn Chétchathaig*' in Edel Bhreathnach (ed.), *The kingship and landscape of Tara* (Dublin, 2005), pp 49–69; Brian Lacey, *Cenél Conaill and the Donegal kingdoms, AD500–800* (Dublin, 2006), pp 175–85.

enduring story so that the relationship between Tara king and contending saint soon became regarded as star-crossed. It may have been because of his crucial participation at Cúl Dreimne that Columba was excommunicated by a synod held in Diarmait's kingdom (*VC* III 3). His close association with the winning of battles for kings who support him probably dates from around this point. But the main reason for the air of uncertainty that surrounds Diarmait is best captured by this unsettling question: how could this Southern Uí Neill king, the celebrant of the last pagan feast of Tara who was opposed by Columba's prayers and kinsmen at Cúl Dreimne, yet have been praised by Adomnán in *VC* as *totius Scotiae regnatorem deo auctore ordinatum*? The juxtaposition of a pagan character and God's ordination has always appeared contradictory to scholars and has never fully been explained. So, too, is Adomnán's desire to declare Diarmait imperial overking of all other Irish rulers. What lies behind this astonishing volte-face? A number of things surely, but some important part of the rationale must lie in the above citation of Isaiah for this is a *uniquely* authoritative witness to the existence of the queerest of royal creatures, a divinely mandated pagan emperor who is the rightful and holiest king of kings. Adomnán's conceptualization of Diarmait, therefore, must pivot on these factors. Cyrus is the ruler chosen by God to do justice, to 'build my city' and to 'let go my captives' (45:13). The great of the world shall belong to him: 'they shall walk after thee, they shall go bound with manacles: and they shall worship thee, and shall make supplication to thee' (45:14). Both provocative aspects of Adomnán's assertion about Diarmait – 'ordination' and hegemonic rule – are thus uniquely justified through Isaiah's prophecies about Cyrus of Persia, who frees the Jews. Since that dual anomaly is matched by other unusual combinations in both Isaiah and *VC* – the prophet who is called from the womb, who makes the islands hearken and teaches them his law – the borrowing of Isaiah's concepts by Adomnán seems demonstrable. Given Adomnán's emphasis on Columba as the prophet who goes to the islands, the connection is not a surprising one. Adomnán is quite consciously tailoring the events of Columba's call and career to fit an OT prototype. As we shall see, moreover, other seers will be co-opted in order to maintain and extend that template.

Further evidence supports this view that Adomnán borrowed the biblical model and employed it to develop his extraordinary conception of a divinely sanctioned national overkingship. The evidence appears in *VC* I 36, which refers to the ordination of the pagan Diarmait to be king of all Ireland. It is not so much an argument as a statement on Adomnán's part of a fait accompli that is, significantly, tied to a killing. Adomnán's intellectual route to his proclamation is important to consider, however, because it illustrates the manner of his thinking, and because he applies the same essential formula to Oswald of Northumbria in *VC* I. The Diarmait chapter must thus be cited in full.

[I 36] *The blessed man's prophecy about Findchán, founder of the monastery called in Irish Artchain on the island of Tiree.*

Once, this priest called Findchán, a soldier of Christ, brought with him from Ireland to Britain a man of the race of Ulster and of royal stock yet wearing a cleric's habit. His name was Áed Dub, and it was intended that he should remain for a number of years as a pilgrim in Findchán's monastery. This Áed Dub had been a very bloody man and had killed many people, among them Diarmait mac Cerbaill, ordained by God's will as king of all Ireland. This same Áed, having spent some time in pilgrimage, was ordained priest in Findchán's monastery, but the ordination was invalid even though a bishop had been brought. This was because the bishop had not dared to place his hand on Áed's head until Findchán (who had a carnal love for Áed) had first laid his right hand on his head in confirmation.

When this ordination was later made known to the saint, he took it ill, pronouncing thereupon this fearful judgment on Findchán and Áed, now ordained, saying: 'That right hand which Findchán, against the law of God and of the Church, laid on the head of a son of perdition will soon grow rotten. It will give him great pain, and be dead and buried before him though he will live many years after his hand is buried. Áed, however, who was ordained unfittingly, will return as a dog to his vomit; he will again be a bloody murderer and in the end, killed by a spear, he will fall from wood into water and die drowning. He deserved such an end to life long ago for having killed the king of all Ireland'. The blessed man's prophecy concerning both of them was fulfiled. First, the right fist of the priest Findchán became rotten and preceded him into the earth, being buried on the island *Ommon*. The man himself, in accordance with St Columba's words, lived on for many years. Áed Dub, priest in name only, returned to his old wickedness and, being pierced by a treacherous spear, he fell from the prow of a ship into the waters of a lake and perished.[38]

---

38 *VC* I 36, pp 138–9. *Beati profetatio viri de Findchano prespitero illius monasterii fundatore quod scotice Artchain nuncupatur in Ethica terra. ALIO IN TEMPORE supra memoratus prespiter Findchanus, Christi miles, Aidum cognomento Nigrum, regio genere ortum, Cruthinicum gente, de Scotia ad Brittanniam sub clericatus habitu secum adduxit, ut in suo apud sé monasterio per aliquot perigrinaretur annos. Qui scilicet Aidus Niger valde sanguinarius homo et multorum fuerat trucidator. Qui et Diormitium filium Cerbulis totius Scotiae regnatorem deo auctore ordinatum interficerat. Hic itaque idem Aidus post aliquantum in perigrinatione transactum tempus accito episcopo quamvis non recte apud supradictum Findchanum prespiter ordinatus est. Episcopus tamen non est ausus super caput ejus manum inponere, nisi prius idem Findchanus Aidum carnaliter amans suam capiti ejus pro confirmatione inponeret dexteram. Quae talis ordinatio cum postea sancto intimaretur viro egre tulit. Tum proinde hanc de illo Findchano et de Aido ordinato formidabilem profatur sententiam, inquiens: 'Illa manus dextera, quam Findchanus contra fas et jus eclesiasticum super caput filii perditionis inpossuit, mox conputrescet et post magnos dolorum cruciatus ipsum in terram sepelienda praecedet. Et ipse post suam humatam manum per multos superstes victurus est annos. Ordinatus vero indebete Aidus sicuti canis ad vomitum revertetur suum. Et ipse rursum sanguilentus trucidator existet, et ad ultimum lancea jugul [a]tus de ligno in aquam cadens submersus morietur. Talem multo prius terminum promeruit vitae, qui totius regem trucidævit Scotiae'.*

Quae beati viri profetia de utroque adimpleta est. Nam prespiteri Findchani dexter prae pugnus putrefactus in terram eum praecessit, in illa sepultus insula quae Ommon nuncupatur. Ipse vero juxta verbum sancti Columbae per multos post vixit annos. Aidus vero Niger, solummodo nomine prespiter, ad sua priora reversus scelera dolo lancea transfixus de prora ratis in aquam lapsus stagneam disperiit.

At first sight, this narrative appears artless and transparent, a simple anecdote about Findchán and the doings of Áed Dub, his killing of Diarmait and Columba's subsequent curse. But that cannot be so since no convincing explanation is given for Columba's rage at Diarmait's death and still less for the highly peculiar nature of his malediction. After all, the killing of kings is not unusual in Columba's time (or later) and there is no great reason to curse a killer (beyond kinship or personal friendship), especially since, for all that we know, the violent death in question may have occurred in the accepted norms of contemporary combat. Elsewhere in *VC*, Adomnán depicts Columba as thoroughly indifferent to the deaths of kings, even when they had been decapitated by their enemies (I 12). And in Diarmait's case, one would rather expect a blessing of his killer instead of a curse because of lingering Columban enmity deriving from Cúl Dreimne and the holy man's later 'wrongful' excommunication by a synod held in Diarmait's territory. These are warning signs that forbid the acceptance of any surface reading that treats the text as naïve disclosure. They encourage the view that I 36 is actually a coded statement – a set of indicators to some other meaning designed for select readers – and the only question is: how does one decipher the code? As we have seen in other cases, Adomnán's code is biblical and typological and here focuses directly on his understanding of 'ordination'. His chapter concerns two ordinations and their consequences – one, the first to be mentioned, is about Áed the Black's ordination that is clearly unlawful and regrettable, while the second is an elision to a magniloquent pronouncement that Diarmait is the rightful ruler of the entire country who has been ordained to rule by God Himself. The punishment for one offence is loss of a hand, while that for the killing is a condemnation to the exotically supernatural threefold death (spear, water and curse). Adomnán's descriptions in the second case only make sense, however, if he perceives it to be sacral punishment for a sacral crime. His interpretation pivots on the assumption that Diarmait is a kind of Cyrus *redivivus*; he is a pagan king whom God has nonetheless chosen to anoint through a miraculous infusion of protective grace, a mystical bestowal of the same unction that one receives at a Hebrew royal inauguration rite. It is this modelling on far-ruling Cyrus that also legitimates Adomnán's statement that Diarmait is *totius Scotiae regnator*. The evidence dovetails exactly, since it not only explains how a pagan king could be ordained to rule by a God whom he rejects, but also accounts through its modelling for the idea of an imperial governance over many other kings. At the same time, it provides a convincing rationale for Columba's otherwise surprising reaction of rage and malediction. It occurs because the killing of such a divinely appointed emperor is a true moral enormity; it transgresses against the foundational biblical injunction of *nolite tangere christos meos* to become an outrageous attack on God and people. No one may assault an anointed king and continue to live, since the OT holds it an act of such intrinsic evil that it brands the attacker and all who aid him as irredeemable outlaws.

Because Adomnán has here drawn upon the two-faceted imperial model of anointed Cyrus while combining it in Ireland with a concept of inviolability that rests solely on a concept of protection created by a royal anointing, it is quite certain that he was thinking of biblical unction when he referred to Diarmait mac Cerbaill as an 'ordained' king. That is not the case with Findchán's ordination of Áed Dub, however, which is described as a non-canonical hand-laying and refers to an unworthy priest rather than a ruler. Columba was roused to anger by this act (*viro egre tulit*), which he regarded as violating 'the law of God and of the Church'. Adomnán's employment of the same term, *ordinatio*, for each consecration is thus not intended to suggest any equivalency of applied usage in administration, since, were it otherwise, Áed Dub would have been regarded as specially honoured by God, and that is obviously not Adomnán's view. It is the terminology itself that misleads, but its ambiguity is narrowed and rendered precise by the evidence of the precedent that it appeals to. In both cases, a sacred act of consecration that changes status has been performed, but, in this time and culture (as in our own), the word used to describe it is loose enough to encompass a variety of different means of achievement. This interpretation is confirmed by the roughly contemporary attitudes expressed in the *Collectio Canonum Hibernensis*, which, for example, refers to two kinds of ordination in its opening to the book *De regno*, refers to four types in *De principatu*, and goes on to declare that evil rulers may not be degraded if they have been anointed.[39] That is the rule even in the debatable case of Saul, whom God Himself is perceived to have anointed, but then subsequently rejected because of his sinful disobedience. Even in such a case, Saul's successor David refused to attack him because of the sacral nature of his anointed character.[40]

The major anomaly of *VC* I 36 is thus explainable once the Cyrus model is introduced and once one recognizes that the assumptions of the *Hibernensis* on the matter of ordination essentially reflect those of Adomnán. Other details of this chapter's narrative are also relevant, however, since they reinforce the basic thrust of the evidence. Consider that I 36, regardless of where it falls in the manuscript, is basically a companion piece to III 5, which centres on the inauguration to kingship of Áedán mac Gabráin of Dál Riata. There are two reasons for linkage: first, each focuses on a royal ordination and that sets it off from other materials; second, they are joined by a similar pattern of word repetition. In the Áedán chapter, Adomnán marks his special interest in Columba's act of hallowing through this device and does so further with repeated references to a book carried by an angel. One or two mentions are not enough; he hammers away at his chosen features of book and ordination until he judges them to be fixed in the reader's consciousness. He does the same in the Diarmait chapter, but now turns his focus to 'hands' – to the bishop's hand, to

39 Hermann Wasserschleben (ed.), *Die irische Kanonensammlung* (Aalen, 1966), pp 76, 131, 129.
40 Ibid., p. 139.

Findchán's hand, to his right hand, to his diseased hand, to his hand that is buried with him. He wishes us to fasten our attention on those hands and the sinful deeds that they do. By implication, of course, Áed Dub's hand, that which has slain an anointed king, is doubly cursed but is now not worth specifically mentioning because he is to die a hard death in any case. Even here, however, Adomnán is obsessed by anointing precedents and his addition of the threefold-death motif is probably inspired by the context that surrounds them.

One must turn to the OT and to 1 Reges for a solution. Chapter 24 of that book describes a situation in which Saul is following David with three thousand men in order to kill him. But David and his men are hidden in a cave, and an opportunity to turn the tables on his tormentor arises when Saul uses the cave to answer a call of nature. David's followers urged him to execute the king but all he would do was to secretly cut off the hem of Saul's robe. Even at that, 'David's heart struck him' and he said to his men:

> The Lord be merciful unto me, that I may do no such thing to my master the Lord's anointed, as to *lay my hand* upon him (my emphasis), because he is the Lord's anointed. And David stopped his men with his words, and suffered them not to rise against Saul.

Instead, going out of the cave, David called out to the king and, when he turned, lowered himself to the ground to worship him. He begged Saul not to listen to those who said that David wished to hurt him. In the next six verses, David constantly reiterates the message. Even though 'the Lord hath delivered thee into my hand', I spared thee, for 'I will not put out my hand against my lord because he is the Lord's anointed'. Even when I cut off the hem of thy robe, 'I would not put out my hand against thee'. Hence there is no evil nor iniquity 'in my hand'. If the Lord judge between me and thee, 'my hand shall not be upon thee'. In an old proverb, it is said that 'from the wicked shall wickedness come forth: therefore my hand shall not be upon thee'. May the Lord judge therefore and 'deliver me out of thy hand'. More such references follow, but it is perhaps unnecessary to cite them. Chapter 25 goes on to make some more general allusions to this theme of life, hand and righteousness, but the matter of the conflict comes to a head in Chapter 26. Once again, Saul is insufficiently guarded and David and his companion Abisai secretly enter the king's camp:

> So David and Abisai came to the people by night, and found Saul lying and sleeping in the tent, and his spear fixed in the ground at his head: and Abner and the people sleeping round about him. And Abisai said to David: God hath shut up thy enemy this day into thy hands: now then I will run him through with my spear even to the earth at once.... And David said to Abisai: Kill him not: for who shall put forth his hand against the Lord's anointed and shall be guiltless? ... The Lord be merciful unto me that I extend not my hand upon the Lord's anointed. But now take the spear which is at his head, and the cup of water, and let us go. (26:7–11)

When the two men reached the opposite hill, David turned and shouted back to Abner, Saul's uncle and general who was charged to protect him from harm. He proclaimed that Abner is a negligent guardian of the king, a man who failed his duty, and therefore he and his soldiers are sons of death.

> And David said to Abner: Art not thou a man? and who is like unto thee in Israel? why then hast thou not kept thy lord the king? for there came one of the people in to kill the king thy lord. This thing is not good that thou hast done: as the Lord liveth, you are the sons of death, who have not kept your master, the Lord's anointed. And now where is the king's spear, and the cup of water, which was at his head?

Saul himself calls back and answers hypocritically. David replies that 'if the Lord stir thee up against me, let him accept of sacrifice: but if the sons of men, they are cursed in the sight of the Lord, who have cast me out this day …'. 'Behold', said David, 'the king's spear: let one of the king's servants come over and fetch it. And the Lord will reward every one according to his justice and his faithfulness: for the Lord hath delivered thee this day into my hand and I would not put forth my hand against the Lord's anointed'. (26:19–23)

Here, in short order, are many of Adomnán's themes that appear in VC I 36. Here too are the insistent repetitions of hand/anointing that prompted his imitation of hand/ordination. Add further the inspiration for the motif of the curse to the threefold death.[41] The presence of the latter is provoked by the spear at Saul's head, by the cup of water, by Abisai's wish to run Saul through 'with my spear', and perhaps by the knowledge that Saul did indeed die by a piercing (30:4). Of course, these are prompts to a theme and not exact identities; a cup of water is not a body of water and there is no reference to Saul's falling from a boat. Nonetheless, such differences do not outweigh the sequence of cumulative correspondences. This is emphatically underlined by the fact that reference to a curse is a feature of the source text itself. Thus David harshly rebukes, or curses, Abner for not properly guarding Saul – he declares that he and his men are 'sons of death' – and then goes on to say that those who speak against him to the king are 'cursed in the sight of the Lord', *maledicti sunt in conspectu Domini*. Adomnán's pattern of adaptive imitation of I Reges is thus demonstrable and that pattern is also keyed to Isaiah's reference to an anointed pagan emperor.

One has the sense that more is meant by this chapter, however, for other questions easily intrude. Why, for example, did Adomnán follow the circuitous path of first describing the wrongful ordination of Áed Dub rather than moving directly to God's mystical anointing of Diarmait mac Cerbaill, which surely is more central to his purpose (as I see it) of a reformation of Irish kingship along OT lines? Several answers are possible. One is that the fact of Áed's priesthood

---

41 Among many studies, see Brian Ó Cuív, 'The motif of the threefold death', *Éigse*, 15–16 (1973–6), 145–50; Joan N. Radner, 'The significance of the threefold death in Celtic tradition' in Patrick K. Ford (ed.), *Celtic folklore and Christianity: essays for W.W. Heist* (Santa Barbara, CA,

was well known and had perhaps become part of a scandal that had helped to shape thinking about the demise of the last pagan king of Tara. Reference to a killer's wrongful action could then structure a narrative in which, by starting with the theme of falsity, the lesson of ultimate veracity could more clearly be drawn. Adomnán may also have aimed at encouraging his educated readers and hearers to think in typological rather than literal terms. By his emphasis on the hand/ordination pairing, he may have been signaling an insistence that they envision the hand/anointing paradigm of biblical inviolability that could confer protection on selected overkings. No hand might touch them. Columba's curse then showed that such rulers would always be defended and avenged by the watchful Iona prophet. Their anointing in life would naturally be the prerogative of the same holy man who had avenged them in death. Reciprocity demanded this; as it had been in the past, so should it be in the future. An emphasis on the divinely granted inviolability of Tara kings achieved through holy oil *and Columba* would then be a key message of the episode.

The theological dimension should not be ignored. Adomnán says that Áed Dub was a frequent killer, that God's chosen king was only one of his victims, and that sometime after his wrongful ordination he returned to being a 'bloody murderer'. His hands had been devoted to evil for a long time and that made him unfit for priestly office. Likewise, aside from any irregularity in the actual ordination, its validity had been undermined by the fact that Findchán's motivation for advancing it was 'carnal' rather than spiritual. As a result, the right hand that he had laid on Áed's had become diseased. Here, one must remember that the priest is a type of Christ, that his life is intended to be an imitation of Christ, and that his hand is the one that consecrates the bread and wine of the Eucharist into the body and blood of Christ. In the OT, Christ is prefigured as both priest and king, the 'anointed one' or messiah, and in the NT is presented as the fulfilment of all messianic hopes.[42] Priest and anointed king are thus theologically related, for the latter is a special type of Christ. His anointing instils in him the *living* spirit of a divinity so that it is forbidden to touch him in anger. Even to curse him with words alone merits death in the same way as a cursing of God (2 Reges 19:21; Lev 24:15). For a priest, whether of disputed status or not, to turn his Christ-consecrating hand against an anointed king, another type of Christ, is thus a shocking idea; it is a moral perversion, an act of sacrilege of near epic proportions. In addition to the historical perspective, it is this item of unexplained but understood typology that may have caused Adomnán to treat the ordinations of *VC* I 36 together.

Although Adomnán does not think of Áed Dub's priestly ordination as including an unction – as we have seen, the term can cover a variety of different ritual acts – the rationale and associations that he made will indeed have a future,

1983), pp 180–99.   42 Amid a large literature, see J. Roy Porter, 'Oil in the Old Testament'; Jeffrey John, 'Anointing in the New Testament' in Martin Dudley and Geoffrey Rowell (eds), *The oil of*

and that perhaps merits a brief mention. Within about a generation or so of Adomnán's death, the Merovingian *Missale Francorum* was compiled, either in the region around Poitiers or in the Seine valley area.[43] It prescribes anointing for a priest, but for his hands (*Consecratio manus*) and not his head. It is thus not the style of priestly anointing mentioned most famously in Exodus 30:25–31 that is being followed, but, apparently, the same references to the work of hands that figures in *VC*.[44] Thus, in the *Item alia* that follows in the missal and begins *Unguantur manus istae*, it is Samuel's anointing of David as king and prophet that is cited and the oil is to be applied in the form of Christ's cross. It thus seems to be the priest/king typology that is seen as foundational, together, perhaps, with the idea of sanctification through oiling from Exodus in order that Aaron and his sons 'may do the office of priesthood unto me'. Although, as members of Christ's body, all of his followers are made kingly and priestly through baptismal and confirmational anointings, the situation here is different because it is directed to an office to be fulfiled.[45]

Another way of appreciating the network of meanings that may arise from these considerations is to query the introduction of the threefold-death motif. This is part of a durable pagan kingship mythos and stands out for that very reason since Adomnán allows no other such dangerous concept to infiltrate his narrative. Why then select this particular one and connect it so closely with Columba and an anointing concept? The reason, we can now perceive, is because Adomnán has found a workable legitimating source for it in the symbols and curse by David in 1 Reges. But the threefold death, it must be remembered, is only one half of a mythos that otherwise encompasses the life of the ruler that begins as such at his inauguration. That detail suggests that Adomnán is thinking according to the Irish paradigm by which the sacral beginning of a reign is

---

gladness: anointing in the Christian tradition (London, 1993), pp 35–46, 46–77.   **43** Leo Cumibert Mohlberg (ed.), *Missale Francorum* (Roma, 1957), pp xxiv–xxvi; Bruno Kleinheyer, *Die Priesterweihe im römischen Ritus: Eine liturgiehistorische Studie* (Trier, 1962), pp 114–22.
44 Mohlberg, *Missale Francorum*, p. 10:
   CONSECRATIO MANUS. Consecrentur manus istae et sanctificentur per istam unctionem et nostram benedictionem, ut quaecumque benedixerint benedicta sint, et quaecumque sanctificauerint sanctificentur: per dominum.
   ITEM ALIA. Unguantur manus istae de oleo sanctificato et crismate sanctificationis: sicut uncxit Samuhel Dauid in regem et prophetam, ita unguantur er consummentur in nomene dei patris et filii et spiritus sancti, facientes imaginem sanctae crucis saluatoris domini nostri Iesu Christi, qui nos a morte redemit et ad regna caelorum perducit.
   For the liturgical background and comparanda, see farther Arnold Angenendt, '"Mit reinen Händen": Das Motif der kultischen Reinheit in der abendländischen Askese' in *Herrschaft, Kirche, Kultur: Beiträge zur Geschichte des Mittelalters. Festschrift für Friedrich Prinz zu seinem 65. Geburtstag* (Stuttgart, 1993), pp 297–317; Yitzhak Hen, *Culture and religion in Merovingian Gaul, AD 481–751* (Leiden, 1995), pp 43–61; *The royal patronage of liturgy in Frankish Gaul: to the death of Charles the Bald (877)* (London, 2001), pp 21–64.
45 Janet Nelson, 'The Lord's anointed and the people's choice: Carolingian royal ritual' in David Carradine and Simon Price (eds), *Rituals of royalty: power and ceremonial in traditional societies* (Cambridge, 1987), pp 137–81 at pp 149–53.

followed at its conclusion by an appropriate sacral ending. Adomnán now signals his acceptance of the latter half of this Irish formula (because of certain elements in the fated Saul story) and offers to replace the former with biblical anointing and its conveyance of a sanctified inviolability. He thus offers personal safety to kings in lieu of traditional prestige. The Irish sovereignty/fertility goddess will mate with anyone suitable and is never without one husband in the shadow of another.[46] Irish political theory encourages insecurity at the top but can be stabilized by a drawing on scripture. If one is intent on making this case, then the murdered(?) Diarmait mac Cerbaill might well be the best figure to begin it with. Notice also Adomnán's desire to *manipulate* the concept of the threefold death. This is suggested by the fact that he applies it to a king's killer rather than to a king himself, which would have been traditional usage. To do so, he had to subtly doctor the record on Áed Dub mac Suibni by stating that he was a man of the race of Ulster and of royal stock (*regio genere ortum Cruithnicum gente*), when, in fact, Áed had probably become king of Dál nAraidi in 563, two years before he killed Diarmait, and then king of Ulaid in 581 until his death in 588.[47] The idea of royal lineage alone is a deliberate downgrading to make Áed Dub seem worse, and less, than he was. Adomnán knew better, but he felt constrained by the nature of his message: namely, that the killers of anointed kings should suffer but not the kings themselves because they had God's, and now, demonstrably, Columba's protection.

Various other aspects of the biblical paradigm interested Adomnán and probably influenced his portrayal of sacral rulers in conflict. From what we have seen, a model featuring a slain king avenged by a holy man was insufficiently attractive to Adomnán. For the sake of Columba's status and that of Iona, he required a biblical precedent involving two kings that turned on a concept of sacrality; one of the two must be deficient and the outcome must be manifestly affected by a prophetic leader in direct communication with God. We know this to be so since the 'hand' and curse references of I 36 point directly to Adomnán's source. The feuding kings of the model were Saul and David, both of whom had been anointed by Samuel the prophet/judge, although the prophet had later declared Saul to be rejected by God because of disobedience. Saul, the deficient king, was the aggressor, although an uncommitted observer might be pardoned for supposing that the feud was Samuel's fault and was actually the case of an arguably good king opposing and arguably high-handed holy man. The bloody strife that followed could just as easily be ascribed to Samuel (and his God) as to

---

46 Proinsias mac Cana, 'Aspects of the theme of king and goddess in Irish literature', *Études celtiques*, 7 (1955), 76–144, 356–413, and 8 (1958–9), 59–65; Edel Bhreathnach and Kevin Murray (eds), '*Baile Chuinn Chétchathaig*: edition' in Edel Bhreathnach (ed.), *Kingship and landscape*, pp 73–94; Charles Doherty, 'Kingship in early Ireland' in Bhreathnach (ed.), *Kingship and landscape*, pp 3–31. 47 Ailbhe MacShamhráin and Paul Byrne, 'Kings named in *Baile Chuinn Chétchathaig* and *The Airgialla Charter Poem*' in Bhreathnach (ed.), *Kingship and landscape*, pp 159–224 at pp 189–92.

Saul. Motifs of sacrality, prophetic decision-making, royal death and the motif of the threefold death (because of spear, water and curse) all linger in the background and inevitably reminded Adomnán of Columba and Diarmait at Cúl Dreimne, and Columba's departure (flight?) from Ireland. Samuel too fled to a distant place of refuge, to Najoth in Ramatha. Here, he protected David and presided over his own 'company of prophets'. Saul, in the meantime, was hunting David in order to kill him but was himself touched by the Lord. He was on his way with his men to Najoth when a miracle occurred: 'the spirit of the Lord came upon him' and Saul 'prophesied' for the remainder of his journey. Once he reached Samuel, the distraught king 'stripped himself also of his garments, and prophesied ... before Samuel, and lay down naked all that day and night'. This gave rise to a proverb: 'What! Is Saul too among the prophets?' (1 Reges 19:20–24). The conflict has now reached a far higher pitch because both prophet and king are divinely inspired. Each was capable of reaching into the supernatural sphere and performing in a supernatural manner. At this point, one is not only reminded of the threefold-death mythos and the career of the historical Columba, but also of the inherent comparability of Saul and Áed Dub. Just as a supernaturally inspired Saul followed Samuel to his refuge at Najoth, so did Áed Dub, on pilgrimage and seeking the office of priest, follow Columba into the sphere of his Iona refuge, at least as far as Tiree. Parts of myth, Bible story and historical revisionism are so thoroughly intertwined in this *VC* narrative that it is clear that Adomnán cannot, or does not wish to, separate them. The mere thought of Diarmait mac Cerbaill in relation to Columba may have aroused a cascade of emotions that gave rise, eventually, to the text of I 36 as we now have it.

The unusual mixture and treatment of materials in I 36 may owe something to the inherently contradictory set of statements that are made in the Bible about Saul. They are profuse and often surprising. They stem from the fact that Saul's traditional laudatory story was downgraded and rewritten in the interest of David's dynasty by scribes who, nonetheless, wished to maintain the basic heroic framework along with many of its details. What they wrought has been the bane of commentators ever since. As a scriptural scholar, Adomnán would have been troubled as well. Partly in reference to the inconsistencies, perhaps, is his remark in III 18 about mysteries of scripture that are 'most dark and difficult'. One of these mysteries meant that Saul could be treated in a variety of contrasting ways. Although he was a legitimately anointed king, the chosen of the Lord, neither Yahweh nor his prophet Samuel had wanted a secular ruler and both later decided that they had chosen wrongly. They rejected him on the basis of a technicality that would have demoted most of the kings of the OT. Depending on one's intent, therefore, Saul could be understood as either the anointed one or the rejected one; he might even be treated as a semi-pagan or Cain-like figure. In his ecclesiastical history, for example, Bede would compare him to the pagan, but otherwise admirable king Aethelfrith who fortunately ravaged the Britons (HE I 34). Adomnán has something of this same sentiment in mind – he identifies strongly with Samuel – but cannot of course pursue it consequentially because it would result in a series of contradictions that would undermine his project of eulogizing Diarmait and revenging his death in the current interest of his Iona community. The topics that appear in the sources that he *certainly* uses, therefore – a debatable anointing, a conflict in which a prophet takes sides between kings, a deficient ruler's ability to prophesy truly in a politico-religious context, a theory of inviolability contingent upon royal unction, and a curse against a background of reference to water and a spear – all combine to produce a series of politico-theological perceptions that he distills into one short and heavily freighted chapter. These considerations explain much about why he wrote in the way that he did, even if not wholly, and even if the full range of his sentiments with regard to Diarmait and to the political situation that prompted him to invoke his shade, are not yet recoverable. Nonetheless, Adomnán clearly felt compelled to draw upon these sources because they are the ones that describe God's way of dealing with anointed kings and their enemies. His plan is manifested in his scriptural choices. While the potential range of materials is huge, his selection among them is rather narrow and that is evidence in itself.

The threefold death is thus a tradition of pagan kingship that can lawfully be carried over into a new regime of Christian kingship because elements that legitimate it can be found in the Samuel/Saul/David saga. Its presence suggests an acceptance of the Irish end-of-reign thematic, but, because accompanied by what we now recognize as an inviolability-through-anointing concept, also indicates an advocacy of a biblical ritual for the inauguration of an Irish overking. It occurs here at the intersection of historical events and Adomnán's persistent need to exorcise the ghost of Diarmait mac Cerbaill. As William Sayers has persuasively argued, the pagan conception probably originally involved a ruler's offence against justice, which then resulted in his dramatic rejection by the elements and the 'sovereignty' goddess who represented them.[48] In time, clerics succeeded in modifying the pattern, so that contentions between kings and clerics came to be the chief dynamic, which gradually marginalized pagan figures, and broadly succeeded in effacing the signs of offences against any other forms of supernatural authority. The church then reserved for itself the right to judge the behaviour of kings and dynasties, promote the accommodation of church and state, and fix the destiny of rulers through curse and prophecy in both the present life and the next. What we can now recognize is that Adomnán was one of these early churchmen (if not perhaps the earliest who wrote about it) who sought to subvert this traditional kingship theme. He did it by deploying the

---

48 William Sayers, 'Guin & crochad & gólad: the earliest Irish threefold death' in Cyril Byrne, Margaret Harry and Pádraig O Siadhail (eds), *Celtic languages and Celtic peoples* (Halifax, NS, 1992), pp 65–82. The following sentences are basically a paraphrase of Sayers, p. 75.

usable elements of the Samuel/Saul saga so that his new Christian prophet could become the judge of kings (Columba is the one who declares Diarmait to be ordained by God), and the judge of their opponents (Columba is the one who curses Áed Dub to a mystical ritual death) while also subtly threatening the right of any other intruding abbot or bishop who wishes to accommodate a 'king' (however ambiguous he is about Áed's status) without his permission. VC I 36 is thus important to Adomnán because he can here advance the unction and inviolability themes while depicting Columba in the role of the sovereignty goddess of the kingdom hitherto connected with the judgment and inauguration of rulers.[49] His new Christian kingship ritual thus comes into being with an adjusted traditional myth already attached to it, with a divinity who will support it in warfare through his champion, and with a prophet who alone has the right to administer it.

As an important side-effect of this finding, the meaning of *ordinatio* as used by Adomnán achieves a sharper and more distinct profile in I 36: Áed Dub's killing of Diarmait is especially revealing because it enables a kind of intellectual triangulation of a conceptual pattern. In *Iona, Tara and Soissons*, I argued that the biblical concept of kingship as a sacred office in which the king may not be attacked because he is God's anointed (*nolite tangere christos meos*) lies behind this anecdote about saint, king and the cursing of a killer ('he deserved such an end to life long ago for having killed the king of all Ireland').[50] This seemed plausible because a definition of *ordinatio* as anointing appears in the roughly contemporary Iona-connected *Hibernensis* and because Adomnán also introduces a revolutionary Christian ritual of king-making in which *ordinatio* is again the term employed. Unfortunately, although I was then aware of the Cyrus reference, I did not think to link it with the prophetic theme itself or with VC III 1 on the unborn prophet. Now that that is done, any possibility of interpretative looseness is eliminated because the non-anointing variables can be excluded. No other explanation can make sense of the bizarre appearance in VC of a pagan 'ordained' king, one not ordained by the saint, but whom it is nonetheless sacrilegious to kill. The nature of the source-text, when combined with the 'hand' references and Columba's cursing of Diarmait's killer, both drawing from 1 Reges, constitute proof that the concept of royal anointing is uppermost in Adomnán's thinking. Adomnán had thus deliberately set out to showcase the anointing concept in practice in order to demonstrate its potential usefulness to rulers. Indeed, Diarmait had to be present so that this idea of applied prophecy-cum-anointing could function, since Adomnán had to be able to invoke the example of a pagan high-king from Columba's own time in order to execute the

---

49 I continue here with reference to the sovereignty goddess to avoid confusion, but I believe it more likely that a smith or 'druid-smith' representing Goibniu was the controlling figure in the pre-Christian mythos of kingship and king-making until he was largely eliminated by Christianity. Unlike the goddess, he was less susceptible to a leaching of original symbolism and had to be denied outright: see Enright, *Sutton Hoo sceptre*. 50 Enright, *Iona, Tara and Soissons*, pp 14–15, 56–7.

parallel that he wished to contrive. The thesis that the *Hibernensis*' understanding of *ordinatio* as an act of anointing is present in *VC* is thus vindicated.[51] A strong presumption is thereby also established that the same is true in regard to the Oswald and Áedán instances, since no compelling reason exists for Adomnán to change the meaning of this lexical item that he is the first to apply to Irish and north British rulers. In addition, as we shall see in part 4 of the present chapter, the application of the unction theory also explains Columba's protective and minatory behaviour in the cluster-of-princes chapters to be investigated. It is thus clearer than before that the king-making and victory-bringing acts described in *VC* are the consequences of a carefully considered and developed theory of royal anointing tied to a concept of prophetic imitation in the islands.

A potential objection may be referred to, however, in order to avoid any confusion. As unlikely as that may now seem, it might be supposed that because Diarmait's anointing as king of all Ireland was spiritual and not physical, then the principle invoked by the reference was purely a mystical one as well. That interpretation is excluded because Adomnán furnishes an example of the biblical theory in practice when he physically consecrates Áedán while using the same terminology. In addition, Adomnán follows an anointing narrative (1 Reges 16:10–14) when he designates Áedán's son as his successor (and that, too, is cited in the B-text of the *Hibernensis*).[52] As he has absorbed the lessons of the

51 Michael Richter's current views to the contrary appear in 'Die frühmittelalterliche Herrschersalbung und die *Collectio canonum hibernensis*' in Matthias Becher and Jörg Jarnut (eds), *Der Dynastiewechsel von 751: Vorgeschichte, Legitimationsstrategien und Erinnerung* (Münster, 2004), pp 211–20. This remarkable article is a belated attempt to review *Iona, Tara and Soissons*, along with some of its reviewers between 1986 and 1990. Richter is dissatisfied with their generally positive reception of the book and believes that, because of a better understanding of the complexity of Irish history, he can improve on their judgment. However, he exhibits no special knowledge of its complexity. With two exceptions, the basic issues discussed by Richter had all been raised and then answered in my book. Of the exceptions, the first concerns Cumméne Find, whose fragment in *VC* I did not discuss. Richter speculates that Adomnán based the key chapter III 5 on his now lost work. That is conjecture. It is here refuted, but for specific problems see below, nn 52, 74. The second exception centres on the idea of an abbot anointing a king and likely Frankish disfavour of such a concept. Richter states that it is a point 'den ich nirgendwo problematisiert gefunden habe' (p. 218). There is good reason for this. Since Adomnán's unction was a complete innovation in the Insular world, no rule existed as to who should perform it. After all, Samuel himself had been neither abbot nor bishop. What counted was that he was an inspired *prophet* who had been directed to intervene by God and that is exactly how Adomnán presents Columba and his ordination of Áedán. As for the Franks, while it is quite possible that one or some of them had read *VC* and seen it as a model for kingmaking in Francia (based on present findings, that is now a more solid possibility), what I argued as most probable was that this message was carried in the *Collectio canonum hibernensis*, a canon law book inherently more authoritative and likely to attract attention because it answered continental needs in other ways. The *Hibernensis* alludes to Samuel anointing Saul, and the question of abbot or bishop plays no role. For the Franks, of course, it was canonical support for the biblical ritual itself that was important. Richter is unclear about these issues, far more so than the reviewers of the book whom he patronizes.   52 Bearing the heading *De eo quad eligitur in regnum frater iunior prae fratribus senioribus*, the chapter that follows is basically a citation of 1 Reges 16:10–14. This excerpt from his unpublished edition of the B-text was kindly given to me by the late Maurice Sheehy. It appears in *Iona, Tara and Soissons*, p. 27.

Samuel/Saul precedents, however, and as he views them as divinely established lawful guides, he cannot here anoint the son because the biblical case depended upon Saul's rejection of the prophet's will. Adomnán indirectly indicated that it is precisely this principle that is operative because he makes his choice depend on Áedán's son exhibiting a love of the prophet in VC I 9:

> 'The one whom the Lord has chosen will run directly to my arms'. They [the sons] were called, as the saint instructed and Eochaid Buide went as soon as he entered and leant on the saint's bosom (*in sinu ejus recubuit*). The saint kissed and blessed him and said to the father: 'This one will survive to be king after you, and his sons will be kings after him'.

Like his father, who is shown as following the saint's will when he calls his sons, and who otherwise seems to have been a stalwart friend, it is Eochaid Buide's display of affection and symbolic gesture of reliance on the prophet that makes him throneworthy. It all follows the best biblical pattern for prophet–king relations. But notice that in this instance, as in the others, the unction connection is determinative. In this example, the pattern invoked is meant to confirm the saint's intention of further reliance on the anointing rite because it follows the pattern of David's anointing as a king. In that instance, the Lord had disavowed Saul and had ordered Samuel to take oil with him to Bethlehem in order to anoint a new king, a successor from among the sons of Jesse. As with Eochaid Buide in the *vita*, Samuel viewed a parade of sons and chose the youngest. The spirit of the Lord then alighted upon David but 'departed from Saul, and an evil spirit from the Lord troubled him' (16:1–14). In VC I 9, Adomnán is creating the biblically patterned royal succession precedents that he means to exploit. Otherwise, the chapter is superfluous.

It is by the explication of such small but significant details as the boy at the saint's bosom that we can glimpse the shape of the abbot's design. As in the Samuel/Saul material (although not so decisively in the case of other prophets), it is the anointer of the king who is able to set policy and, ultimately, to decide on royal replacements. One should not be surprised that the biblical source-passage for the Eochaid Buide episode is copied into the B-version of the *Hibernensis*. It is a further instance of the Iona group's influence in this matter of the proposed introduction of a new Christian kingship ritual. That is the lynch-pin of the programme. The anointing rite is essential because without it the prophetically based abbatial ideology that textual analysis reveals – in the process of counter-point between VC episodes and biblical sources – cannot be made operational. It is the ritual that holds the potential to actualize the coded messages that are present in the work as a unit.

By looking to the biblical source passages and then comparing them to those of VC, we have watched Adomnán's intellectual adaptation under way. We have thus developed a clearer picture of how the hagiographer set out to manipulate the theme of the call of the prophet and have also seen why he regarded certain passages of Isaiah as instrumental for his purposes. We have also begun to frame an enhanced understanding of those purposes, of the reasons why the classic OT keynote of guiding prophet and assenting ruler converge in two clusters and several chapters of VC. They are trimmed to fit the cultures of Ireland and northern Britain. Like Eochaid Buide's tender steps into the security of Columba's protection, they are part of a carefully drawn but apparently miscellaneous set of scenes whose cumulative effect is to reveal the divinely sanctioned rightness of the saint's statements and actions. God approves of all Columban precedents, explicit and implicit. But I am in danger here of leaping ahead, since it has yet to be shown that the remainder of VC III supports this interpretation or, indeed, that VC III 1 actually begins a cluster of connected episodes. As the next step in these demonstrations, let us now examine the motif of the cloak of 'glorious honour'.

Mantles, 'sons' and divine calls

This *peplum*, *sagum*, *pallium*, all terms used to describe it, is clearly a miraculous garment signifying authority as it spreads and grows greater 'so that it seemed to be broader than the plains and to exceed in measure the mountains and the forests'. It reminds us of Joseph's famous cloak of many colours, and especially of Columba's own robe as he is described in the programmatic VC I 1, where he appears to Oswald, 'afterwards ordained by God as emperor of all Britain':

> While this King Oswald was camped ready for battle, he was asleep on a pillow in his tent one day when he had a vision of St Columba. His appearance shone with angelic beauty, and he seemed so tall that his head touched the clouds and, as he stood in the middle of the camp, he covered all of it except one far corner with his shining robe.

Here, too, a dream, this time of the mother's adult son, whose shining mantle has grown large enough to cover most of an army's camp. And those not covered, apparently, are the small number destined to die in the morrow's battle against Cadwallon. There seems little doubt that Adomnán means us to think of this garment as the splendid robe of God's prophet, since we have seen that the context in III 1 is the foreshadowed call of the prophet, since we are told that Columba is 'a son of such flower that he shall be reckoned as one of the prophets', and since I 1 presents Columba as a prophet foretelling victory.

This mantle of the prophet of VC III 1 is a further indication of Adomnán's purposes with regard to Columba, for it has a number of important associations in both Old and New Testaments. When Mt 7:15 warns of false prophets 'who come to you in the clothing of sheep' but are inwardly like ravening wolves, he seems to be recalling a practice of holy men dressing in clothing of sackcloth but also of hairy cloaks of sheepskin or goatskin.[53] This appears to have been a kind of prophetic uniform and is not infrequently referred to in the OT. Thus, when Saul went to consult the spirit of Samuel, he recognized him by his mantle: 'And she said: an old man cometh up, and he is covered with a mantle. And Saul understood that it was Samuel ...' (1 Reges 28:14).

This prophet's mantle could also become symbolic of royal authority. When Samuel proclaimed that the Lord had rejected Saul because of his disobedience, Saul grasped the skirt of Samuel's mantle as he turned away, and it rent: 'And Samuel said to him: the Lord hath rent the kingdom of Israel from thee this day, and hath given it to thy neighbour who is better than thee' (1 Reges 15:28). Similarly, the prophet Ahijah the Shilonite tore his new mantle into twelve pieces (3 Reges 11:29–38) and gave ten of them to Jeroboam to show that the Lord intended to make him ruler of ten of the Hebrew tribes. Of course, neither of these mantles is remotely comparable in beauty and mystery to the spectacular robe temporarily given to the saint's mother (representing the time Columba spent in her womb perhaps), but that is surely because Adomnán needs an enhanced miraculous version suited to his argument about Columba's status and breadth of authority.

The prophet's mantle features prominently in one other set of biblical narratives, however, and these are especially notable because they directly tie the cloak to the authority wielded by a prophet. Furthermore, these narratives provide a key for the interpretation of the episodes that follow in *VC* III 2–4. The core references are to the Elijah/Elisha stories from 3 and 4 Reges.

Elijah the Tishbite (the name may mean 'settler') is a major prophet cast in the mould of Moses and is a figure much beloved by the Hebrews who awaited his return for centuries (see also Mal 4:5).[54] For scholars of a certain theological bent, however, he and his disciple Elisha present interpretative inconveniences, because nowhere else among the prophets does one find such an exuberant saga-like collection of outright miracle stories. These are (perish the thought) much like medieval hagiography. For present purposes, the salient passages are found in 3 Reges 19:19–21 and 4 Reges 2:1–18. In the first instance, Elijah is found exhausted in the desert after fleeing from Jezebel's wrath, is fed by an angel and soon has a vision of the Lord. He leaves thereafter in search of the farmer's son Elisha, whom he finds ploughing with twelve yoke of oxen: 'and when Elijah came up to him, he cast his mantle upon him'. Apparently, Elijah simply continued walking for Elisha had to run after him in order to ask permission to

---

53 Otto Böcher, 'Wolfe in Schafspelzen: zum religionsgeschichtlichen Hintergrund von Matth. 7, 15', *Theologische Zeitschrift*, 24 (1968), 405–26. James Bruce states (*Prophecy, miracles, angels*, p. 133) that 'The image is of a robe, a vestment denoting rule, the ultimate ruler being the Lord God, King of Kings, who would one day come'. I agree with the first part, but suggest that it is actually the rule of the prophetic 'father' over other prophets that is being signaled. See below. 54 See, for example, Witherington, *Jesus the seer*, pp 80–103.

kiss his father and mother before departure. Elisha returns, kills his oxen for a farewell feast for the people of the village and then 'followed Elijah, and ministered to him'. This is not a 'call' narrative – or at least not a typical one – since the call is indirect, given to Elijah about Elisha but not to the man himself. The story is thus important because it is more like a succession episode that explains how prophetic authority is transmitted; hence, I suggest, its utility for Adomnán in *VC* III 1. Commentators also often point out that the entire Elijah/Elisha saga is markedly intertextual and recalls Moses/Joshua materials (see also Deut 34:9). The means of transmitting power is by the cloak of the leader of a prophetic company. As Volkmer Fritz observes: 'the mantle is filled with the power of its owner: in the gesture Elisha becomes Elijah's property and is forced to serve him. The mantle symbolizes the new bond and marks the change of affiliation'.[55]

We learn more about the mantle in the narrative of Elijah's ascent to heaven and Elisha's inheritance of leadership. Yahweh has now resolved to take Elijah in a whirlwind. As they continue their journey, the latter repeatedly tells Elisha to remain behind, and, on each occasion Elisha takes an oath that he will not do so. Enter the 'sons of the prophet', who now assume a distinctive role. As we saw, these were attached to shrines or to holy men whom they followed and there is some link between them and Elijah even though they are not mentioned as sharing his recent journeys. Elijah is too eccentric a 'settler' to be bound by them.

> The sons of the prophets, that were at Bethel, came forth to Elisha, and said to him: 'Dost thou know that this day the Lord will take away thy master from thee?' And he answered: 'I also know it: hold your peace'.

These prophetic groups are thus depicted as possessing genuine mantic talent. Shortly afterwards, the sons of the prophets 'that were at Jericho' came out to make the same statement and they, too, received the same answer. As Elijah and Elisha went to cross the Jordan, 'fifty men of the sons of the prophets followed them, and stood in sight at a distance'. Elijah now performs a Red Sea-type miracle, in that he 'took his mantle and folded it together, and struck the waters, and they were divided hither and thither, and they both passed over on dry ground'. Both men know that the time of parting has arrived. Elisha asks his 'father' for a gift, 'I beseech thee that in me may be thy double spirit'. He asks, in other words, for the double portion that goes to the eldest son in Hebrew law. And when the fiery chariot and fiery horses parted this 'father' and 'son', Elisha 'took up the mantle of Elijah, that fell from him'. On returning to the Jordan, he duplicated the father's procedure and parted the waters with the mantle that he now wore:

---

55 Volkmar Fritz, *1 & 2 Kings: a Continental commentary* (Minneapolis, MN, 2003), p. 200.

> And the sons of the prophets at Jericho, who were over against him, seeing it [the mantle] said: The spirit of Elijah hath rested upon Elisha. And coming to meet him, they worshipped him, falling to the ground.

It is clear that Elisha has now gained command of the company for they press him to allow a search for Elijah but will not conduct it without his permission. The 'sons of the prophets' thereby appear as the ratifying body who recognize the bearer of the mantle as the prophet before all others. He has become their prophetic 'father' with the authority that the term implies.[56]

A major part of the meaning of VC III 1 can now be explicated. In the OT family of prophets, it is the first-born son with the double portion and the mantle who becomes the head of all other prophets in the country of the one true God. Hence, the hagiographer's creation of a symbolic cloak of 'glorious honour' for the mother of the future prophet who must receive it before her son is born – the angel brings it 'one night' after Columba's conception 'but before his birth' – if the additional OT pattern of Jeremiah and Isaiah, prophets 'from the womb', is to be a valid part of the instructional recipe. Adomnán requires the spirit of these other prophets not only because he wishes Columba to be the prophetic father without equal, but because he wished to align, co-opt and then appeal to their call narratives and the particular commands that they received from God. These enable him to claim for Columba the right to evangelize and to govern 'through all the provinces of the ocean's islands' as per the prophecy of Patrick's disciple in VC Second Preface. This is in full keeping with the symbolism of the mantle that expanded 'greater and greater so that it seemed to be broader than the plains and to exceed in measure the mountains and the forests'. It represents the great kingdom of Columba's rule and the extent of his protection just as his miraculously expanded robe in VC I 1 covered all but a fraction of an army camp. Patrick's close follower becomes the spokesman of this message because the familia of Patrick is being called upon to give its assent to the protection of this mantle and to accept the generous guidance of its bearer, the leading prophet. The gentle phrasing of the disciple's words is meant to be a token of Adomnán's benign intentions when they do so.

This narrative of the mantle given to Columba's pregnant mother is thus a device that enables Adomnán to succinctly formulate a message of both power and purpose as legitimately inherited from a multiplicity of towering prophets: Jeremiah, Isaiah, Elijah, Elisha and, of course, Samuel, recognized by Saul because of his mantle. The abbot's co-option of a prophetic phalanx enables him to expand the emphasis of his anointing theme, not only Samuel/Saul but also Isaiah/Cyrus, manifested in chapters about the theoretically inviolable Diarmait, the 'predestined' (and hence prophetically known) Áed Sláine, and the equally prophetically designated Áedán mac Gabráin and his son. The bearer of the

---

56 Williams, 'Prophetic "Father"', 344–8.

mantle can thus properly function in a biblical succession as the divinely 'called' and divinely 'sent' anointer of the kings of 'all Ireland' and 'all Britain'. Nor should one think of Elijah and Elisha as being uninvolved in this greater scheme simply because they are depicted as frequent desert wanderers. Although neither man was attached to court or shrine, each was of a respected background in regular contact with kings and could announce their deaths and future reigns (see also 4 Reges 19:15–16).

If the mantle chapter has been explicitly designed to indicate that Columba is the divinely commissioned law-bringer to the British Isles, it may also be the case that Adomnán sees himself as participating in the venture, not just as abbot and continuator of Columba's sacred task, but as a kind of belated 'secretary' to the prophet who writes down his inspired words. There is a hint of this attitude in the preface to Book III, where he refers to his 'short and succinct account of St Columba's prophetic revelations, set down in writing *with the help of God*' (my italics). Coming fresh from an immersion in the prophetic literature, I would no longer wish to interpret this remark as a commonplace sentiment. Just as Baruch served as the famous secretary of Jeremiah (and Adomnán would have been far more attentive to such a connection than are we) so is it plausible to suppose that if Columba is a prophet who participates in the same kinds of commands as Jeremiah then so does Adomnán participate in the same precedents as Jeremiah's secretary when he describes and records them. I am also inclined to this view because Adomnán shows himself to be deeply interested in the writing and miraculous associations of books in the *VC*. Scholars do not tire of remarking this connection.[57] What has been universally missed, however, is the fact that Columba's status as a prophet in the biblical succession, as Adomnán insists that he is in III 1 ('he shall be reckoned as one of the prophets'), almost requires that books and writing play a role in his constructed persona. It is only when studying the prophets that one comes to appreciate the great significance of literacy in their works. I have already referred to Samuel in this regard, but consider also these links: Yahweh tells Isaiah to 'take thee a great book, and write in it with a man's pen' (8:1). He says much the same to Jeremiah: 'write thee all the words that I have spoken to thee, in a book' (30:2). Similarly, Habakuk announced the judgment of the Chaldeans on boards, Zachariah saw a book flying (5:1) and God forced Ezekiel to eat an entire scroll (2:8–9). Prophets and book-production are thus fellow-travellers. It is perhaps not the only reason for *VC*'s emphasis on this topic, but it is one that is quite probably related to Adomnán's primary thesis about his master's status, since he too was given a heavenly book (in III 5). It shows once more how decisively the theme of biblical prophecy and prophets has influenced the whole of the text. Adomnán may well understand himself to be a participant in a divinely willed chain.

---

57 As I did myself in *Iona, Tara and Soissons*, pp 20–1.

43

One prominent motif from the mantle chapter (III 1) has yet to be discussed. That is its decoration 'with what looked like the colours of every flower' (*in quo veluti universorum decorosi colores florum depicti videbantur*). This should probably also be seen in relation to the angel's remark that Columba's mother will bear 'a son of such flower that he shall be reckoned as one of the prophets' (*talem filium editura es floridum qui quasi unus profetarum dei inter ipsos connumerabitur*). I am afraid that I know of no other close precedent for the 'colours of every flower' aspect of this cloak, although Joseph's robe of many colours of Gn 37:3 is an obvious candidate. But Joseph is not a prophet, the context is not comparable and his beautiful robe does not seem to denote a divinely granted authority. A few other possibilities exist, but none could be called persuasive. Curiously enough, however, it does seem possible to clarify the origin of Adomnán's conception even if we cannot offer a complete explanation for the fullness of his usage.

In *Amra Choluimb Chille*, that very difficult poem of *c*.600, we are told of Columba:

> By his wisdom he made glosses clear.
> He fixed the Psalms,
> he made known the books of Law
> those books Cassian loved[58]

'Cassian' is John Cassian (*c*.360–*c*.435), whose *Institutes* and *Conferences* exercised a wide and permanent influence in the medieval West.[59] In his view, the ascetic, the monk living in a disciplined community, is the image of God on earth, and he devotes deep attention to explaining the best ways of work, prayer, contemplation and self-control in such a structured setting. Adomnán greatly admired him. It is, I think, in the first book of Cassian's *Institutes*, where he treats 'of the dress of the monk', that we find a likely answer. The first short chapter begins, significantly, with a reference to Elijah and Elisha, who are, we are told, the forerunners and originators of the Christian monks who should, as soldiers of Christ, always walk with their loins girded. Elijah was recognizable by his girdle of leather and by his hairiness and so were other figures of the New Testament like John the Baptist, Peter, Paul and 'others of the same rank'. Even in the OT, such figures 'displayed the flowers of a virgin life and an example of chastity and continence' (*qui in ueteri testament uirginitatis iam flores et castimoniae continentiaeque praefigurabat exampla*). In his even briefer chapter VII, Cassian goes on to speak of the sheepskin, goatskin and staff, which is the uniform of the

---

58 Thomas Owen Clancy and Gilbert Márkus, *Iona: the earliest poetry of a Celtic monastery* (Edinburgh, 1995), pp 106–9. The edition of Whitley Stokes on which this text and translation is based is 'The Bodleian *Amra Chohaimb Chile*', *Revue Celtique*, 20 (1899), 31–55, 132–83, 248–89, 400–37. 59 Owen Chadwick, *John Cassian* (Cambridge, 1968); A.M.C. Casiday, *Tradition and theology in St John Cassian* (Oxford, 2007).

Egyptian monks carried by them in imitation of those 'who foreshadowed the lines of the monastic life in the Old Testament'.[60] These garments signify the destruction of all wantonness and carnal passions. In these passages, one finds reference to the two crucial prophets, to a special kind of ascetic dress and to the 'flowers of virgin life'. Although the flowers are purely metaphorical and mentioned only in passing, the coincidence of the connection with the high-status prophets Elijah/Elisha and monasticism seems too apropos to be coincidental. Adomnán has apparently taken this combination of the girdle, flowers and goatskin of biblical anchorites and adapted it to suit his grander theme of a flowery mantle of succession, which will pass from the prophets Elijah and Elisha to the saint. Columba is the epitome of this quality of flowers, but whether it still represents chastity in Adomnán's view, or something else such as, perhaps, the spirit of prophecy, is uncertain.

One may now turn to a consideration of III 2–4, whose contents will be briefly described and then interpreted together. Each chapter, it will be argued, serves essentially the same goal. In III 2, Adomnán refers to an occasion when Columba's 'foster-father', Cruithnechán, 'a priest of admirable life', was returning after office in the church when he witnessed a fiery ball of light poised over the face of the child. He recognized, says Adomnán, that the grace of the Holy Ghost was being poured from heaven upon the boy. III 3 is a longer and more interesting narrative. Many years after this, says Adomnán, alluding to the ball of light episode, Columba 'was excommunicated for some trivial and quite excusable offences by a synod that, as eventually became known, had acted wrongly'.[61] The saint himself appeared at the assembly that had been convoked against him. St Brendan, the 'founder of the monastery of Birr', was there also and, when he saw Columba approaching, 'he rose quickly to meet him, bowed his face and kissed him with reverence'. When he was berated for these honorific gestures by the elders of the synod, Brendan replied that if they

> had seen what the Lord deigned to disclose to me today, concerning this chosen one whom you refuse to honour, you would never have excommunicated him. For in no sense does God excommunicate him in accordance with your wrong judgment, but rather glorifies him more and more.

How does God glorify him, the elders ask, when we have excommunicated him 'for a good reason?'. 'I saw a very bright column of fiery light going in front of the man of God whom you despise, and holy angels as his companions travelling over the plain. Therefore, I do not dare to spurn this man whom God, as I have

---

60 Jean-Claude Guy (ed. and trans.), *Jean Cassien: Institutions cénobitiques* (Paris, 1965), pp 36, 46. And again in *Conferences* XVIII 6 Cassian refers to the 'flowers and fruits of the anchorites' who imitate John the Baptist and Elijah and Elisha.   61 Binchy, 'Fair of Tailtiu', 122–3; Alfred P. Smyth, *Warlords and holy men: Scotland, AD80–1000* (London, 1984), pp 91–3; Sharpe, *Adomnán*, p. 353, nn 355, 356.

had visible proof, has predestined to lead the nations to life' (*quem populorum ducem ad vitam a deo praeordinatum video*). After Brendan's statement, the elders dropped their charge; they dared not to continue but instead honoured Columba 'with great reverence'.

In III 4, Adomnán refers to an occasion when Columba visited 'his master the holy bishop Uinniau, who was an old man'. When the saintly bishop saw him approach, he noticed that an angel of the Lord was walking by his side. He drew this portent to the attention of nearby monks, telling them that Columba 'has deserved to have as the companion of his journey an angel out of heaven'.

Although it is possible to read each of these episodes as individual statements affirming a regard for Columba's holiness, I venture to suggest that they are better interpreted as a group, viewed in accord with Adomnán's intentions as demonstrated by previous findings concerning the nature of the mantle chapter. As we have seen, a close examination of the motifs presented indicates that that narrative is pointedly constructed to show Columba as a major prophet who inherits the status and focused powers of a series of biblical ancestors gifted by unusual grace and talent. The mantle is the sign proving that inheritance. While significant in itself, however, the Elijah/Elisha story indicates that something additional is necessary; the grant of the mantle requires a collective recognition of the newly acquired status of 'father' of the prophets. In 4 Reges, the wearing of the mantle is accompanied by a miracle that is witnessed by the 'sons of the prophets' who then acclaim Elisha and worship him. It is this pattern of collective approval that Adomnán feels compelled to recall, although he does so through a series of individual vignettes. Notice, however, that the collective approval of the 'sons' is more closely represented in III 3 when the synod of elders apparently reversed their position and chose instead to honour Columba 'with great reverence' (*sed etiam valde venerati honorarunt*). It may be useful here to point out that the Elijah/Elisha saga seems to have been viewed as emblematic for monks. For this we have the evidence from John Cassian, whose writings were revered by Columba himself. So too by other monastic founders. In his *regula monachorum*, for example, Columbanus is recalling the pattern of both Cassian and the Bible when he declares that monks must absolutely disdain all riches 'knowing that greed is a leprosy for monks who copy the sons of the prophets' (*monachis imitatoribus filiorum prophetarum*).[62] Even more significantly, perhaps, the Elijah/Elisha example, along with that of John the Baptist and other desert fathers, is seen as the beginning of monasticism in the *Hibernensis: De monachis*, cap. 2, is headed *De exordio et auctoritate monachorum*.[63] The themes invoked were thus well known on Iona, and in monastic circles generally.

After inheriting his mantle, Elisha had immediately proceeded to perform a miracle witnessed by the now assenting, worshipping, and subordinate prophets.

62 G.S.M. Walker (ed. and trans.), *Sancti Columbani Opera* (Dublin, 1957), pp 126–7.
63 Hemnann Wasserschleben (ed.), *Die irische Kanonensammlung* (2nd ed., Leipzig, 1885), p. 147.

This has become Adomnán's compass for his construction of VC III 2–4. He begins a series of what may be described as status recognition episodes at this point with his vignette of Columba beneath a fiery ball of light as witnessed by his foster-father, a venerable holy man just returned from prayer. Cruithnechán is overcome by the sight and stands trembling: he 'bowed his face to the ground' and 'stood in awe', for 'he recognized that the grace of the Holy Ghost was poured from heaven upon his foster-son'. Adomnán continues this theme in III 3, where Columba's exalted position is proclaimed by a saintly monastic founder whose rising, bowing and reverential kiss are accompanied by his drawing the elders' attention to Columba's escort of angels. Next comes St Uinniau (or Finnio or Finbarr),[64] a renowned scholar and bishop with whom Columba had studied scripture (see also II 1). He witnesses Columba's companion angel and, like Brendan at the synod of elders, draws it to the attention of nearby ascetics. Coming after Columba's angelic designation in the womb, we thus find a miracle accompanied by a statement of divine approval from heaven and this is followed by two scenes of leading sixth-century saints, each of whom initiates what becomes a collective witness of Columba's exalted status by, we might say, the contemporary 'sons of the prophets'. VC III 2–4 is thus a sequence of texts arising from the biblical description of the homage received by Elisha after his inheritance of Elijah's mantle. Although Adomnán is not presenting an exact biblical duplication, he clearly wished to exploit the closely similar scriptural principle of a ratification of prophetic leadership. The prophet recognized in this way became the chief prophet of the country.

VC III 5 remains to be discussed, but already it appears to be the culminating chapter of a series. Before turning to III 5, however, the central III 3 episode featuring St Brendan of Birr and the antagonistic synod deserves further scrutiny. Scholars have long been uncertain about Columba's motivation in leaving Ireland in 563 when he was already around forty-one years old.[65] This was 'two years after the Battle of Cúl Drebene' (I 7) or 'in the second year following the Battle of Cúl Drebene' (Second Preface). His departure is also set in relation to this hostile forum of Tailtiu or Teltown (Co. Meath), since we are told that it was 'during this period' that the saint and his twelve disciples crossed to Britain (III 3). Diarmait mac Cerbaill was involved in both instances, since the synod met in his territory and his influence on its members is to be expected (notwithstanding his paganism). We have seen that the annals attribute Diarmait's defeat at Cúl Dreimne to the force of Columba's prayers, and much later legend connects the saint's departure for Britain with a decision for either a personal or synodally enjoined exile in order to atone for the deaths caused in the battle. Adomnán himself, however, does not make that connection. But

---

64 Sharpe, *Adomnán*, p. 317, n. 210; Pádraig O Riain, 'St Finnbarr: a study in a cult', *Journal of the Cork Historical and Archaeological Society*, 82 (1977), 63–82. 65 See Herbert, *Iona, Kells and Derry*, pp 27–8; Smyth, *Warlords*, pp 92–3.

neither does he say much about Columba's first forty years of life and what he does say lacks a sense of authenticity. The miracle highlighting Cruithnechán's testimony in III 2 is a fair example. It does have a purpose, but it is one that requires knowledge of OT prophecy to interpret rightly, and informs us more about Adomnán's contemporary politico-theological intentions than it does about Columba's career as boy or man. It seems probable, therefore, that Adomnán is deliberately suppressing information, or at least seeking to counter negative views about Columba's career that are widely known.[66] Were that not the case, he would hardly have informed us about the surprising (and indeed shocking) fact that Columba had been excommunicated (while implying that the sentence had subsequently been lifted) and insisting that it had been for 'some trivial and quite excusable offences' while yet allowing one of the elders of the synod to declare that it was 'for a good reason'. Such a public concession would not have been made if the known facts were certainly exculpatory. In these circumstances, Adomnán's best strategy would be the one that we actually read in the VC, in which he calls those offences of Columba's excusable and then shows that God favours and upholds the saint by the far higher tests of divine miracle and saintly witness. Moreover, if we suppose this to have been the case, it ties in well with the Diarmait mac Cerbaill material as a whole, since Adomnán has certainly gone out of his way to mend fences and allay distrust in that quarter. He has exaggerated Diarmait's status and divine support, and depicted Columba as cursing his killer and giving invaluable prophetic advice to his son. This is easier to understand if we suppose that Columba's actions against his Uí Néill relative had indeed constituted a cause célèbre that had continued to negatively affect relations, even if only as an unhappy memory, in subsequent generations. Adomnán is thus now bidding for a deeper peace and mutual aid. It helps, of course, that this approach is also in keeping with Adomnán's emphasis on Columba as the supernatural guardian of kings who can win battles for them. Cúl Dreimne certainly suggests that capacity. The concepts of unction, supernatural protection and reconciliation work well together.

In addition, Adomnán's allusions to the Teltown synod provide an artful means of confusing the historical issue of Columba's 'expulsion' by linking it to a scripturally founded process of divine approval for Columba's departure to Britain. It can turn vice to virtue and woe to weal. Brendan's last words in III 3 are the key to understanding this point, because his witness of an extraordinary column of light and an angel are declared to be 'visible proof' that God has predestined Columba 'to lead the nations to life'.[67] Once considered carefully, it

---

66 Smyth, *Warlords*, p. 93: 'It is impossible to escape the obvious conclusion that Columba's departure for Scotland, marking as it did such a radical change of direction in his life, was in some way connected with his pardon at the Teltown Synod. ... Such an assembly would most likely impose a penance after readmitting Columba into the church'.　67 *Hunc itaque spernere non audeo quem populorum ducem ad vitam a deo praeordinatum video* (*VC*, p. 470). Both the Andersons and

can be seen that this statement is important in several ways. First, it reads very much like an adjusted replay of the Patrician disciple's remarks in the Second Preface, where Mochta makes a 'marvellous prophecy', a revelation of the Holy Spirit, showing that Columba will become famous 'through all the provinces of the ocean's islands, and he will be a bright light in the last days of the world'. Here, after all, are founders of two different monastic familiae, sons of the prophet, each of whom are glorifying Columba, and prophesying that he is meant to go to other islands and nations. Adomnán surely wishes to convey the impression that those passages are not simply his opinion but rather those of venerable saints, with varying interests, whom God has deliberately sensitized to his will regarding Columba's mission. Such revelations cannot be wrong. These two prophecies in turn link up with the angel's giving of the prophets' mantle in III 1, and with the heavenly voice that follows it, in which Columba's mother is told not to be distressed because her son will be 'reckoned as one of the prophets': he is 'destined by God to lead innumerable souls to the heavenly kingdom'. Each of these three prophecies seems to be part of a defensively eirenic strategy which maintains the position that whatever the Teltown synod decided or did not decide is actually immaterial, and so is the question of the saint's behaviour before it, because Columba simply acted as God's predestined instrument to be employed in the greater task of evangelizing the nations. Although Adomnán does not explicitly say so, his exploitation of the theme of prophet 'from the womb' also adds weight to the argument that Columba's call to greater service overseas does indeed render his earlier offences 'trivial'. He *could* be considered to be like Jeremiah, whom God drove and compelled to act contrary to his own tortured will: 'before thou camest forth out of the womb, I sanctified thee, and made thee a prophet unto the nations'. Although the coercive element is absent in Isaiah, the combined elements of predestination, islands and a new law for peoples is even clearer there: 'Give ear, ye islands, and hearken ye peoples from afar. The Lord hath called me from the womb'. He has given me 'to be the light of the Gentiles'. Isaiah, of course, is the prophet who makes possible Adomnán's idea of a pagan anointed king in the manner of Cyrus. Hence Adomnán has already connected Isaiah's message to Diarmait, and in III 3 he has again recalled this link in an even subtler manner, because he related it to Columba's departure from Ireland for an entirely separate and laudable reason – not because of any decision by Diarmait's synod, but because God had specifically created him for the purpose of spreading the 'law'. With the pagan but mystically anointed Cyrus, Yahweh had inflicted a shocking lesson on his people. He was not only the God of a single royal house, that of David: he could also effectively employ any king or any dynasty to carry out his ends. This is part

Sharpe translate *populorum* as 'nations' rather than 'peoples', a decision borne out by the symbolic growth of the mantle in III 1 and Columba's move to Scotland thereafter.

of the great universalizing message of Second Isaiah. Adomnán has taken it to heart. He seeks to apply this universalizing concept to Ireland and Britain, where, in addition, he seeks to establish biblical techniques of royal installation because that is part of the 'law' he is called to uphold.[68]

By such careful adjustments of the past, the sensitive political memories of many in Ireland might be amended, since the figures of militant saint and sacral king would no longer need to serve as the icons of suspicious factions or camps. Not everyone would be satisfied, of course, but many would, and the gesture of offering a different memory was a useful emollient agent in itself. Two things now appear clearer, however: the Battle of Cúl Dreimne must have been a pivotal event in sixth-century Ireland, for ideological reasons if for no other, and the arguments and stories of the opposing sides were probably still powerful marshalling slogans nearly a century and a half later. Whatever may have been the interpretations of earlier times and earlier texts, the evidence suggests that, by the time Adomnán was writing, he viewed the interests of Iona as being served by a palliation of the feelings about the saga-encrusted conflict. As part of that aim, any punitive or penitential associations that had existed or been attached to Columba's move to Britain had to be combated.

The prophetic universalizing theme of Isaiah thus operated at multiple levels for Adomnán, since it could potentially change the nature of the debate among quarrelling monastic families and their allies, and channel it in a way congenial to Iona. Lest one suppose that this point is pressed too far, however, it is salutary to note that the same theme, somewhat more chiselled down to human size, is found also in the Elisha saga. Let us pause to review it a bit more since it can lead us to an enhanced perspective. Elisha is not just a wandering miracle-working prophet – he performs more miracles then any of his kind in the Bible – he is also an overtly political figure, who takes sides. He is, in fact (along with his company of prophets), a crucial power-broker in the politics of the time as he schemes to overthrow the surviving members of the Omride dynasty.[69] He plays an active role in rebellion. He accompanies armies and aids them by miracle and by prophecy of victory (4 Reges 3:1–19). There is much in his political activities that reminds one of the politico-religious constellations surrounding Columba, Cenél Conaill and Diarmait, as it is members of the Omrides like Ahab and Jezebel who promote pagan worship until they are opposed by Elijah and then Elisha. One wonders if the historical Columba (whose life is hardly discussed until after Cúl Dreimne) might not have associated Diarmait with king Ahab of Israel, and Diarmait's *feis Temro* with Ahab's marriage to Jezebel of Tyre, with

68 von Rad, *Old Testament theology*, II, pp 238–62. All commentaries will discuss this change. Adomnán thinks of Ireland and Britain as 'the islands of the ocean' and says so in *VC* II 46, although he may think of 'our islands' as being more specifically Ireland and northern Britain. In general, see Thomas O'Loughlin, 'Living in the ocean' in Cormac Bourke (ed.), *Studies in the cult of St Columba* (Dublin, 1997), pp 11–23. 69 J. Maxwell Miller, 'The Elisha cycle and the accounts of the Omride wars', *Journal of Biblical Literature*, 85 (1966), 441–54.

her offensive fertility cult. It is an attractive possibility. Be that as it may, however, Adomnán wanted to get past it, although still keeping a more elevated pagan connection by capitalizing on the anointed Cyrus of Persia. Something of the universalist theme (of Yahweh the true God of all nations and not just Israel and Judah) also occurs, for example, when Elisha is responsible for Hazael's accession as king of Syria (4 Reges 8:7–15) because 'the Lord hath shown me that thou shalt be king of Syria'. Elijah is said to have anointed him. Here, the mantle-bearing prophet creates kings outside the Hebrew lands. More significant still is the example of the healing of Naaman, which shows Elisha acting in the capacity of a prophet to the Gentiles. Naaman is a high-ranking Syrian commander whom the Lord has turned to his purpose, 'for by him the Lord gave deliverance to Syria'. Naaman seeks help for his leprosy, and is advised by a captive slave-girl from Israel to consult Elisha for a cure. Naaman decides to do so, although he must first overcome political difficulties in order to pass through Israel. Once there, the prophet appears to insult him by working through a servant, but Naaman is persuaded to forego his anger and to follow Elisha's directions. He is cured, and rushed to reward Elisha, declaring: 'In truth, I know there is no other God in all the earth, but only in Israel' (4 Reges 5:1–18). He requests permission to remove two loads of earth and states that henceforth he will offer sacrifice only to the Lord even though he must also serve his master in the rituals of Remmon (a Syrian Baal).

At first glance, this narrative may not appear to have any lasting significance, but it is actually of crucial interpretive value. A surprising thing in the account is that God, who will later act through the foreign king Cyrus, also acts here to give victory to an alien general. And he guides this foreigner to healing by way of a captive girl in poor circumstances, a motif which may have aroused a special interest in Adomnán who was known for his sympathy for endangered women. The taking of soil from Israel is also related to reverence for Yahweh, as foreign soil is considered unclean in his worship (see also Am 7:17; Hos 9:3). By taking soil, therefore, the worship of Yahweh can be made possible anywhere or everywhere and it thus assumes a theological quality touching on universalism. To appreciate the full meaning of this episode to Adomnán, however, one must also know that it features in Luke's Gospel. It occurs at a pivotal moment, at the very beginning of Christ's public ministry (4:16–28). The context is important. Like an earlier prophet, Jesus has recently come out of the desert and his fame has begun to spread. On the Sabbath, he entered a synagogue, rose up to read from the book of Isaiah the prophet, and turned to the place where it was written that 'The spirit of the Lord is upon me'. He is called to preach such things as 'deliverance to the captives' and a setting at liberty of those that are bruised. Then he returned the book and said 'this day is fulfiled this scripture in your ears'.

> And he said: Amen I say to you, that no prophet is accepted in his own country. In truth I say to you, there were many widows in the days of Elijah in Israel ... And to none of them was Elijah sent, but to Sarepta of Sidon, to a widow-woman. And there were many lepers in Israel in the time of Elisha the prophet: and none of them was cleansed but Naaman the Syrian.

At these words, those in the synagogue were filled with anger. They drove him from the town and sought to kill him. The reason lay in his declaration that in days of need, Elijah was sent to a woman from Sidon only and that Elisha cured only Naaman the Syrian. Jesus is here using Elijah and Elisha to justify his own undertaking of a mission not just to Jews but to Gentiles everywhere. It is here that we find Adomnán's rationale. To follow in Elisha's footsteps, to take up his mantle, is to be taken directly to Christ and to his mission to lead Gentiles to a new kind of law. As Christ was here ejected from the synagogue by uncomprehending zealots who wished to harm him, so had Columba been ejected from the synod held in Diarmait's lands because, as Luke has it, 'no prophet is accepted in his own country'. Like Christ, Columba's mission was to Gentiles and included all peoples, and not just the Irish. Like Christ, and like Isaiah, he had been predestined to do so 'from the womb'. As Christ's public life begins in these circumstances, so does Columba's departure for Britain; it is in their common acceptance of this predestined burden of mission that the Saviour and his prophet become known to the world.

At the risk of labouring the point, and in order to avoid possible misunderstanding, it may be allowable to restate some main points. In VC III 1–5, Adomnán has artfully contrived a sequence of linked chapters in order (among other things) to craft a biblically legitimated framework to justify the controversial nature of Columba's career and his claims to premier authority. Beginning with the mindfully selected emphasis on prophetic name and character, he leads us to the concepts of a prophet from the womb graced with the mantle of Elijah and Elisha, a theme also connected to the rule of monks, since monks are the contemporary 'sons of the prophet'. As in the OT recognitions, saints and monastic founders in the VC then testify to the holiness and worthiness of the chief prophet, who, it is stated, is 'predestined to lead the nations to life'. This mainly hostile synodal context in turn is keyed to the malicious reaction to Christ's teaching in the synagogue, where he contemplates Isaiah and exile as he begins his public mission. To follow these intertextual motifs thus leads to the concept of universalism that hinges on the idea of an anointed pagan great king and thence to Christ himself. Among other things then, Diarmait's 'ordination' must be understood as 'anointing', since the knot of subtle allusions to Cyrus/Diarmait and to Christ/Columba/prophet/exile constitutes so intricate an authenticating constellation as to defy any thought of accidental reflection on the part of Adomnán. And to it may be added items that seem to have been of special interest to Adomnán – to the woman in distress, for example, the captive slave-girl and the widow of Sidon, and the allusion to the release of captives for which he was famous. These, too, resonate in a most peculiar way, almost incidental but not quite. It is not just prophetic intertextuality, then; a perceptible sound of the author's own career may perhaps be thought to echo, as it strikes the biblical wall to appear in his VC chapters, a justification for his own deeds mixed with those of his saintly predecessor, and associated with those of Christ and the prophets. Adomnán refers to himself a number of times in VC, but there may be more of him in the character of Columba than we can now tell. He is perhaps not entirely acting as Baruch did for Jeremiah. At any rate, it is now clear that his thought possessed a genuine subtlety and depth, and it is easy to understand why it was preferred to that of Cumméne Find, if indeed that author's book ever contained anything of comparable substance. Adomnán was a true innovator. The problem with his writing in VC, however, is always the same: in his desire to be succinct, Adomnán compresses his thought to the point where a literary excavation of textual strata is necessary in order to elucidate his full meaning.

In one sense at least, many of the principal problems attending Adomnán's views on kingship have now been explained in a way that helps to illuminate the mind and intentions of the author. However, the task is far from finished. We should thus now resume our analysis of the whole of VC III 1–5. In III 1, the first step in a sequence, Adomnán depicts Columba as having been sanctified or designated as the premier prophet with the implication, conveyed through the mantle and the angel's words, that his life's work will lie in creating a great spiritual kingdom in Ireland and Britain. That is his destiny. Chapters 2–4 are sign-texts proving this sanctification or designation in various ways. But it must now be emphasized that neither the mother's dream nor angelic comments constitute a true divine 'call'. That requires the assent and participation of the prophet himself. It can be foreshadowed by a miraculous act, as it is in VC, but the biblical pattern requires that it be completed in other ways. In earlier discussion of this 'call' phenomenon, I have provided a number of examples of its operation but a brief discussion of its more-or-less formal scriptural schema will help us to understand how Adomnán adapted it. Such is useful also because there are links between III 1, III 2 and III 5 that have not yet been explained but that cast new light on our texts, illustrating Columba's progression towards achieving his task – that is, towards becoming the prophet who carries out God's will in respect of the nations.

Although there are many varieties of call narrative, and several scholarly interpretations of the whole and its parts, the call of Jeremiah contains a full repertoire of elements or stages in succession. The case of Jeremiah has already been briefly examined, and I do so here, following the work of Habel and Aune,[70]

---

70 Habel, 'Form and significance', 297–323; Aune, *Prophecy*, pp 97–9.

53

only to illustrate the almost liturgical process of 'installation', which will then aid in describing the means by which Columba was called. It must be kept in mind, however, that there are many variations within the general scheme by which God chose to call his prophets. First comes the Divine Confrontation (1:4): 'And the word of the Lord came to me saying ...'. Next, the Commission: 'I ... made thee a prophet unto the nations'. Now, an Objection: 'And I said: ah, ah, ah, Lord God: behold, I cannot speak, for I am a child'. Yahweh provides Reassurance at this point: 'And the Lord said to me: Say not: I am a child: for thou shalt go to all that I shall send thee: and whatsoever I shall command thee, thou shalt speak'. Then, a Sign of the commissioning: 'And the Lord put forth his hand, and touched my mouth: and the Lord said to me: Behold I have given my words in thy mouth: Lo, I have set thee this day over the nations, and over kingdoms, to root up, and to pull down, and to waste, and to destroy, and to build, and to plant'.

It is believed that this schema recalls the commissioning of a messenger in the monarchies of the ancient Middle East. As many scholars have pointed out, the messenger always has a specific goal and the message a specific content. Neither is dispensable. The messenger/prophet, therefore, is commissioned for a targeted purpose. Sometimes it is the reiteration of the familiar topics of repentance and a return to right worship. At other times, as in the case of Jeremiah, the prophet is directed to the nations and to build and plant, although in this case four of the six terms employed refer to destruction. But what then was Columba's purpose and why did Adomnán choose it? The fact is that Adomnán seeks to do several things at once, all to be described in the shortest space possible. He wants to legitimate Columba's status and deeds in the strongest way that he can, but, for whatever reason, he apparently desires to ration his words. His first self-assigned task is to shape Columba as an authentic prophet of biblical stamp. Since the saint had spent the second half of his life in overseas nations, he must be depicted as recalling Jeremiah and Isaiah, who refer significantly to 'nations' and 'islands', and who are also similar in being the only two prophets 'from the womb'. The divine import of Columba's overseas 'assignment' must also be stressed, because Adomnán wants to counter the politically harmful memory of the saint as a king-opposer who was excommunicated and perhaps exiled after Cúl Dreimne. That memory may not always have been injurious, but it has become so, for whatever reason, and Adomnán hopes to propagate a new one. The theme of universalism, useful in many ways, aids to this end through its use of the shocking figure of the Yahweh-supported pagan king – 'This saith the Lord to my anointed Cyrus, whose right hand I have taken hold of, to subdue nations before his face, and to turn the backs of kings' – which arrives like a god-sent message to Adomnán. Both Diarmait's historical hostility, and Columba's perhaps unhappy departure in the wake of condemnation by allies or relatives, can all be retroactively made good, favourably turned, if the universalist theme already linking Isaiah and Columba be further applied to Diarmait and his son. The vital kingship theme from the OT – which not only ties succeeding prophets to each other, but also to both kings and pagan emperors – is thus carefully transposed to VC in order to create a greater symmetry with biblical texts. This labyrinthine manipulation of prophet–king texts in the run-up to III 5 is strong evidence of the centrality of the relationship in Adomnán's thought.

Important as Isaiah and Elijah/Elisha are, however, none can provide the full range of clear and direct power linkages that Adomnán wishes to form the background terrain to his drama. To more strongly highlight that series of connections, he requires the lightly camouflaged persona of still another prophet – Samuel, whose associations with kings encapsulate the crucial lessons. One of these lessons is that which shows the prophet as victory-bringer in battle; another is that of the prophet as royal protector and advisor; a third is that of the prophet as rightful leader of a band of prophets, the symbolic ancestors of Iona monks; a fourth lies in the fact that Samuel has been granted the power to create a new kind of extra-tribal ruler through anointing; and a fifth lies in his ability to renounce and disinherit him while then choosing a successor. Beyond these advantages lies the exalted status of Samuel, who is, far more than any of his kind in the Bible, with the possible exception of Moses, a ruler in both the spiritual and the secular spheres. He is not only the head of all prophets: he is linked to the Ark, is the guardian of the central amphictyonic cult at Shiloh and is the judge of all the land. As I Reges 7:15 puts it: 'Samuel judged Israel all the days of his life'. Thus Samuel remains all-powerful even after the creation of a king. This imperial judge/prophet combines all the qualities that an aristocratic abbot could want, and his choice as model tells us a lot about the abbot's purpose.

The influence of the Samuel model is already present in VC III 1, and continues in III 2, for while one set of Adomnán's chosen vectors leads to mantle/prophetic succession and the concept of prophet from the womb, another leads to the narrative about Samuel's mother and her commitment of her son to the priesthood. In III 1, Adomnán's focus is somewhat surprising because it is on Columba's mother rather than the saint. A second rationale for this design becomes clearer when one finds that the first chapter of I Reges also begins by centring on 'Anna',[71] the bearer of the holy man. It is worth pointing out that such a concentration enables Adomnán to avoid the topic of Columba's historical childhood and youth. A scheme of biblical patterning, in other words, enables the author to sidestep the whole issue of Cenél Conaill/Uí Néill lineage relations and the problem of Cúl Dreimne politics. That is, perhaps, not a wholly negligible reason for Adomnán's approach and may also have had some bearing on his decision to write a miracle-based rather than a chronologically oriented

---

71 I Reges 1:2–20.

vita in the first place. Be that as it may, the story of Anna is important because she is the means of creating a prophetic call. Anna was a childless wife much mocked by her husband's other wife, who was fruitful. Giving herself over to prayers, she made a vow to devote her issue to Yahweh if she could bear a son. Eventually, the priest of Shiloh, Heli or Eli, tells her that God has granted her petition. Then, while her child 'was as yet very young', Anna handed him over to Eli to be trained to minister to the Lord. At Shiloh, we are told, the little boy was 'girded with a linen ephod' and his mother made him a little coat, which she brought to him on the appointed days (1 Reges 2:18–19). Neither an ephod nor a coat can be easily compared to a mantle like that of Elisha, but it is nonetheless probable that, in pondering the deeper scriptural meaning of those lines about a prophet whom a king would later identify because of his mantle, Adomnán should recall the story of Anna providing a garment for her son in the Temple. It enables a path of narrative development that focuses on womb and prophetic succession rather than on Columba's youth and manhood. Eli the priest thus becomes the child's guardian or foster-father, as Samuel serves him as the son given to the shrine. It is this concentration that, in *VC* III 2, helps to inspire allusion to Cruithnechán, described as 'St Columba's foster-father'. Returning from church (his shrine one supposes), Cruithnechán witnesses a fiery ball of light over the child Columba's head, and recognizes it as the grace of the Holy Ghost being poured from heaven. This chapter is thus comparable to chapter 3:1–14 of 1 Reges, where the call of young Samuel is described. I shall turn to that momentarily. Notice first, however, that a very important shift has here taken place. While Adomnán obviously has the basic Samuel narrative in mind – hence the motifs of mother/son, garment and heavenly visitation – he now turns away from the canonical Samuel sequence to insert something parallel but not closely similar (although it is possible to think of this miracle as the Holy Spirit communing with a child). Why? He could easily have continued to follow the Samuel-in-the-Temple story and have 'called' Columba at this juncture, while inserting the mantle episode subsequently if he wished. One possible answer is that Columba would then have been a 'called' and 'sent' prophet from childhood, and he would thus have had God's direction when later acting against Diarmait the king at Cúl Dreimne. But that would have contradicted the touch-not-my-anointed message of *VC* I 36, where Adomnán has Columba cursing Diarmait's killer for attacking 'the king of all Ireland'. It would have undermined his own universalizing ideology of royal anointing while focusing attention on exactly that phase of Columba's life during which he had, as logic now suggests, opposed the interests of the Southern Uí Néill. On the other hand, Adomnán's desire to maintain the Samuel story-line as much as possible is indicated by the nature of the implicit Eli/Cruithnechán comparison, which, through the device of inserting the explicit presence of the Holy Spirit, is made as close to a call-narrative as Adomnán can allow himself. By delaying Columba's call to III 5, moreover, Adomnán has determined to establish the closest connection with the act of prophetic king-making. His planning for this began with III 1.

In 1 Reges 3, we are told that the 'word' of the Lord was rare in the days of Eli, and that scarcity is, apparently, because Eli behaved unjustly in not judging his corrupt sons. The boy Samuel is now sleeping 'in the Temple of the Lord, where the ark of God was'. The Lord then calls Samuel but the boy mistakes the voice for Eli's, and runs to the old priest to ask him what he wants. Eli replies that he did not call him, and tells him to return to sleep. This pattern is repeated three times until Eli understands that it is Yahweh who is speaking. He tells Samuel that if he hears a voice speaking again he is to say: 'Speak, Lord, for thy servant heareth'. Now Yaweh himself comes to stand in the Temple and repeats Samuel's name twice. He declares that He is going to make an end of the house of Eli because of the wickedness of his sons. Upon Eli's questioning next morning, Samuel reluctantly relays God's message. Thereafter, as Samuel grew, 'the Lord was with him and not one of his words fell to the ground' (1 Reges 3:19).

This call-narrative is a truncated one. It includes the Divine Confrontation and Introductory Word. The Commission seems vague or incomplete, however, because Yahweh simply says: 'Behold I do a thing in Israel and whosoever shall hear it, both his ears shall tingle'. From what follows, it seems that the Commission is simply to relay God's judgment to Eli; the message is given to Samuel but is for Eli. The Objection, Reassurance and Sign are also missing. That is not especially surprising since they are also omitted in some other calls. The 'call' is a valid one; it is simply not fully reported. 1 Reges 3:20 states that 'all Israel from Dan to Bersabee knew that Samuel was a faithful prophet of the Lord'. Samuel's tasks cannot have been fully defined by the Shiloh verses. His career does not end with Eli's fall. On the contrary, it is actually devoted to warfare and to the creation and removal of kings by the new ritual of anointing, which he describes in a book that is presented to Yahweh. In fact, it looks as if the partial Shiloh description is later amended and supplemented after Saul had established himself as king and won significant battles:

> *Et dixit Samuhel ad Saul me misit Dominus ut unguerem te in regem super populum eius Israhel nunc ergo audi vocem Domini haec dicit Dominus exercituum recensui quaecumque fecit Amalech Israheli quomodo restitit ei in via cum ascenderet de Aegypto nunc igitur vade et percute Amalech et demolire universa eius* ... (1 Reges 15:1 – 3)

> And Samuel said to Saul: The Lord *sent* [my emphasis] me to anoint thee king over his people Israel: now therefore hearken thou unto the voice of the Lord: thus saith the Lord of hosts: I have reckoned up all that Amalec hath done to Israel: how he opposed them in the way when they came up out of Egypt. Now therefore go, and smite Amalec, and utterly destroy all that he hath.

In these verses, Samuel declares that he had been 'sent' by God to be the anointer of Saul, so that it seems now clearer that this task was intended as part of his original commissioning in the Temple. In other words, the installation of kings by the new ritual of anointing is the reason he has been called to be a prophet. It is combined with directing the ruler to do battle with Israel's enemies and, as we shall see, with the guardianship and protection of rulers who, unlike the tribal leaders of the old amphictyony, have been hallowed to be kings of all Israel. Such kings are greater lords with special tasks. All these topics are also major themes in VC (along with royal inviolability). It is now increasingly obvious that Adomnán cannot have intended any omission of unction, since that would mean that the prophesied 'law' that Columba was destined to bring the nations was unbiblical and hence reprehensible.

Columba's 'call' in later life is designed to avoid the problem of Cúl Dreimne politics and is set in III 5 in direct proximity to king-making.[72]

> Of the angel of the Lord who was sent to St Columba to bid him ordain Áedán as king, and who appeared to him in a vision while he was living in the island of Hinba.

> Once, when the praiseworthy man was living in the island of Hinba, he saw one night in a mental trance an angel of the Lord sent to him. He had in his hand a glass book of the ordination of kings, which St Columba received from him, and which at the angel's bidding he began to read. In the book, the command was given him that he should ordain Áedán as king, which St Columba refused to do because he held Áedán's brother Éoganán in higher regard. Whereupon the angel reached out and struck the saint with a whip, the scar from which remained with him for the rest of his life. Then the angel addressed him sternly: 'Know then as a certain truth, I am sent to you by God with the glass book in order that you should ordain Áedán to the kingship according to the words you have read in it. But if you refuse to obey this command, I shall strike you again'.

> In this way, the angel of the Lord appeared to St Columba on three successive nights, each time having the same glass book, and each time making the same

---

72 *De angelo domini qui ad sanctum Columbam in Hinba commorantem insula per visum apparuit, misus ut Aidanum in regem ordinaret.*

ALIO IN TEMPORE, cum vir praedicabilis in Hinba commoraretur insula, quadam nocte in extasi mentis angelum domini ad sé misum vidit, qui in manu vitreum ordinationis regum habebat librum. Quem cum vir venerandus de manu angeli accipisset ab eo jusus legere coepit. Qui cum secundum quod ei in libro erat commendatum Aidanum in regem ordinare recussaret, quia magis Iogenanum fratrem ejus dilegeret, subito angelus extendens manum sanctum percussit flagillo, cujus livorosum in ejus latere vestigium omnibus suae diebus permansit vitae. Hocque intulit verbum: 'Pro certo scias' inquiens, 'quia ad té a deo misus sum cum vitreo libro, ut juxta verba quae in eo legisti Aidanum in regnum ordines. Quod si obsecundare huic nolueris jusioni, percutiam te iterato'.

Hic itaque angelus domini cum per tris contenuas noctes eundem in manu vitreum habens codicem apparuisset, eademque domini jusa de regis ejusdem ordinatione commendasset, sanctus verbo obsequtus domini ad Iovam transnavigavit insulam, ibidemque Aidanum hisdem adventantem diebus in regem sicut erat jusus ordinavit. Et inter ordinationis verba de filiis et nepotibus pronepotibusque ejus futura profetizavit, inponensque manum super caput ejus ordinans benedixit.

demand that he should ordain Áedán as king. The holy man obeyed the word of the Lord and sailed from Hinba to Iona, where Áedán had arrived at this time, and he ordained him king in accordance with the Lord's command. As he was performing the ordination, St Columba also prophesied the future of Áedán's sons and grandsons and great-grandsons, then he laid his hand on Áedán's head in ordination and blessed him.

Like that of Samuel, this call occurs at night when Columba is asleep to the world in *extasi mentis*. Like Samuel also the message must be repeatedly stated before it is carried out. The Divine Confrontation is with an angel sent by God, as was the case with the warrior prophet Gideon. The Introductory Word is described in the angel's bidding that Columba read from the book, and the Commission in the command that he should ordain Áedán as king. Like Ezekiel, he appears to have been given a book that is not returned, but unlike that prophet, he does not have to eat it. Columba's initial unwillingness to bow to God's will parallels the Objections of several prophets, like Jeremiah or Moses (Ex 3:11, 4:10), for example. Jeremiah, that other 'womb' prophet, expressed his objections throughout his life and would berate God because he had overpowered him. Columba, on the other hand, carries it as far as a lashing, and his Reassurance lies only in the angel's emphasis that he should 'know then as a certain truth', that I am sent to you by God with a glass book. In a peculiar way, these objections are a sign of Columba's future strength as a prophet. Like a wild animal whose taming requires great effort by his master, the effort is eventually repaid by a stronger devotion. According to Habel's analysis of the call narratives, this is the assertion of the prophetic 'I', which 'becomes an important part of the prophet's role'.[73] Moses, for example, chides God, argues with Him and demands to see His face. God will meet him half way because his very stubbornness is an aspect of his usefulness as a messenger (Ex 33:12–23). Adomnán has accepted this inference of the greater the trouble, the greater the value. And God does leave his Sign on Columba, even more than on Ezekiel, whose mouth had been touched with a live coal by an angel. For his part, the saint gets a tangible scar from the angel's whip, a scar that 'remained with him for the rest of his life'.

The first half of *VC* III 5 is thus most fully understandable as Adomnán's version of a scriptural call narrative designed to equate Columba with an outstanding king-making prophet and to vindicate the implications of the previous four chapters of his sequence. Even the otherwise puzzling scar and book references are explainable in this context. The former belongs to the legitimating sign aspect of the call. Even though the behaviour of the saint (and the angel) is extreme, it is actually a way of indicating Columba's high status in God's eyes and such behaviour, although admittedly less radical, does have significant precedents in the calls and colloquies of major prophets. Adomnán

73 Habel, 'Form and significance', 308.

certainly viewed it in this light, since otherwise he would not have highlighted the episode in such a prominent way in his work. Books, too, occupy a prominent place in the calls and lives of some of the prophets; indeed a number are called 'the writing prophets' by scholars. In the present case, the book is especially significant because Samuel had written one about Saul's installation, and because the book is here coupled with motifs from Samuel's 'call' and with God's command that he anoint the first Hebrew king.[74] The entire pattern is internally consistent and meant to be suggested in Áedán's anointing, the first such

---

74 David Woods argues otherwise in 'Four notes on Adomnán's *Vita Columbae*', *Peritia*, 16 (2002), 40–67 at 62–7. I should like to thank the author for sending me an offprint of this work on publication. It must be stressed that no evidence exists to demonstrate that Adomnán actually follows Cumméne Find's account of any earlier sacring, Áedán's or anyone else's. Assuming that Dorbbéne is simply copying and not paraphrasing or modifying his excerpt – a large and unprovable assumption – it does not follow that Cumméne's work referred to an *ordinatio* rather than, say, a blessing or prophecy that might perhaps have alluded to a future kingship for Áedán. And if perchance Cumméne did refer to such, it need not have been to the same type of ritual as in III 5. Since Adomnán wrote in a different time and politico-theological context, it is probable that he would have treated any such event differently. One must not forget that Adomnán decided to write a *new* book about Columba, that he deliberately chose to exclude the information in the fragment, and that Dorbbéne thus acted against his will when he inserted it. Indeed, Woods finds an inconsistency between III 5 and the excerpt and concludes that it 'does not support the whole of Adomnán's account of the ordination by Columba of Áedán'. I add that a second possible inconsistency lies in the fact that the fragment refers to an alliance with the sons and grandsons of Áedán and claims that it exists because of the scourging that Columba endured for Áedán's sake. An angel is thus a common factor. According to Adomnán's text, however, Columba endured the scourging for Éoganán's sake and not for his brother. That is a strange basis for an alliance with the descendants of Áedán. But Adomnán resolutely ignores all of this material. He does so in order to concentrate wholly on the Columba–angel interaction and the ordination that follows it. It is thus obvious that these were the things most important to him. Because Adomnán was creating a new narrative in which older details or statements had to be abandoned, any possible deductions from Cumméne are irrelevant to his plans in his *vita*. Woods is wide of the mark when he argues that Samuel's book containing the *legem regni* does not reflect the process of the prophet's king-making and thus would not also have been reflected in the words of the *liber vitreus*. In order to do so, he must ignore demonstrations that Adomnán draws on the figure of Samuel for his descriptions. He must also ignore the key corresponding fact that 1 Reges 10 describes the *first* creation of a Hebrew king through the innovation of prophetic anointing. Samuel calls an assembly of the people to witness his new procedure and there is no break between his descriptions and his act of writing them into law (1 Reges 10:17–25). Since, moreover, prophets thereafter continued to anoint kings, it is difficult to suppose that such was not part of the law that Samuel the judge created. Nor does Woods face up to the striking uniqueness in Adomnán's actions. Since the Iona ritual is the first prophetic king-making in the islands, how did Columba know what to do? How did he know how a Christian prophet goes about creating a king? Adomnán shows himself to be perfectly aware of the problem and solves it by having the angel command Columba to ordain and then to declare that he must do it according to the words in the book *ut juxta quae in eo legisti Aidanum in regnum ordines*. The remainder of Woods's essay is based on guesswork treated as fact. He is sure, for example, that the 'words' of the glass book actually mean that a list of 'names' was contained in it. Likewise, he is sure that Cumméne is Adomnán's 'main source'. The key question, he holds, is whether Adomnán necessarily understood the term *ordinatio* 'in the manner that Cumméne had originally intended'. He goes on to suggest how it was that Adomnán had misunderstood the way in which Cumméne had 'originally' employed the term. Other intuitions follow. Sadly, this is no more than speculation about a book that Adomnán worked hard to replace.

reported act in the Iro-British sphere. Adomnán's deep interest in reinforcing Columba's links with Samuel is then shown by what follows in the latter part of III 5. As I have written about this matter at some length elsewhere,[75] I will not now burden the reader with repetition. Suffice it to say that the peculiar site, timing and actions of the king-making are all precisely crafted to recall the legitimating model behaviour of Samuel and Saul in I Reges 9–10. It is thus deliberately and particularly for the making of kings according to divine ordinance that Columba has been 'called' and 'sent' like an OT prophet to the 'isles of ocean'.

A mirror for a guardian of princes

It insufficient to connect only III 1–5 together with I 9, 14, and 36 to the figure of Samuel and to the lessons drawn from the *Books of Kings*. Since I have now demonstrated that Adomnán chose to directly link God's 'call' to Columba with the task of king-making, it is not unlikely that other aspects of his relations with Irish, Dál Riata and Northumbrian rulers or would-be rulers would share in the same biblical framework. That is due to the overarching nature of the concept of the 'called' and 'sent' prophet who is thereby bound to his lifelong particular message. A preliminary investigation indicates that such is indeed the case and it casts a new light on Adomnán's construction of the character of his prophet and on all of the kingship material in *VC* (with perhaps the partial exclusion of Pictish examples).[76] I 7–8 and I 9–15 are the chapters that are most clearly implicated. Adomnán had already grouped them together in his chapter headings to his first book. I 7–8 are called *Profetationes ejus de bellis* and I 9–15 are together entitled *De regibus*. It seems reasonable to consider them in concert, however, since they follow each other in the text and since the battles all involve kings. Likewise, I 1 must be associated with them since it is called a 'summary' chapter, which focuses on both topics, kings and battles, as well as the 'spirit of prophecy' and particularly Columba's powers in their regard. In what follows, then, I shall look to these chapters in particular while pausing occasionally to point to some of the ways in which they complement or relate to the material on Áedán, Diarmait and especially the themes of royal unction and succession.

What is it that Columba – more than any other saint – can do for kings? That is the question that Adomnán is primarily and most anxiously eager to answer in these episodes. He already moves to do so in I 1, where he has Columba promise rulers victory in battle when they call upon him. This ability of the saint's is the result of a unique grant of power by God:

---

75 Enright, *Iona, Tara and Soissons.*   76 On which, see now James E. Fraser, 'Adomnán, Cumméne Ailbe and the Picts', *Peritia*, 17–18 (2003–4), 183–98.

> Some kings were conquered in the terrifying crash of battle and others emerged victorious according to what Columba asked of God by the power of prayer. God who honours all saints gave this special privilege to him as to a mighty and triumphant champion, and it remained as true after he quit the flesh as it had been in this present life. (I 1)

This special privilege, *hoc tale praevilegium*, is mentioned again in the immediately following sentence, where Adomnán provides an example of 'this special honour' granted to Columba by the Almighty from heaven. The saint's chosen recipient is king Oswald of Northumbria on the day before his battle against Cadwallon, 'the most powerful king of the Britons'.[77] Columba appeared to the king in a vision so that he seemed to be an angelic giant, so tall that his head touched the clouds and wearing a shining robe that covered all except one corner of the king's camp. 'The blessed man revealed his name to the king and gave him these words of encouragement, the same the Lord spoke to Joshua, saying, "Be strong and act manfully. Behold, I will be with thee"'. The saint then gave directions to the king, telling him to leave his camp at night, 'for the Lord has granted me that at this time your foes shall be put to flight and Cadwallon your enemy shall be delivered into your hands and you shall return victorious after battle and reign happily'. Oswald listened carefully and 'just as he had been told in the vision', he marched forth from his camp with a small force against many thousands. 'A happy and easy victory was given him by the Lord'. Cadwallon was killed in the battle; Oswald returned as victor 'and was afterwards ordained by God as emperor of all Britain'.

The two chapters that Adomnán dedicates to battle prophecies then take up the same theme. I 7 reads like a second introduction to the subject. It is entitled 'A prophecy of the saint about the crash of battles far away':

> Two years after the Battle of Cúl Drebene, when the holy man first set sail from Ireland to be a pilgrim, it happened one day that, at the very hour when the battle Móin Daire Lothair was fought in Ireland, the saint gave a full account of it in Britain, in the presence of king Conall mac Comgaill. He described the battle and named the kings to whom the Lord gave victory, Ainmire mac Sétnae and the two sons of Mac Ercae, Domnall and Forgus. Likewise, he prophesied of a king of the Cruithni called Eochaid Laib, who was defeated but escaped in a chariot.

In this chapter, Adomnán is making the implicit claim that Columba is sensitized even to faraway battles, knows the identity of the participants, can discern which of them receives the divine grant of victory and can even 'prophesy' the way in which one defeated ruler leaves the field. It is thus a variation and expansion of the message of I 1 about the saint's power to win battles even when a small force

---

77 Clare Stancliffe, 'Oswald, most holy and most victorious king of the Northumbrians' in Clare Stancliffe and Eric Cambridge (eds), *Oswald: Northumbrian king to European saint* (Stamford, CT,

confronts a much larger one. It is designed to show that Columba's abilities cross all geographical and temporal bounds, and include a full reservoir of mantic knowledge about royal affairs that make him the perennial sage of dynastic conflict, the master of kings at war. It is thus an appropriately chosen introduction to the group of prince chapters that follow and expand Columba's portrait in other ways. I 8 is different only in detail. It describes king Áedán's battle with the Miathi, followed by Columba's prophecy about the king's sons in which Eochaid Buide is chosen and blessed. In I 8, the saint becomes supernaturally aware of the events of the battle. He calls the brethren together and they kneel to 'pray fervently to the Lord for this people and for king Áedán, for even now they are going into battle'. Columba is then also aware when the battle is won, and knows that it is not a happy victory since many of Áedán's men were killed 'as the saint had also prophesied'.

One other nearby chapter, I 12, which belongs to the cluster of princes group (I 9–15), may perhaps also be pressed for evidence here, since it carries the same overall message only now turned negatively. While one day walking through a rough and rocky district, Columba heard his companions conversing about the affairs of two Irish kings. He turned to them and said: 'My dear sons, why do you gossip idly about these kings? For both of those you mention were recently killed by their enemies, and their heads cut off. Sailors will arrive today from Ireland and tell you this'. On that day, 'the saint's prophecy about the dead kings was fulfiled'. Adomnán here proclaims a stark lesson that is the obverse of the victorious battle stories mentioned earlier. The saint is still pictured as omnisciently aware of the affairs of rulers, but unless apparently they have done him reverence, they are shown to be of no consequence. He refers to them dismissively and they are defeated and decapitated in battle – they die, in other words, under the exact conditions where Columba possesses the permanent and unique supernatural power to save their lives and grant them victory. There can be no doubt of Adomnán's intent here, since this chapter stands out among the princes' cluster where, as we shall see later, Adomnán takes pains to show Columba as aiding those that he can prophetically sense are willing to honour and obey him. However, let us first deal with this issue of warfare and prophetic patronage.

First-time readers of VC are almost always struck by Adomnán's stress on Columba as a victory-bringer in battle, a link established immediately in the $vita$ where the power is identified as a 'special privilege' granted to 'a mighty and triumphant champion'. Scholars, on the other hand, generally seem not to have viewed this saint/battle-champion connection as a crux requiring any special explanation. They are often familiar with the theme from later texts, those relating to Columba's $Cathach$ for example,[78] and repeated readings of the $vita$

1995), pp 33–84.   78 On which, see Raghnall Ó Floinn, 'Insignia Columbae I' in Bourke (ed.), $Studies in the cult of St Columba$, pp 136–41.

63

can easily cause one to lose the sense of wonder and make it seem commonplace. Adomnán's opinion is emphatically to the contrary; he explicitly presents the power as unique. It separates Columba from all other saints and marks him as the prophet of warfare, the existential sphere of kings. This power has a precise source in the Bible, however. It derives from 1 Reges and the career of the prophet Samuel.

At the beginning of Samuel's career is God's decision that the priesthood had become corrupt. Yahweh thus declares: 'And I will raise me up a faithful priest, who shall do according to my heart, and my soul, and I will build him a faithful house, and he shall walk all days before my anointed' (1 Reges 2:35). The Lord then 'calls' Samuel to serve in a way, as I have already shown, that forms part of the model for his 'call' to Columba to ordain Áedán. 'And all Israel from Dan to Bersabee, knew that Samuel was a faithful prophet of the Lord' (3:20). At precisely that time, the Israelites were greatly afflicted by the Philistines and grieved at their bad treatment and serious military defeats. Samuel spoke to a gathering of the people and said that if they put aside their false gods to serve the Lord alone, 'he will deliver you out of the hands of the Philistines' (7:3). He then began to pray and to offer sacrifice (7:5, 9). Learning of this gathering, the Philistines decided to attack it:

> the Philistines began the battle against Israel: but the Lord thundered with a great thunder on that day upon the Philistines, and terrified them, and they were overthrown before the face of Israel. And the men of Israel going out of Masphath pursued after the Philistines, and made slaughter of them till they came under Bethchar. ... And the Philistines were humbled and they did not come any more into the borders of Israel. And the hand of the Lord was against the Philistines all the days of Samuel. ... And Samuel judged Israel all the days of his life. (7:10–15)

In 7:8, the Israelites had said to Samuel: 'Cease not to cry to the Lord our God for us that he may save us out of the hand of the Philistines'. As the succeeding verses demonstrate, Samuel had answered their petitions and in doing so had shown himself to be the prophet and judge who could gain victories from God. He had become a dependable battle-helper for his people. But they also wanted more than this and begged Samuel to 'make us a king, to judge us, as all nations have'. Samuel opposed this desire but in the end acceded to God's order to 'hearken to their voice, and make them a king' (8:22). Thereafter is described Saul's search for his father's lost asses, which unknowingly brings him to the holy man. The Lord announces his coming to the prophet:

> Tomorrow about this same hour I will send thee a man of the land of Benjamin, and thou shalt anoint him to be ruler over my people Israel: and he shall save my people out of the hand of the Philistines: for I have looked down upon my people, because their cry is come to me. (9:16)

Saul then comes looking for 'the house of the seer'. On the following day, Samuel makes him king:

> And Samuel took a little vial of oil, and poured it upon his head, and kissed him and said: Behold, the Lord hath anointed thee to be prince over his inheritance, and thou shalt deliver his people out of the hands of their enemies, that are round about them. And this shalt be a sign unto thee, that God hath anointed thee to be prince. (10:1)

Not long after that, Saul begins his career by slaying the Ammonites 'until the day grew hot, and the rest were scattered, so that two of them were not left together' (11:11).

Several points require emphasis. First is a recognition of the conception that the fact of being a prophet of Samuel's type is here directly and causally linked to the art of gaining victories in battles. When Samuel prays for this, God answers him. Adomnán's claim of this 'special privilege' in a chapter that also describes Columba's coming to enjoy the 'spirit of prophecy' is thus a deliberate act of patterning to an existent model. It is neither Adomnán's conception, nor a native Irish one: it is biblical. A battle-prophet already exists in the OT. Moreover, when the Israelites request Samuel to give them a king, it is not simply to judge them but in order that their king would 'go out before us, and fight our battles for us' (8:20). And when the Lord ordered Samuel to anoint Saul, it was done so that 'he shall save my people out of the hands of the Philistines'. This express military rationale occurs again when the anointing takes place and Saul is told that defeats of the enemies round about shall be in themselves a sign to him of his proper status. This complements the fact that Adomnán is careful to provide a victory for Áedán among his cluster of princes (I 8). The motif of victory-bringer, the intervention of the 'called' prophet, and the unction that the prophet performs are all links in the same identical chain. They belong within the same structure. Adomnán understood them in that light, and to seek to separate them is to misinterpret his text.

Additional evidence strengthens the argument. Although the Oswald episode in I 1, for example, has not hitherto been examined from this perspective, it is, I suggest, one that well encapsulates Adomnán's intentions. Let us look to it within the context of his ideal biblical model. In I Reges 7, Samuel the judge answers his people's call for help in battle by praying for them. As a condition for delivery from the Philistines, they have to give up their pagan practices. And so 'the children of Israel put away Baalim and Astaroth, and served the Lord only'. Even after their delivery, however, and much to Samuel's chagrin, they persist in a clamour, an 'evil' desire, that he give them a king. The prophet did so only reluctantly because, as Yahweh had wished, the prophet's guidance alone should have been sufficient. In his ire, Samuel punished them by calling down a storm of thunder and rain, so that 'you shall know and see that you yourselves

65

have done a great evil in the sight of the Lord, in desiring a king over you' (12:17). The frightened people besought Samuel to beg the Lord's forgiveness on their behalf. Samuel relented and blessed them. He declared that in spite of their sin in seeking a king, he would not 'cease to pray for you, and I will teach you the good and right way' (12:23). This is a crucial passage because it shows that Samuel (who has his own corrupt sons to support) means to maintain his judge's power regardless of the popular will. Yahweh can tolerate a king, but it is not what he really wants. One can only feel sympathy for Saul, a man 'of the least tribe of Israel', and his kindred 'the least among all the families of the tribe of Benjamin' (9:21). He is about to become a victim. If Saul had ever laboured under the impression that he could lead independently of the prophet, he was sadly mistaken. Samuel aims to keep him on a leash and docile. Although Saul did his honest best and 'slew the Ammonites until the day grew hot', he was always constrained by the power of he who possessed the only acceptable access to the divine will. One example refers to the Philistines. Despite the new king's exertions they remained in the ascendant. While preparing for a great battle against them, Samuel and Saul hatched a plan in which the former agreed to meet the king at the cultic site of Galgal, where the prophet would offer a holocaust to the Lord. Saul gathered a force in the meantime and waited the appointed seven days for Samuel. The problem was that the size of the Philistine army of over 36,000 men was constantly growing while Saul's much smaller army was losing courage, so that 'the people slipt away from him' (13:8). 'And Samuel came not to Galgal'. In the end, forced by necessity because of declining numbers, Saul offered the holocaust alone only to see Samuel appear thereafter. Saul courteously 'went forth to meet him and salute him' and tried to explain that because of defections and Samuel's delay, he had no choice but to offer the necessary sacrifice. The prophet offered no explanation for his delay but immediately decreed that the Lord had removed Saul from his kingship and chosen another:

> Thou hast done foolishly, and hast not kept the commandments of the Lord thy God, which he commanded thee. And if thou hadst not done thus, the Lord would now have established thy kingdom over Israel for ever. But thy kingdom shall not continue. The Lord hath sought him a man according to his own heart: and him hath the Lord commanded to be prince over his people, because thou hast not observed that which the Lord commanded. (13:13–14)

In this story of Saul waiting with his men for battle with the Philistines, one finds the origin of the Oswald episode and the popular conversion that accompanies it in *VC* I 1. Appearing first in that narration is the inclusion of the victory-bringing prophet motif, which derives from Samuel's prayers for victory over Israel's enemies in 1 Reges 7. In that chapter it is joined to a religious reformation and a cessation of Jewish paganism. Adomnán connects both themes

66

to his anecdote about Oswald, who, like Saul against the Philistines, faces a much superior force in Cadwallon's British army, but finds that his whole people are strengthened by Columba's words: they 'promised that after their return from battle they would accept the faith and receive baptism. For up to that time the whole of England was darkened by the shadow of heathendom and ignorance'. Despite his much inferior force, Oswald then wins 'a happy and easy victory' given him by the Lord. Unlike Saul, he has listened to God's commands as relayed by his prophet. And that is decisive. It is actually Oswald's obedience, his surrender of will to the saint, that is crucial. Hence in the *VC*, although it is easy to read over it too quickly, Columba adds the unusual detail that Oswald shall 'this coming night go out from your camp into battle'. It is 'at this time', declares the saint, that the Lord will grant victory. The time requirement is mentioned in a third instance, when the reader is told that on 'that same night, just as he had been told in the vision' Oswald marched out with his small force. In its own way, this command for an extraordinary night-time going into battle is just as noteworthy as the fixed time for Saul's meeting with Samuel. It establishes a condition of adherence to the will of the prophet as a criterion for throne-worthiness. But it is only when one learns to compare the *VC* story with that in 1 Reges that one is able to determine that such is the emphasis desired by Adomnán. Otherwise the chronological repetition in the text could easily seem to be a stylistic detail or iteration alone. Kingship is in Samuel's gift, however, and in 1 Reges it is now to be given to another whom the Lord has chosen. In *VC*, on the other hand, it becomes a statement that, after the battle, Oswald was 'ordained by God as emperor of all Britain'. Adomnán has here adjusted the biblical version in order to give it the positive spin that he desires but, as his use of the OT time motif shows, he remains true to the principle of Samuel's power: the voice of the prophet is the voice of God, and kingship is won or lost depending upon the leader's attention to it. In this famous *VC* anecdote, therefore, Adomnán has again drawn his inspiration from 1 Reges. He has deliberately done so because Samuel's behaviour is his model. It is a model that enables him to integrate an abandonment of paganism with a prophet's battle-championship while adding a notable victory against great odds with the prophetic privilege of naming (or un-naming) a prominent ruler. While some differences obviously exist in the two accounts compared, these cannot obscure the presence of the recognizable pattern.

Despite the instructive outlining of parallels, however, a possible objection to my conclusions might lie in the fact of their alleged generality, i.e. that the idea of a holy man promising a leader victory and then hailing him as king thereafter, or unkinging him if he behaves wrongly, is not an unusual enough set of motif to enable the view that they arise from a single source. They might actually be the purely original invention of the hagiographer. That cannot be a plausible objection in the case of the Oswald episode because the five identifiable related motifs – a popular conversion, a victory against great odds, a prophetic victory-bringer, an established time constraint and a real or apparent granting or ungranting of kingship – are too uncommon when all appear together. In addition, such possible criticism fails because other kingship references in VC are again tied to the behaviour of the prophet Samuel, in the cases of Áedán and Diarmait mac Cerbaill, for example. The Oswald episode can thus now be recognized as one strand in Adomnán's network of deliberately constructed kingship interventions based on the Samuel/Saul/Cyrus model and affecting rulers who are presented in VC as specially 'ordained'. The concept of *ordinatio* thus demonstrably lies at the centre of Adomnán's thinking about the most powerful kings. In applying it, he may also have had in mind the fact that Saul's creation as king replaced an older system of rule, that Israel was subsequently divided into more than one kingdom, and that God had anointed Cyrus as the greatest of over-kings. This borrowed theme of the prophetic battle-champion can also be applied to other rulers who are not ordained, however, as we have also seen.

This finding in the Oswald case is important for any overall interpretation of Adomnán's intentions in VC. But what about the theme of obedience to the prophet, which I have stressed in the explication above? Is that too 'political' a view of the circumstance, as some scholars might see it? Consider anew, from this viewpoint, another adaptation (as I maintain) – the case of Áed Sláine (114) in which Columba warns this man whom God has 'predestined' for the 'kingship of all Ireland' that he will lose this divinely granted prerogative if he commits the sin of family murder.[79] In this brief chapter, capable of several different interpretations because its purpose is not explicitly declared, it is only possible to understand Adomnán's full meaning if one applies the lesson of the Samuel/Saul paradigm. Examine it without such reference and it could be simply a case of an inspired holy man providing a warning, something that any saint might do for a prince. It then floats like a leaf in a shallow pond along with other apparently unrelated stories about kings. Apply the Samuel model, however, and it becomes clear that Adomnán's true message is only partly about a warning against family bloodshed. It is rather, or is in addition, a pointed illustration of the need for obedience to the prophet. It shows that disaster comes to kings who ignore his pressing advice. *Mutatis mutandis*, Áed Sláine has here become the embodiment of the untrusting and impatient side of Saul, that part which acts independently of the prophet's will and is thus essentially disobedient. Áed fails his glorious destiny, despite being a son of the ordained king of all Ireland, because he refuses to comply with Columba's wishes, and is thus comparable to Saul, who disobeys Samuel and undermines his own future: 'And if thou hadst not done thus, the Lord would now have established thy kingdom over Israel for

---

79 Ailbhe MacShamhráin and Paul Byrne, 'Prosopography 1: kings named in *Baile Chuinn Chétchathaig* and *The Airgíalla charter poem*' in Bhreathnach (ed.), *Kingship and landscape*, pp 159–225 at pp 182–4.

ever. But thy kingdom shall not continue'. The same model of Samuel's prophetic oversight is drawn upon. Whereas it is God's prerogative to predestine to kingship or empire, Columba is God's agent in the matter and hence, like Samuel when he operated in the world, he is the sole legitimate judge of a prince's candidacy or tenure. Oswald is a suitable emperor because he follows Columba's directions exactly; Eochaid Buide will be a suitable over-king because he shows his future character when he runs to Columba's arms and leans on his bosom. Áed Sláine, on the other hand, will not listen, and thus he is like Saul, who can rule only in a limited way after his disobedience. In none of these examples is it explicitly stated that the king must listen to the Iona abbot, but that stricture is intended as an inherent aspect of the message. It is later employed by Dorbbéne through his insert in III 5.[80] To explain why this is the case is not to overemphasize a political interpretation but to recognize and clarify the nature of the text. Is it reasonable to suppose that Adomnán chose to depict Columba's dealings with kings frequently because the issue of relative authority was only a secondary issue in his thought?

Adomnán's concern to show a Columban presence at royal succession is amply demonstrated by the Áed Sláine and Eochaid Buide interventions, one favourable and one monitory. It is essential to note that, in such cases, Columba is continuing to act according to the OT principle that a prophet is to be an assayer of princes. As in the citation above from Jer 6:27–30, he acts as the 'strong trier' set by God who is to 'prove' the nature of people and princes in order to establish whether they are like brass or iron or 'reprobate silver'. Like the smith who makes trial of royal sons in the Tara kingship mythos, he tests them to know if the bellows have failed and if the founder has melted in vain. The fire that surrounds the smith of truth will never be far from such a prophetic refiner of sons (see also Mal 3:2–3). Adomnán has here made a dual adaptation, drawing on both native tradition and the Bible. Such examples are interesting for another reason, however, and both appear in that section to which Adomnán gives a somewhat distinctive tone through his assigning it the title *De regibus*. The right question to begin an analysis of these chapters continues to be: what is it that Columba alone can do for kings? One answer is that he can assess their sons; another, as we shall see, continues to be tied to the unction paradigm.

I 9 begins with Columba's 'prophecy about king Áedán's sons': 'Once, before the battle we have just mentioned, the saint questioned king Áedán about a successor to the kingdom'. When the king answered that he did not know who his successor would be, the saint explained the future to him, saying that the three sons that he thought most likely would all be slaughtered by enemies in

---

80 *VC*, pp 474–6. The purpose of the excerpt is an insistence on politico–military alliance. It probably has several sources, but one of them is likely to be the bond established between the bestower and receiver of a sacramental act. See Arnold Angenendt, *Kaiserherrschaft und Königstaufe* (Berlin, 1984), pp 91–165.

battle. 'But if you have other, younger sons, let them now come to me. The one whom the Lord has chosen will run directly to my arms'. They were duly called in 'as the saint instructed', and the little boy Eochaid Buide went immediately and 'leant on the saint's bosom'. Columba 'kissed and blessed him' and told Áedán that 'this one will survive to be king after you, and his sons will be kings after him'. The following chapter, I 10, touches on a similar succession question. It concerns Domnall mac Áedo, a relative of the saint and a future king of Cenél Conaill. At his death in 642, the Annals of Ulster will call him 'king of Ireland'.[81] While 'still a boy', Domnall's foster-parents had brought him to Columba, who was attending the convention at Druim Cett.[82] He was asked to bless the boy, which he did, after he had 'looked at the boy for a while'. 'As soon as he had blessed the boy', the saint declared: 'this boy will outlive all his brothers and be a famous king. He will never be handed over to his enemies but will die at home in his bed, in a peaceful old age, in the friendly presence of his household'.

Of the following three chapters, I 11–13, two depict Columba both blessing and comforting young aristocrats, future kings then highly vulnerable and enduring dismally hard fates, while the third speaks slightingly of two rulers who die in battle. I 11, also set at Druim Cett, refers to Scandlán mac Colmáin, who is apparently that ruler who became king of Osraige and is called Scandlán Mór in *Chronicon Scotorum* s.a. 641. At this time, he is a hostage held publicly in chains by Áed mac Ainmirech, a close relation of Columba's and a king of Cenél Conaill and Tara. The saint 'went to him blessed him and comforted him', saying

> My son, do not be sad; rather be happy and of good comfort. For king Áed, by whom you are held in irons, will die before you, and though you spend some time in exile, you will afterwards be king over your own people for thirty years. Then you will again be a fugitive from your kingdom and for some days live in exile. Afterwards, your people will recall you, and you will be king once more for three short seasons.

I 12 is that chapter already cited in which Columba speaks slightingly of two kings of Cenél nEogain whom he knows to be recently defeated in battle and decapitated. In I 13, the saint offers solace and hope to Oengus mac Áedo Commain, nicknamed Brónbachal, future king of Cenél Coirpri. Driven out of his country, he came as an exile to Iona. Columba 'blessed him and spoke from his holy heart these words of prophecy':

---

81 AU2 642.1: *regis Hibernie.*   82 The purpose of this meeting was probably the forging of an alliance between Áed mac Ainmerech of Cenél Conaill and Áedán mac Gabráin of Dál Riata. Columba seems to have functioned as a mediator: Sharpe, *Adomnán*, pp 270–3, nn 84–8; Francis John Byrne, 'The Ireland of St Columba', *Historical Studies*, 5 (1965), 37–58.

This young man will remain alive when his brothers are dead, and for a long time will be king in his country. His enemies will fall before him, and he will never be delivered into their hands. He will die in peace, an old man, with his friends around him.

I 14 is 'the blessed man's prophecy about king Diarmait's son, called in Irish Áed Sláine'. Although Áed should succeed his father as king of all Ireland, he is warned of the possible loss of his prerogative. I 15 is a prophecy about king Rhydderch of Dumbarton, who appears to be an established ruler and 'a friend of the saint'. He has been made anxious by attacks on him, and 'wanted to learn whether he should be slaughtered by his enemies or not'. Columba declares that 'he will never be delivered into enemies' hands but he will die at home on his own pillow'.

What is the purpose of this special section about kings? Several observations seem pertinent. Most immediate is the point that, contrary to appearances, this is not a random selection of miracles about rulers whose only commonality is royalty provided with prophecy, although it must be said that Adomnán's manner of dividing the *vita* encourages that view among modern readers. Rather, the author has here presented a set of carefully designed vignettes in which he focuses on typical events in the dangerously unpredictable life-cycle of princes, on the ups and downs of fortune's wheel, in order to demonstrate that Columba is the prophet who is specially called to minister to kings, or future kings, at all points in their span of life. Columba can remove that element of unpredictability through his prophecy, and he can encourage and strengthen those whom he trusts to support his community. Eochaid Buide, for example, is a happy boy at home. The saint provides an invaluable service to his father by informing him of his son's future succession, and he then strengthens the boy with his blessing. Domnall mac Áedo, a boy in fosterage, receives a similarly happy treatment. Here, too, the focus is on a statement of royal succession joined to a promise of fame and happy old age. Evidently, boys can be brought to the saint for his judgment at any time. Scandlán mac Colmáin cannot, however, because he is a boy held in irons as a hostage. And so the saint goes to him. He blesses and comforts him and provides a detailed prophecy of a mostly happy future life and an enduring kingship. He, too, will succeed to a throne. The same fate awaits Oengus Brónbachal, who is a 'young man'. When he and his two brothers come in exile to the saint, he is welcomed to a refuge, blessed and heartened. He receives a prophecy that he will be king of his country, that his enemies will be defeated, that they will never capture him and that he will die an old man among friends. Áed Sláine is an exception to the general stance of affirmation. His chapter also concerns royal succession but it is a contingent case. Like the others, this young man receives a vital service in Columba's prophecy, which, in addition, provides an explicit description of what to avoid doing in order to maintain God's plan for his glorious future. But Áed undervalues the gift and thus never achieves the prize. The saint has well understood this lack of respect for his counsel, since he bestows no blessing. King Rhydderch, on the other hand, is a friend of the saint and appears to be a well-established king, and perhaps thus a mature man. He, too, receives a prophetic present, which indicates that it is not just a thing given to boys and the young. His anxiety seems to be that of an older man, and he gets the future that would please him. I 12 is that chapter which delivers the harsh message of rejection; it exemplifies the case of those kings for whom the saint has no regard.

I 9–15 is thus a companion piece to I 1, 7–8, which answers the question as to what Columba can do for kings in battle. But I 9–15 switches the emphasis to a wider perspective, to one that explores the vicissitudes of a royal career through boyhood, young manhood and maturity: in other words, throughout life. It seeks to cover the enduring problems – captivity, hostageship, opposition from relatives, exile, attacks from enemies and the worry of weakness as one grows old. It shows by example how the saint can counter these – by prophecy and blessing, which strengthens the will and health of those wavering or despairing; through words of comfort; through providing a refuge in his community; and through his good counsel that can overcome obstacles. These chapters are essentially a promise of care, nurture and benefit for those in alliance with Iona, and contrariwise, as in I 14 and I 12, a declaration of the loss of kingship to be expected when trust is partial or alliance wanting. The battle-champion motif no longer appears in I 9–15 because it no longer requires stressing; it is now assumed to be a permanent part of Iona's benefits package.[83] Its place is taken by prophecy and blessing, a combination that seems to have been part of king-making in pre-Christian times.[84] When reinforced with the certainty of

---

83 Despite its association with the insurance industry, the phrase is a useful one. I borrow it from Thomas Owen Clancy, 'King-making and images of kingship in medieval Gaelic literature' in Richard Welander, David J. Breeze and Thomas Owen Clancy (eds), *The stone of destiny* (Edinburgh, 2003), pp 85–107. 84 Fergus Kelly (ed. and trans.), *Audacht Morainn* (Dublin, 1976), p. xiv. All that we have seen so far makes it clear that Adomnán is trying to Christianize the traditional pagan inauguration rituals by substituting a biblically sanctioned act by a leading prophet. The iconic figure of Samuel is peculiarly appropriate to such a transitional era in Ireland and Britain, because Adomnán would have been highly conscious that Samuel's own period was presented as transitional in 1 Reges, where the prophet's status was also perceived to be changing (1 Reges 9:9, 18–19). Here, we are told that 'in times past, in Israel' one consulted God through a 'seer' who is 'now called a prophet'. Indeed, on the day before he anointed Saul, Samuel identified himself as 'the seer'. And this is a concept easily related to the Irish *filid*, who also may have played a role in inauguration in various kingdoms. See Kim McCone, 'A tale of two ditties: poet and satirist in *Cath Maige Tuired*' in Donnchadh Ó Corráin, Liam Breatnach and Kim McCone (eds), *Sages, saints and storytellers: Celtic studies in honour of Professor James Carney* (Maynooth, 1989), pp 122–43 at p. 136; T.M. Charles-Edwards, *Early Christian Ireland* (Cambridge, 2000), p. 192, n. 42. What gives force and direction to such observations, however, is not so much Columba's poetic links to the *filid* as in *Amra Choluim Chille* or the way in which his prophetic powers might resemble *imbas forosnai*. While neither is irrelevant, it is rather the fact that Samuel is seer/prophet, judge and kingmaker that is most significant for Adomnán. All three aspects must be seen in coordination

Columba's divinely granted inspiration, therefore, it looks as if the acts constitute a designation, a way of creating a *tánaise ríg* or an heir-designate.[85] Certainly, that function is theoretically present, since, in each of the four cases where Columba delivers a prophecy with a blessing, kingship is the eventual result, and the entire section of chapters is entitled *De regibus*, even though four of the protagonists are not actually kings. When Columba then moves to create a king in fact, Adomnán adds the term *ordinatio* as a sign that something additional and more powerful is occurring in the ritual. In this cluster, therefore, a number of themes are present, but it is probably at least partly meant as an inducement for support not only to kings but to those members of a royal kin-group who may wish to become kings. Columba can guarantee their goal, but he can also choose between them as Samuel did among the sons of Jesse and the saint did among the sons of Áedán. These blessings are thus part of Adomnán's programme for a reformed regime.

One aspect of the present cluster that is especially interesting, however, is that Adomnán is now revealed as a 'root-and-branch' man. He not only wishes to foster and dominate an OT king-making rite, he also wishes to Christianize the entire process of dynastic selection and to establish control from its commencement, that is long before the final ritual is carried out. Like Samuel, he means to be a permanent supervisor of royal affairs. It is a duty that flows from his 'call', and his condition as assayer of princes. It must always be remembered that it is only the Iona saint who is supernaturally licensed to operate in this way. No other community may participate, except with his indulgence, since the 'called' prophet with the mantle is the chief prophet, and since the 'call' sequence already investigated establishes that he has been divinely 'sent' to create kings. His words and plans have been approved and predestined by heaven so that other prophets, even authentic ones, such as those who mistakenly predicted victory for king Ahab in 3 Reges 22, will be proven wrong if they contest his statements.[86] Only Columba may nurture princes because only he has been commissioned to do so.

1 Reges continued to provide Adomnán's main legitimating rationale. This would have been clear to the biblically learned members of the Iona brotherhood, since they would have quickly noted that Columba's designation of Eochaid Buide, in the first chapter of *De regibus*, is a thinly veiled version of Samuel's choosing of one boy, David, out of many sons to succeed Saul (without

against a background of politico-religious transformation, which Adomnán shows Columba as bringing about. A useful means of demonstrating this is through an analysis of *VC* I 36, where Adomnán himself connects biblical ritual, biblical concepts and pagan Irish tradition.   85 A recent discussion is Megan McGowan, 'Royal succession in earlier medieval Ireland: the fiction of tanistry', *Peritia*, 17–18 (2003–4), 357–81. Her argument would have benefitted (as in her n. 86) by further following *Iona, Tara and Soissons* and discussing the designation of Eochaid Buide by Columba.   86 So much for Armagh, whose prophet is modelled after Moses among others. See Enright, 'Royal succession and abbatial prerogative', 93–4.

an unction, since Áedán had not disobeyed the prophet). As already seen, the notable difference between the texts lies in VC's highlighting of the boy's gesture of love for Columba. By placing this obviously source-based episode at the beginning of I 9–15, Adomnán signals that it is going to establish the interpretive context for what follows. And so it does. The princes' cluster is present in part so that Adomnán can establish the way in which Columba cares for afflicted royals and their followers, who are caught up in the perennial conflicts surrounding dynastic transitions, a situation in which any of a large number of relatives in lineage segments would be eligible to become kings themselves and would thus be driven to frequent contentions in order to establish dominance and fully accepted heirship. The story of David's choosing, viewed in terms of complicated family and dynastic consequences, is ideal for this purpose, since it describes a readily recognizable regime. David is taken into the home of Saul, becomes the royal armour-bearer, and is like a foster-son (see also Domnall mac Áedo in fosterage who will outlive his brothers), in that he is the covenanted brother of Jonathan, Saul's heir, who tries to protect him. David wins famous victories and is loved by the people, but the jealous king drives him into exile and then hunts him for years in the wilderness. During these years, David grows to manhood, suffers greatly and sometimes despairs (like Scandlán in chains and Oengus Brónbachal, who comes in exile to Iona). But he is helped by the priest Achimelech and Gad the prophet, who may have accompanied him. At one important juncture, however, David sought help from Samuel, who was then presiding over his company of lesser prophets: 'But David fled and escaped, and came to Samuel in Ramatha, and told him all that Saul had done to him: and he and Samuel went and dwelt in Najoth' (1 Reges 19:18). It is thus Samuel who provides refuge for the rightful king-to-be in Najoth, in the same way that Iona abbots will make their island a refuge for princes like Oswald and his men and Oengus Brónbachal and his brothers.[87] The theme of the safety of princes is thus a pointedly selected and trenchant one for Adomnán. What we see in addition is the rationale for the concept in Samuel's power to choose among sons, and then anoint one thereafter. While Columba has anointed Áedán and designated Eochaid Buide, Adomnán has here expanded the model and given it a broader nurturing function which may perhaps be linked to the universalizing theme in Isaiah and its adjusted imitation in VC.

But can it be shown that Adomnán means to relate the concept of anointing to his protection/patronage thematic based on the Samuel/Saul/David saga? The answer seems likely to be positive, since both have been causally united from

---

87 Sharpe, *Adomnán*, p. 275, n. 94: 'It is not without interest to note that Iona was already in the saint's lifetime a refuge for rulers, or their heirs, temporarily displaced in the political strife of Ireland. In the seventh century, it would serve the same role for exiled Northumbrian royalty'. This historical reality can thus provide one basis for Adomnán's identification of Samuel and Najoth with Columba and Iona. It may have been significant for contemporary aristocrats.

the origin of the practice in 1 Reges. Adomnán evinces no uncertainty about it because he appeals to the principle in the Diarmait episode in I 36. As has been shown, the *nolite tangere christos meos* theme there expressed is drawn directly from an episode in the hunting of David story, while the second aspect of Columba's cursing of Áed Dub reflects an adaptation of David's curse of Abner (for leaving the anointed Saul in harm's way) from the same set of passages. The prophet who provides a place of refuge for a prince has also been included. But Adomnán's net is even more tightly woven around his model, because Diarmait's sacrality is patterned on the anointed character of the pagan Cyrus, whose status as ruler of an empire – the 'shepherd' whose right hand the Lord has taken hold of – is the reason for the peculiarly grand formula *totius Scottiae regnatorem a deo ordinatum* being applied to the Uí Néill ruler. Sacrality, inviolability, empire and anointing are here joined at the hip. It is thus certain that *ordinatio* refers to anointing in the case of Diarmait mac Cerbaill. On the strength of that demonstration, the same must be true of Oswald of Northumbria, called *totius Britanniae imperator a deo ordinatus*, whose miracle of victory was mediated by a victory-bringer modelled on the figure of Samuel, the battle-prophet. In the case of Áedán (where the fact that Columba is the anointer and not God might cause confusion), the same *ordinatio* terminology is again applied, and so it would seem to follow that the same ritual concept is being invoked. It is further manifest because the acts and descriptions of the Áedán chapter have been deliberately keyed to the narrative of Saul's encounter with Samuel and to his oiling that follows. Moreover, since Adomnán has already used the acts of prophesying and blessing separately to designate the one who succeeds a king in the cluster of princes chapters (where an unction is almost ostentatiously omitted for Eochaid Buide), it is inherently probable that some additional ritual element is envisioned for the creation of an over-king like Áedán. Inviolability, the theoretical result of prophetic anointing, is that element envisioned by Adomnán in I 36.

These deductions are then substantiated by the demonstration that Columba the prophet has been selected by God according to an OT scheme whereby he is 'called' and 'sent' for a particular purpose, in this case to be the maker of kings. No prophet so scrupulously trimmed to a template could possibly act outside the enjoined pattern. Indeed, by the narrative imitations already referred to, Adomnán shows that he has no intentions of doing so. That is now part of the larger demonstration proving that Adomnán draws all of his kingship themes (with the exception of the threefold death) from biblical prophet–king inter-actions and from prophetic sources. Columba is the Irish version of a Hebrew prophet. He remains faithful to the accepted model for such a personage, but he is also perfectly suited to the Insular context; indeed, Adomnán has taken extraordinary pains to provide a biblical justification for his every act. What moderns see as innovation, Adomnán saw as the restoration of God-willed continuity, and he wanted to make that clear to his readers. I 1, 7–8, 9–15, 36 are thus inseparable from the sequence of III 1–5. These sixteen chapters contain the most important prophet–prince interactions in VC and many of the complex multiple links between them have now been delineated. In itself, that structure is a remarkable constellation of coordinated adjustments that enables the Iona abbot to marry insular history and culture to a Samuel/Saul/David model and to Second Isaiah. It seems likely that Adomnán began with the concept of the mantle-bearing prophet and thereafter developed the strategy of fitting Columba's behaviour to the divine plan for government suggested by a reading of 1 Reges. That book was most valuable because it described the means by which a prophet should act to control kings, warfare, succession and society. But many possibilities exist because, as the Law of the Innocents shows, Adomnán had been committed to a grand reform agenda for a long time. Having now witnessed Adomnán's deep admiration for Samuel, and having seen that his conception of prophet–king relations is most often keyed to Samuel's precedents, behaviours and opinions, one is required to ask the following questions of those scholars sceptical of the unction hypothesis: Why would Adomnán choose to omit Samuel's oiling from his own imitative sacring when it is one of the key repetitive rituals that a prophet performs in all the texts that Adomnán methodically and deliberately draws upon? It is the constant precedent. On what grounds could it be considered irrelevant, unwelcome or inapplicable? Could kings be considered inviolable or even truly made if their creation in a Christian act did not follow the OT ritual that conferred that quality? I am unable to find a single reason why Adomnán would have wished to modify this aspect of the biblical pattern that he otherwise earnestly wished to introduce. To do so, it seems to me, would have been to undermine the legitimacy of his own arduously constructed textual connections, since his premier justification for creating them is the manner in which they reflect God's chosen model for rulers. The evidence lends no support to any such rejection. Rather, it points to the precise opposite. Let us briefly look to some additional signs.

In a little-known law text consisting of twenty canons entitled *Canones Adamnani*, Adomnán advocates the making of OT distinctions between clean and unclean food.[88] In one case (canon 7), he refers to the 'law' in doing so and the context makes it clear that he is thinking of Mosaic law. Interestingly, canon 16 forbids a husband to take another wife even when his original wife has become a harlot or married another. It relates well to Adomnán's interest in marital problems as evinced in VC II 41, for example, and also to the theme of protecting women, which Adomnán famously advocates in his Law of the Innocents.[89] It is not completely clear that Adomnán wrote these canons as they stand, but there

---

88 For the *Canones Adomnani*, see Ludwig Bieler (ed. and trans.), *The Irish penitentials* (Dublin, 1963), pp 176–8.   89 Máirín Ní Dhonnchadha, 'Birr and the Law of the Innocents' in Thomas O'Loughlin (ed.), *Adomnán at Birr, AD697: essays in commemoration of the Law of the Innocents* (Dublin, 2001), pp 13–32.

is no reason to doubt the attribution of their substance to him. All are squarely based on scripture, with especial attention to Genesis, Exodus, Leviticus and Deuteronomy. Consider also a peculiar reference in III 6 of the *VC*:

> Once when St Columba was living in Iona one of his monks, a Briton, dedicated to good works, was taken ill with a bodily affliction and came close to death. The holy man came to visit him in his last hour, standing for a time beside his bed and blessing him. But he soon left the monk, for he wished not to see the man die. The end came as soon as the saint had left the house.

As he left the deceased, Columba paused to look up towards heaven to see the soul of the Briton being carried by angels. This episode is initially puzzling, for it seems to accord ill with Adomnán's efforts to depict a kindly and dependably charitable saint. Adomnán's rationale is to be found in Lv 21:1, which forbids a priest to incur an uncleanness by witnessing death except of his close kin, and which in 21:11 forbids a high-priest from witnessing death, even of his father and mother. Now, the fascinating point, of course, is not just that Columba observes a special detail of OT law but rather that Adomnán should have chosen to make an issue of the fact by devoting a selected episode to demonstrating the punctilious exactitude of his allegiance. He thus held it as decidedly important that Columba be viewed as binding himself to biblical precedent. And then, moreover, in order to demonstrate divine approval of that faithful stance, Adomnán pauses to remark that the monk died only when the saint had left the hut. Adomnán clearly intends to show that Columba was a stickler for the law. One may also point to *VC* I 1, where Adomnán refers to a miracle of Columba's and declares that it would be possible to find a great many witnesses and not just the two or three which would be 'enough to satisfy the law'. He repeats the point in II 45 in regard to another miracle, and states that 'the law requires two or three witnesses'. These references are not to Irish law (as one might expect), but rather to the law of Moses expressed in Deut 19:15: 'one witness shall not rise up against any man ... but in the mouth of two or three witnesses every word shall stand'. Interestingly, this view is also expressed in the *Hibernensis*, which begins by stating that no one may be condemned by one witness and then goes on to cite Deut 19:15 and 17:6 in support.

Such evidence says a great deal about Adomnán's character, and reveals a thoroughgoing allegiance to the OT as a legal standard, a touchstone for virtuous behaviour.[90] We find an abbot who relies on it so strongly that he portrays his hero as keeping the Sabbath when he is dying, leaving a follower's deathbed in order not to become ritually unclean, advocating an adherence to Jewish dietary

---

90 In this, Adomnán was very much like the rest of the Irish. Raymund Kottje, *Studien zum Einfluss des Alten Testaments auf Recht und Liturgie des frühen Mittelalters (6.-8. Jahrhundert)* (Bonn, 1970); Donnchadh Ó Corráin, Liam Breatnach and Aidan Breen, 'The laws of the Irish', *Peritia*, 3 (1984), 382–438.

prohibitions, and declaring that levitical requirements concerning witnesses are necessary for a judgment. Is this the character of an author who would choose to base Columba's ordination of Áedán on Samuel's unction of Saul but then, contrary to his revered source, omit that single act that the Bible everywhere regards as constitutive? And, if one nonetheless maintains that he did so, what warrant or rationale can be offered for the deliberate omission? Simply to ask these questions on the heels of the evidence is to show the utter improbability of Adomnán's improvization of a king-making ritual that excluded an oiling as part of a hand-laying. The *ordinatio*/unction agreement that is established for Diarmait also applies to Áedán. Little room for manoeuvre is allowed in this opinion, since the basic lesson of the prince-centred chapters is that Adomnán is the opposite of eclectic. In this area, his motifs and lessons are drawn around a very few OT themes.

The prophet's reform plan

What are the implications of these 'call' and kingship chapters for Adomnán's thought in *VC*? Any assessment must be tentative because so much of the work continues to require an interpretive unravelling, and I suspect that that cannot be satisfactorily done until all of the situations (and not just allusions) presented in it have been analysed in terms of the biblical texts and portraits that he draws upon. Some of it in turn will probably require comparison with the materials of the *Hibernensis* (which I continue to view as a work ultimately inspired by Adomnán and his Iona contemporaries). The fundamental tendencies of the sixteen chapters that I have examined, however, become clearer when read within the context of the OT model according to which they have been devised, trimmed or calibrated. Adomnán's desire to hold this standard is an object-lesson in itself.

The most important thing about Adomnán's Columba is that he is a prophet inspired by the Holy Ghost, who has been commissioned according to the sacred pattern established for the greatest prophets of the Bible. Adomnán is not far from saying this himself when he writes that Columba is comparable to the prophets Elijah and Elisha and to the apostles Peter, Paul and John (II 32). Like them, 'he has a seat of everlasting glory in the heavenly homeland as himself a prophet and apostle ...'. He will sit with them in the company of the Holy Trinity. Adomnán thus leaps over a host of possible comparisons with famous but lesser saints. Nothing will do him but the prophets and the apostles and among those only the foremost. One must, therefore, abandon any probative thinking that finds such comparisons hyperbolic. To think so is to lose contact with Adomnán's personal mindset, and to discount wrongly what he apparently sincerely believes about his communities' founder. Columba is not someone for whom the divine 'call' of a biblical prophet is outlandish, nor is his commission to bring the 'law' to the nations or to assay princes any surprise. He is perfectly suited to do so, because God has stamped him with the same true impression that enables such tasks. He will naturally resemble others who bore this stamp in the past, while the 'law' that he is to proclaim – which I take to mean the exact divine teachings as they appear in both Old and New Testaments together with the sacred authority of the 'sent' prophet who declares them – will automatically reflect God's decrees. As humble as Columba seeks to appear, his spiritual/ miraculous power is colossal. His God-given jurisdiction is over all the isles of ocean. Any other jurisdictions that have been established since his death, in Northumbria, for example, are illicit because Columba proclaimed the only acceptable law for the islands when he was alive, and Columba's mandate has been rightly and duly passed to his successors. Any deviations since his time must thus be uprooted and the 'law' re-established.

The part of the 'law' examined here mostly concerns kings. To rightly comprehend Adomnán's views on kingship, one must first absorb the lesson that God has little affection for secular leaders or for the institution of kingship. Gideon the prophet, for example, had led the people to a great victory over the Midianites. The men of Israel wished to make him a king (Jdg 8:22–23):

> Rule thou over us, and thy son, and thy son's son: because thou hast delivered us from the hand of Midian. And he said to them: I will not rule over you, neither shall my son rule over you, but the Lord shall rule over you.

This sentiment, that God rules directly or through his prophets, priests and chosen servants, also governs Yahweh's original opinion regarding Saul's proposed kingship, although he later reluctantly changed his mind and allowed Samuel to anoint him. Samuel, we remember, was so outraged by the popular insistence on having a king, which he interpreted as a direct affront to God, that he punished the people for it, and only gradually relented. His problem then became that of controlling the new king and making him behave according to God's will, an effort that failed and resulted in Saul's replacement. In theory, however, the king was bound to an egalitarian Hebrew tradition in a variety of ways. He must be native born, for example, must accept a low tax-yield, may not seek alliances through foreign wives, and must study the laws of royal office under the instruction of levitical priests.[91] In other words, kings are meant to be under the tutelage of prophets and priests. Prophets create them, chastise them and have the power to bless and curse them. That is why Elijah, to whom Adomnán compares Columba, can cause the overthrow of a dynasty, and why Columba possesses the power to avenge a king's killer by cursing him. Divine law trumps human law, and prophets like Gideon, Joshua and Samuel carry it out.

---

91 See, for example, Joshua A. Berman, *Created equal: how the Bible broke with ancient political thought* (Oxford, 2008).

That such is Adomnán's fundamental approach to kingship is demonstrated by the facts that he takes such pains to follow an OT 'call' sequence in creating a prophet, that he depicts the prophet as making a king according to a newly introduced OT pattern, and that he continues to follow that template when he counsels rulers, provides a refuge for them, and rejects them when they are unworthy. Columba is a victory-bringer because Samuel is and Gideon is, not because he is a saint, which is the wrong way to look at the matter, but because he is a biblical prophet in the islands. And Columba has a 'book' (in this case of the 'ordination of kings') because Samuel has one, and so does Joshua and many other prophets. A prophet needs a book, and the words within it – 'you should ordain Áedán to the kingship according to the words you have read in it' – reveal the nature of his commission as a prophet. Columba's commission is to anoint, designate, judge, protect and counsel; it is part of the new regime envisioned by Adomnán.

And I emphasize 'envisioned by Adomnán' and not, as some now wish to suppose, by Cumméne Find, whom they want to interpret as the author of all of *VC* III 5 and not just of the excerpt inserted by the copyist Dorbbéne in the Schaffhausen manuscript of *c*.713. Given the total absence of any supportive evidence, that hypothesis has never appeared likely, but it has nonetheless persuaded some of those opposed to the unction argument, since it has the concomitant virtue of making Adomnán less of an innovator and propagandist, while also weakening the level of linkage between the usages of *ordinatio* when applied to kings. Such a view is no longer tenable, since it has now been shown that III 5 is not a chapter that stands alone; it is part of a sequence. Hence, defenders of the Cumméne Find hypothesis would now have to argue that he is the author of five chapters rather than one. In such a case, the slender reed that can hardly bear the weight of one episode must now carry the burden of four more. But the problems then continue to proliferate since the unction model on which III 5 is founded is the same one that explains the creation of the victory-bringing prophet in I 1, 7–8, the prophet who protects and rejects rulers in I 9–15, and the prophet who represents anointing as a replacement for pagan charisma in I 36. Even worse complications follow. The Cumméne Find authorship hypothesis thus leads to a near absurdity – one which is easily dispensed with, however, since recent attempts to lever his small fragment into a greater significance have been driven by little more than a desire to counter a thesis.[92] The evidence here assembled indicates that in *VC* we are dealing with the

---

92 T.M. Charles-Edwards has sought to show that the 'principal Old Testament background' to Columba's ordination of Áedán is to be found in Isaac's dealings with Jacob and Esau and Jacob's with Judah and the sons of Joseph. He believes that *VC* III 5 was written 'according to Cumméne'; that the Iona practice shows up again in the *Life of Columbanus* by Jonas; and that *ordinatio* means simply an elevation to higher status. See T.M. Charles-Edwards, 'A contract between king and people in early medieval Ireland? *Críth gablach* on kingship', *Peritia*, 8 (1994), 107–19; idem, *Early Christian Ireland*, pp 313, 360–1. On other occasions, however, Charles-Edwards can refer to the

strategic programme of a single outstanding mind that has carefully studied all of the effects linked to prophetically administered royal anointing in the Bible, and has chosen to construct around them a theory of politico-theological reformation to be applied in Ireland and Britain. This programme was designed to be implemented, but as far as we can tell, never achieved that fruition.

The historical Columba was an accomplished leader and may have been a genuinely inspired visionary saint. I like to think so. Adomnán, too, was a devout and holy man, perhaps the outstanding ecclesiastic of his age; but much of what he wrote and what he said about what he wrote is not credible, especially when applied to the chapters explored above. In part, these reflect a biblical instruction and patterning. In part, they are essentially propaganda, in that the construction of Columba's persona is tailored to enhance the standing of his community. Nor, except in a few remarks, are the fuller implications of Columba's managerial persona developed. And that is notable. The iron fist of prophetic oversight for kings is present but kept subdued so that a positive message may prevail. Some of the message is that alliance with Columba brings great advantages to rulers. The saint likes and honours kings and chooses to work his will through them. His designations and anointings are always beneficial because they are in accord with God's plan, and his counsels, protection, tutelage and prayers for victory constitute a permanent advantage for his royal clients. Such alliance may sometimes be created through the ritual of royal anointing, since that is in accord with the law brought by the prophet. It, too, is an advantage for princes, since Columba then pays special attention to the family, defends it when it is attacked, and avenges the ruler if he is killed.

The holy man has thus been 'called' to work through kings, and thereby to renew society and bring it into a right relationship with God, such as is sometimes depicted in 1 Reges and elsewhere in the Bible. His reformation of kingship under prophetic guidance is an instrument to restore an originally biblical right 'order', a concept that is also suggested by the term *ordinatio* in the Áedán episode, which Adomnán employs to include an unction but which goes beyond the ritual to suggest the right arrangement and disposition within a society that the anointed king creates. *Ordinatio* has inherent overtones of *ordo* and is used by Adomnán (eight times in III 5 excluding the insert) so as to express the idea of a prophet who installs a hallowed ruler, who then works with him to bring 'law' to the nation. God's plan is manifest in such a ritual because it is God's choice who becomes king, and not that of people or aristocracy in any kind of contract. Hence God's angel harshly overrules Columba, who had

extract or *fragment* of Cumméne the White in Adomnán's III 5; for example, *Early Christian Ireland*, p. 312, n. 146. Some extended defence of this whole approach is indispensable if one is to question so drastically the personal authorship of Adomnán, who makes no reference to Cumméne, and who places his own foremost emphasis on accounts 'handed down by our elders, men both reliable and informed'. Adomnán's 'diligent inquiry' does include written work, but the Iona monastery probably had written references to the founder other than that in question.

favoured another candidate in III 5, and then grants Columba the power to bless and prophesy the future for the dynasty. *Ordinatio*, therefore, does not solely mean to 'give a person higher rank', or to elevate to a higher status, since in that case one would hardly need a prophet to establish it through supernatural acts. An exclusive sacrality thereby infuses the ruler; he is not, or not any longer, *primus inter pares*. Hence the argument that elevation in rank is all that *ordinatio* means can never be convincing. The term actually denotes an interior transformation of character achieved through a particularly sanctifying ritual in which God participates because the ruler is installed to be the head of a society and to govern it virtuously in accord with the divine ordinance. Admittedly, *ordinatio* can also refer to a ritual without anointing – a providential royal selection by lot, for example, as in the *Hibernensis* interpretation of 1 Reges 10:19–21. But, if that is one legitimate meaning of the term in Irish usage, every situation relating to kings that I have examined in the *VC* shows that it is not the one used by Adomnán.

No one doubts that *ordinatio* is an ambiguous term capable of bearing a number of different meanings. Such being the case, the only way to determine what a writer intends when he employs it is to examine his usages in relation to the sources upon which he draws. That has been accomplished with the following result: when referring to kings ordained by God or by Columba, Adomnán never fails to link that term to the biblical ritual or situation of anointing and, most commonly, to the Samuel/Saul saga. That consistent attachment is the only reliable guide to the content with which he invested the term in these cases. Nor does that pattern occur alone; it is replicated in Adomnán's development of the battle–champion motif, and, in a somewhat more extended way, in the cases of care and protection that Columba extends to princes. All of these are new and unheard-of ways of dealing with Irish and British kingship, and hence, given also the additional evidence presented, must be treated as essential parts of a reform plan based on the OT model. To this evidence may be added the fact that Adomnán's definition of *ordinatio* as including *unctio* also occurs in the near contemporary Iona-connected *Hibernensis*, where it is the first definition given in the book *De regno*. The fact that *ordinatio* can also bear the meaning of a choosing by lot (this is the second definition given) does not detract from the point. In keeping with the Iona reform of kingship project, one may further note that chapters three and four of *De regno*, which follow the ordination references, then present a revised interpretation of the 'king's justice', whereby (as in the mid–seventh–century *De duodecim abusivis saeculi*) the partially pagan conception of cosmic kingship is provided with a Christian theoretical foundation. In keeping with an *ordo* understanding, the ordained ruler now acts to produce the ideal regime of justice in which, for example, theft, adultery and sinfulness are punished and where the kingdom flourishes in peace, health, charity and fecundity because the king is in accord with supernaturally encompassing law. It is this conception of a sanctified king, whose expression of law disposes a society to goodness, that Adomnán seeks to foster. And the *Hibernensis* here again follows a path blazed by Adomnán, since the brief chapter eight of *De regno, De non custodiente regem*, refers solely to David's cursing of Abner, who did not properly care for his anointed lord. This is part of the model for Columba's curse of Áed Dub in *VC* I 36. It is, of course, a telling piece of evidence that not only suggests a relationship between *VC* and *Hibernensis*, but also indicates that the *Hibernensis* chapter *De regno* has taken seriously the definition of ordination as anointing.

A reformation of kingship thus goes a long way towards achieving a new 'law' to govern society, one that is in effect a revised OT paradigm applied to conditions in the islands. Chosen and guided by the Iona abbot, kings and their successors are the instruments that will maintain and enforce this law. Such an innovation naturally requires that the pagan rituals and theory of kingship be abandoned. Although Adomnán does not explicitly mention pagan kingship conceptions, either when writing of Diarmait or of the threefold death, the present analysis shows that *VC* I 36 is the chapter where they are most clearly at issue. It is where Adomnán states his case, however briefly and abruptly. He perceives biblical and Irish paganism as similar phenomena and his reaction to each, as reflected in the anecdotes about the kings mentioned, is to trim his insular prince/prophet interactions to his biblical template. He does so because his biblically formed world-view persuades him that royal anointing and prophetic direction are the divinely mandated rightful means of governing.

Looked at as a whole, *VC* I 36 allows us to draw the following conclusions: first, Adomnán is truly intent on a policy of kingship renovation in a period that he himself recognizes as one of transition; second, his instruments are biblical ritual and prophetic judgment that are meant to replace a series of pagan acts and conceptions; third, he is probably willing to allow a modified form of royal sacrality to continue (perhaps also in the area of the 'king's truth') under church guidance or, perhaps better, under prophetic guidance; fourth, the logic of all cases demonstrates that no ruler may avoid submission to the Iona prophet just as the Hebrew king had to submit to Samuel. The irony of all this reform planning, of course, is that the new royal ritual was adopted in Francia and not in Ireland,[93] although its accompanying *VC* motif of the threefold death continued to flourish like an immortal weed in a garden corner.

This condition of inviolability and supportive curse in I 36 is thus no jury-rigged device for a single case. It is a pivotal aspect of a greater complex in *VC*

---

93 Various arguments continue to be advanced: see Arnold Angenendt, 'Pippins Königserhebung und Salbung' in Becher and Jarnut (eds), *Dynastiewechsel*, pp 179–211; Josef Semmler, *Der Dynastiewechsel von 751 und die frankische Königssalbung*, Studia Humaniora 6, Series Minor ([Düsseldorf], 2003); Franz-Reiner Erkens, *Herrschersakralität ins Mittelalter: von den Anfägen bit zum Investiturstreit* (Stuttgart, 2006).

because it is a natural complement to the message of the nurture of princes chapters, which portrays Columba in the same light as beneficent royal tutor who brings victory to friends and defeat to enemies. If his protection fails, his curse carries a savage permanent punishment. All these elements (down even to the curse) are tied to a prophetic anointing paradigm, and where Adomnán differs somewhat from the OT is in his more intense concentration on the miracle-working nature of the 'called' prophet's power. As a single episode, the Diarmait chapter is a significant indication of what is to come, but it lacks a serious propagandistic punch, and finds one only when it is bracketed within the larger scheme of connected lessons within an affirming series. Part of what I have tried to do in the present work is to restore the series, by showing how and why its intellectual content makes it a coherent structure. But that, in turn, is one aspect of the problem of interpreting the entire *vita* in its curious mode of division. Assuming that Adomnán carefully deliberated writing it in this way, then he seems to have been juggling two intentions, at least. One is his desire to imitate the OT governmental order that we have examined, while the other is his wish to divide the work into three parts so as to design his own version of the distinguished Life of St Martin by Sulpicius Severus, a work held in high regard by contemporaries. Unfortunately, in the arrangements and dispositions required to give shape to that scheme, Adomnán's impressively innovative reformation-of-kingship-in-the-islands message is fractured, its energy dissipated, so that the ideological shock that it had been partly crafted to deliver against rival claims by competing communities is only partially achieved. The painstakingly constructed individual lessons of OT mirroring remain in the chapter details but, uncoupled, they now amount to a sporadic survey of the bricks so that one can hardly recognize any longer the symmetry of the wall. In particular, the direct connection between the prophetic status of Columba and his divine commissioning to be a kingmaker, victory-bringer and guardian of kings has been sadly obscured. In my opinion, however, one can find a legally defined and fuller expression of Adomnán's reform programme in the *Hibernensis*, in books like *De regno* and *De principatu*, whose regulations probably owe a significant debt to his teachings.

CHAPTER TWO

Claims, agendas and a prophetic culture in the Lives of Patrick and Columba

Muirchú moccu Machthéni and Adomnán of Cenél Conaill and Iona are the respective authors of two famous seventh-century Lives, the *Vita S. Patricii* and the *Vita S. Columbae* (henceforth *VP* and *VC*).[1] Given their common interests in scholarship and their trusted positions in monastic organizations of the northern half of a small country, it is probable that the two biographers knew each other personally. The odds are against any amiable meeting of minds, however, as the evidence indicates that their organizations were at loggerheads. Each brotherhood was enthusiastically committed to an opposing agenda that routinely aimed to persuade discrete population groups of the superior power and prestige of its own founding saint.[2] In such a case, even in moments of apparent Christian agreement, few apples could be without a worm. Muirchú was one of the guarantors of the *Cáin Adomnáin* of 697, for example, itself a sign of his high standing among Armagh supporters, but regardless of any agreement about the good to be accomplished by the law, its countrywide promulgation was a splendid sign of the heavenly influence of St Columba and not of St Patrick.[3] That had upsetting theoretical (as well as legal and financial) consequences for Armagh. The conception that the power of a heavenly patron was manifested on earth in his capacity to support his own people, and to dominate their enemies, was held as a truism by all concerned. By this measure, Patrick could be seen as

1 In this chapter, I have preferred the Latin text and translation of Patrick's Life in Ludwig Bieler (ed.), *The Patrician texts in the Book of Armagh* (Dublin, 1979), pp 61–123 [text hereafter *VP*], although I have also consulted David Howlett (ed.), *Muirchú moccu Machthéni's 'Vita sancti Patricii': Life of Saint Patrick* (Dublin, 2006). For Columba, I continue to use the Latin text of *VC* and the English translation of Sharpe, *Adomnán*. The Bible version is the Vulgate: Fischer et al. (eds), *Biblia sacra iuxta vulgatem versionem*; the translation is the Douay-Rheims-Challoner version reset by the Baronius Press (London, 2005). In a few cases, I have silently changed the personal names in the version to those now more familiar: for example, Elijah rather than Elias, and Ezra rather than Ezdras. 2 For the arguments involved, see Doherty, 'Politics of Armagh'; Sharpe, 'St Patrick and the see of Armagh'; de Paor, 'The aggrandizement of Armagh'; Richard Sharpe, 'Armagh and Rome in the seventh century'; Enright, 'Royal succession and abbatial prerogative', 83–104. Still fundamental is D.A. Binchy, 'Patrick and his biographers, ancient and modern', *Studia Hibernica*, 2 (1962), 7–173. 3 Kuno Meyer (ed.), *Cáin Adomnáin: an Old Irish treatise on the Law of Adamnán* (Oxford, 1905); Máirín Ní Donnchadha, 'The guarantor list of Cáin Adomnáin, 697', *Peritia*, 1 (1982), 178–215; eadem, 'The *Lex Innocentium*: Adomnán's law for women, clerics and youths, 697AD' in Mary O'Dowd and Sabine Wichert (eds), *Chattel, servant or citizen: woman's status in church, state and society* (Belfast, 1995), pp 58–69.

85

wanting. From the viewpoint of Muirchú's constituency, therefore, few of Iona's honours could be accepted with equanimity – indeed they had to be actively challenged – since Armagh was also claiming primatial rights of jurisdiction across the country, and these were unlikely to flourish if Columba and his community were perceived to deserve a greater harvest of popular respect, devotion or allegiance.

It is clear that Muirchú's *vita* precedes that of Adomnán and equally so that Muirchú is more aggressive and direct in his propaganda to advance his community. Where the former is sometimes strident, the latter is more subtle and reticent; one seems to threaten with his vengeful saint where the other tends to seduce with his calmer counterpart. Something of the difference in tone may, possibly, also relate to the Synod of Birr, as some recent interpreters now maintain that the *VP* was written about the mid-690s.[4] As it is prudent to assume perhaps a decade of strenuous diplomacy and consensus-building leading up to that great assembly, tiding of its ambitious goals will have aroused an animated atmosphere of interested discussion that could well have prompted Muirchú to enter the fray. Adomnán, on the other hand, may have been writing in 697 and it is widely held that the *VC* should be dated to *c*.700.[5] Few scholars have taken the further step of hypothesizing one *vita* as a response to the other, however, or if they have, did not develop a means of advancing the proposal. Richard Sharpe, author of a recent translation and commentary on the *VC*, appears to have spoken for many when he wrote that 'it is certainly probable that he [Adomnán] meant to present a portrait of St Columba that could stand alongside that of St Patrick', but because Armagh's claims 'were still only claims', Adomnán had no great need to confront or challenge Muirchú's sometimes extravagant statements about power, property or jurisdiction.[6]

And yet it is not easy to construct a significant portrait of Columba to stand alongside Patrick's without in some sense constructing an argument and persona that counters these extravagant claims that were surely affecting Columba's community in the later seventh century. As Tirechán's impassioned accusations demonstrate, the assertions involved cannot simply be regarded as theoretical or harmless because they involved the ownership and allegiance of churches that were currently changing hands amid considerable objection.[7] One possibility,

---

4 David Howlett suggests 'the last seven to ten years of the seventh century', *Muirchú*, p. 184. T.M. Charles-Edwards suggests '*c*.695' in *Early Christian Ireland*, p. 440. These dates stand or fall based upon arguments about events in Britain and their influence on Irish thinking. While plausible and even persuasive, a study in depth remains a desideratum and it must establish a secure date for the *Liber Angeli*. See, however, Charles-Edwards, *Early Christian Ireland*, pp 429–40. 5 Sharpe, *Adomnán*, p. 55; Herbert, *Iona, Kells and Derry*, p. 12; *VC*, pp 7, 19. 6 Sharpe, *Adomnán*, p. 63. 7 He writes, for example, that the community of Clonmacnoise wrongly claims properties 'as they hold forcibly many of Patrick's places since the recent plague'. Elsewhere, he remarks that he sorrows for Patrick 'because the deserters and arch-robber and war-lords of Ireland hate Patrick's territorial supremacy, because they have taken away from him what was his and are afraid; for if an heir of Patrick were to investigate his supremacy he would vindicate for him almost the whole island

then, is that Adomnán's *vita* does indeed constitute a retort but one that is overly subtle and hence no longer easily recognizable as such. Another is that we simply do not perceive his statements as rejoinders because they are couched in a mode of argumentation that is uncommon in modern times. In either case, a fundamental dimension of the debate would then be escaping comprehension. It seems to the present writer that a notable portion of the direct and indirect argumentation in these two Lives centres on the question of the founder as potent prophet, with that term defined operationally as having two interwoven meanings: first, it refers to an actual verbal and behavioural resemblance to prophets of the Old and New Testaments, and, second, to the saint as a miracle-worker whose actions recall such powerful figures. That being so, it would suggest that each of our biographers sought to manipulate his portrait in order to stress an affinity between his hero and his biblical model or models; each might even wish to adapt an OT narrative in order to drive home the lesson. Debate would then be intertextual on at least two levels, with regard to biblical precedent and with regard to the claims or work of the opponent. One respondent might also prefer a more abstract level of argumentation. Such a dispute would be highly indirect, oblique and even ambiguous, and thus difficult for later readers to discern. The clash of opinion might then be reflected mostly in the presentation of the saint or in the handling of certain stressed or repetitive topics. In either case, the treatment of kings (and kingship) would be essential questions at issue and would say much about each organization's approach to matters of power. Their presence in such an oblique polemic would be nearly unavoidable as they are the heads of the bodies that OT prophets are normally 'sent' to correct.[8] They are the natural targets of prophets, and how they are dealt with is both significant and paradigmatic. Because kings possess the power to either thwart or advance the prophet's reforms, the means by which the prophet influences them is a highly important focus that displays the character and inner qualities of his own nature The qualities ascribed to the prophets are thus issues in themselves.

In this chapter, it will be argued that a number of significant scenes in the two Lives reflects this intertextual patterning and biblical mirroring that is present in order to demonstrate that the hero in question is the *most* genuine and potent OT prophetic avatar. His paruchia thus has a right to rule others, in Armagh's arguments, or to maintain its independence and extend its influence in Iona's. One fascinating point is that each biographer has constructed important episodes of his work to imitate the *same* OT prophets and situations; both draw

as his domain'. Bieler, *Patrician Texts*, pp 138f., 142f. See, however, Catherine Swift, 'Tirechán's motives in compiling the *Collectanea*: an alternative explanation', *Ériu*, 45 (1994), 53–82. 8 For prophets and their divine commissioning, see Lindblom, *Prophecy*, esp. pp 65–108; Aune, *Prophecy*, esp. pp 16–23, 81–103; R.R. Wilson, 'Prophecy and ecstasy', *Journal of Biblical Literature*, 98 (1979), 321–37. Helpful in ways that some others are not is Joseph Blenkinsopp, *A history of prophecy in Israel* (Louisville, KY, 1996), pp 30–65.

heavily on the Elijah/Elisha saga. One thus has an unusual opportunity to compare their emphases and thereby to focus more precisely on those points that each writer himself wished to display, to advance or to defend. In conducting a *partial* comparison of those two *vitae*, it is hoped that some new or neglected nuances may thereby be more effectively revealed or better appreciated, and that the issue of one *vita* as a 'reply' to the other may be further clarified even if not settled. One begins then with an outlining of the partly concealed OT patterning in some episodes of Muirchú. That use of the term 'concealment', of course, refers only to modern perceptions, since the clergy of the communities that these *vitae* aimed to inform were saturated with biblical knowledge and lived in an atmosphere intensely alive to the prophetic overtones of even the slightest biblical allusion.

Patrick and Benignus at Tara

Two of the more famous episodes in *VP* involve Benignus, the boy who serves Patrick on his travels and whom the saint would allegedly select as his successor as bishop of Armagh. In one of these, chapter I 20 (19) of Bieler's edition, Benignus is placed in a burning house in order, ostensibly, to establish the truth of Patrick's teachings before king Loiguire and his druids. In the other, I 28 (27), Benignus is given a succession test of visionary power by Patrick himself. Each of these episodes will be scrutinized in an attempt to determine the rationale for its presence in relation to the sources from which it was drawn and which were used to justify it. The first case begins when king Loiguire (Lóeguire mac Néill) at Tara orders that the contest between Patrick and the druids continue: *permitte per ignem*. Patrick decides that

> 'one of the boys in my service together with you [the druid] shall go into a divided and closed house, and you shall wear my garment and my boy shall wear yours, and so you two together shall be set on fire and be judged in the presence of the Highest'. And this plan was accepted, and a house was built for them, half of green wood and half of dry wood, and the druid was placed in the green part of the house and one of the holy Patrick's boys, Benineus (=Benignus) by name, wearing the druid's garb, in its dry part; then the house was closed from outside and in the presence of the whole crowd was set on fire. And in that hour it so happened through the prayer of Patrick that the flame of the fire consumed the druid together with the green half of the house, and nothing was left intact except the chasuble of holy Patrick, which the fire did not touch. On the other hand, happy Benineus, and the dry half of the house, experienced what has been said of the three young men: the fire did not even touch him, and brought him neither pain nor discomfort; only the garb of the druid, which he had donned, was burnt in accordance with God's will.

88

Elsewhere and on a quite different occasion, Benignus must endure still another test at Patrick's wish. Now Muirchú writes:

> I shall briefly relate a miracle of the godly and apostolic man Patrick, of whom we are speaking (something) that miraculously happened to him when he was still in the flesh; this, as far as I know, has been written about him and Stephen only. At one time when he was in his usual place to pray during the night, he beheld the wonders of heaven, familiar to him, and wishing to test his beloved and faithful holy boy, he said to him: 'Please, tell me my son, whether you experience what I experience'. Then the small boy, named Benignus, said without hesitation: 'I know already what you are experiencing. For I see heaven open and behold the Son of God and His angels'. Then Patrick said: 'I see now that you are worthy to be my successor'. At once they walked to his usual place of prayer. As they were praying in the middle of the river bed the boy said: 'I can stand the cold water no longer'. For the water was too cold for him. Then Patrick told him to go from the upper river down to the lower. There, too, however, he was not able to stay very long because, he confessed, he felt the water to be too hot. Unable to stay long in that place, he then went on land.

The main source (but not the only one) of both these episodes is the continued biblical saga of Elijah and Elisha from 3 Reges 18:15–40, 19:19–21 and 4 Reges 2:1–15. In the first case, Elijah arranges a duel of fire between himself and the priests of Baal favoured by King Ahab and Queen Jezebel. These represent the hostile druids of Loiguire. Two pyres are prepared with a bullock for sacrifice on each. Elijah and the priests will call on their gods in order to establish which is able to answer by lighting the pyre assigned. Whereas the wood on the altar of the Baalites is dry, that on the Lord's site is repeatedly drenched with water. This is the functional equivalent of the two sides of the fiery house at Tara, where one half was constructed of green wood and the other from dry.[9] Once God had lit the chosen pyre, Elijah slaughtered the priests of Baal as, in the *VP*, Patrick would kill the druids and 'many' of the people with them. It is hard to imagine anything more alien to the doings of the historical saint as we know him from his letters, but his behaviour is quite consistent with that of Muirchú's chosen model of Elijah.

This pattern of OT imitation extends to the vision test of Benignus and to the movement to the water that follows it. After his victory and personal slaughter of the priests (3 Reges 18:40, 19:1), Elijah flees from the wrath of Jezebel and Ahab and is drawn to a meeting with the Lord. He covers his face with his mantle and hears God tell him to anoint certain kings and to make Elisha his successor. Upon finding Elisha, the prophet simply walked up to him and 'he cast his

---

9 For a complete analysis of this episode, see Thomas O'Loughlin, 'Reading Muirchú's Tara-event within its background as a biblical "trial of divinities"' in Jane Cartwright (ed.), *Celtic hagiography and saints' cults* (Cardiff, 2003), pp 123–35.

89

mantle upon him'. By this mean, Elisha knew that he had been chosen to become a prophet, and so he left his parents 'and followed Elijah and ministered to him' as Elijah had left his servant behind him. After some time, Elijah realizes that he is going to be taken up into heaven and tries to depart without Elisha. Elisha refuses to leave him even though he is constantly reminded that his master is going to the Lord by 'sons of the prophets', that is by bands of wandering prophetic disciples. Elijah now approaches the Jordan and strikes the waters with his mantle so that they part before him. When they had crossed, Elijah asks Elisha what he would have from him, since final departure is imminent. Elisha replies: 'I beseech thee that in me may be thy double spirit'. He asks, in other words, for the double portion that a father gives as inheritance to his firstborn son in Hebrew law. Elijah, however, is uncertain that it can be granted: 'Thou hast asked a hard thing: nevertheless, if thou see me when I am taken from thee, thou shalt have what thou hast asked: but if thou see me not, thou shalt not have it' (4 Reges 2:10). As they walked, 'a fiery chariot, and fiery horses parted them' and Elijah rose in a whirlwind. 'My father, my father', cried Elisha, 'and he took up the mantle of Elijah, that fell from him'. Returning to the Jordan, Elisha tried to cross by parting the waters as his 'father' had done, but failed. Calling upon God and striking the waters a second time with the mantle, he was finally able to cross. 'Sons of the prophet' on the other side saw him with Elijah's mantle and proceeded to recognize his new status, saying 'the spirit of Elijah hath rested upon Elisha. And coming to meet him, they worshipped him, falling to the ground'.

Muirchú's depiction of a vision criterion for succession, in which Benignus too is able to see into heaven, is clearly derived from Elisha's question about inheritance and Elijah's setting of a perception criterion as a result.[10] Other aspects of his chapter point to reliance on the same saga. It is in 4 Reges, for example, that one finds the motif of prophetic inheritance linked to the one who had earlier 'ministered' to the prophet. That is what Elisha had done after Elijah's servant had been left behind – he served Elijah – and, when Patrick orders Benignus into the burning house, he refers to him as one of his servant boys, *unus ex meis pueris*. The pattern prevails again when Patrick and Benignus move to a river after the test has been passed. That is what Elisha does after Elijah has been taken up into heaven. However, Elisha now requires two attempts to perform the same miracle that Elijah had accomplished in one. He is thus a capable successor but does not, or not yet, possess the same level of power and standing with God as his 'father'. That is the lesson that Benignus is shown in the water. He is truly the successor, but is far from being the equal. Not surprising, since he is only a boy! Looking at both citations then, it is clear that

---

10 Also recognized by Thomas O'Loughlin, *Discovering Saint Patrick* (London, 2005), p. 221, n. 187; Howlett, *Muirchú*, p. 174, who notes in addition that the typology of Elisha is made explicitly in his II xiiii.

Muirchú is seeking to portray Patrick in the guise of a biblical prophet and that his picture of Benignus is meant to continue and fix the prophetic pattern for all to see. This confirms other evidence from the text in that Muirchú shows himself to be particularly interested in OT prophets. Moses is most important to him but others are eminently useful. In his second chapter, he refers to Jonas, Moses and Elijah – he has Patrick invoke Elijah twice – and elsewhere he refers to Gideon, Daniel and Elisha. But this demonstration only accentuates the presence of a remarkable anomaly in his work: although he carefully designs both Patrick/Benignus episodes on the Elijah/Elisha saga, he nonetheless chooses to omit any mention of the crucial sign of succession to prophetic office that is achieved in these texts through a temporary placement of the mantle upon the candidate and a final transmission of the mantle thereafter. Any biblically conscious monk of this period would have recognized this condition as a problematic anomaly, especially because Muirchú actually underscores the relational Elijah/Elisha model when he has Patrick directly link the vision test with succession to his own episcopacy. The omitted episode would have brashly stood out; it is a case where silence would have spoken loudly.

Muirchú indubitably considered the matter carefully, however, because he does include this placement-of-a-mantle motif in the burning house episode only that he turns it upside down by placing *his* mantle, Patrick's garment or 'chasuble', over the shoulders of a druid who is about to be burnt. This extraordinary switch cannot have been accidental or otherwise done without any special meaning, because both of our cited episodes relate to *tests* that are each constructed from Elijah/Elisha materials in which the mantle figures prominently. Neither can it be because Muirchú simply wished to demonstrate the truth of Patrick's teaching before Loiguire as Elijah had shown the truth of his claims against the priests of Baal in the faces of Ahab and Jezebel. If that were the case, if Patrick's truth were indeed the *central* issue, then Patrick himself would have entered the house to be burnt (which test, again following Elijah, he had also proposed). He deliberately chose not to do so, and that choice, given Muirchú's model, creates another anomaly, because all of the preceding series of tests have followed the pattern of Patrick alone against the druids alone. In order to accomplish his design, therefore, whatever it was, Muirchú had to switch fields in an unexpected and illogical manner.[11] Instead of Patrick and the druid entering the house together, Patrick declares that 'you yourself [the druid] and one of the boys in my service' shall enter the building to be burnt. He adds that 'you shall wear my garment and my boy shall wear yours'. Unaccountably, and

---

11 The perplexing nature of the switch has been recognized by other scholars since it renders the decisive step in the contest unequal. O'Loughlin suggests that Muirchú may have intended to show that Patrick's power was such that 'he can reproduce it in one of his spiritual "sons"'. But this rationale seems intrinsically weak and is not forwarded with any confidence. It hardly solves the puzzle, since it does not explain why the druid would have accepted the wager of his life against that of a boy deputy. O'Loughlin, *Saint Patrick*, p. 211, n. 126.

without objection to a now almost farcical trial – in which the druid must wager his life but the saint only his credibility, in which the druid must don his opponent's insignia while giving up his own to a servant boy – the contest goes forward on these terms. None of it makes clear sense, either spiritual, magical or narrational, and that is why no existing explanation of Muirchú's purpose can yet be deemed sufficient.

Another surprising but perhaps related anomaly occurs just after this burning house episode in I 21 (20) of Bieler's edition. It concerns Loiguire's conversion and Patrick's prophecy of his future and that of his line. After the druid has been burnt and after Patrick has killed many 'impious people', the saint offers Loiguire an ultimatum: 'If you do not believe now you shall die at once, for the wrath of God has come down upon your head'. The king 'trembled' in great fear and so did his entire city. Calling his advisors, he declared 'it is better for me to believe that to die'. Patrick accepted his reluctant conversion but declared: 'Since you have resisted my teaching and been offensive to me, the days of your own reign shall run on, but none of your offspring shall ever be king'.

As has long been recognized, this is a case of a post-factual prophecy that is nonetheless wrong. Loiguire's line was not a distinguished one but it did produce kings.[12] It is an incredible mistake for Muirchú to make since the Uí Néill lineages were well known and he had deliberately sought out a son of the great Níall Noígíallach (during whose reign, apparently, Patrick had been enslaved) to be Patrick's opponent. Indeed, he had named Níall as *origo stirpis regiae huius pene insolae*, so that he already had a particular interest in that family.[13] Analysed in this manner, a series of surprising oddities are seen to exist that call for some explanation. These include Patrick's false prophecy, the separation of the mantle motif from the vision test only to have it inserted into the burning house episode on the back of a druid, and Muirchú's decision to remove Patrick from the house so that Benignus could be placed there in his stead. Until these puzzles are clarified, no analysis of Muirchú's work is adequate, and no comparison can be properly executed. As far as I can determine, the most promising route to a solution is to treat them as a linked whole and to seek an explanation in Muirchú's interest in the Elijah/Elisha narrative.

Like Solomon, King Ahab married a foreign woman, the influential Jezebel who 'set' him to evil deeds. He built a temple for her and followed her in worshipping Baal. He 'did more to provoke the Lord the God of Israel than all the kings of Israel that were before him' (3 Reges 16:31–33). He persecuted followers of Yahweh, and insulted the prophet Elijah by calling him a 'troubler' of Israel. Elijah replies that it is not he who troubles the land but thou 'and thy father's house'. Ahab's father, Omri, was the heroic founder of the Omride

---

12 On the *Cenél Lóeguire*, see Dáibhí Ó Cróinín, 'Ireland, 400–800' in idem (ed.), *A new history of Ireland: prehistoric and early Ireland* (Oxford, 2008), pp 206–9. 13 Bieler, *Patrician texts*, p. 74.

dynasty, famous in the surrounding lands, but just as religiously disloyal as his son. In the confrontations between Ahab, Jezebel and Elijah, many hundreds of prophets are killed on each side. The slaughter was fierce. Its recollection may in some degree have prompted Patrick's severity at Tara, but it cannot have been determinative in the case of the king, since the saint is actually far harsher on Loiguire than Elijah is on Ahab, who has the excuse of a depraved wife. It is during this struggle that Yahweh directs Elijah to choose Elisha as his successor. Muirchú also follows this cue, although he separates it from the conflict proper in his *vita* and does not connect it with the death of the prophet in 4 Reges. Like Loiguire, who finally accepts the faith, however, Ahab does show some signs of remorse. Hence, although at one point Elijah condemns him, saying 'I will bring evil upon thee, and I will cut down thy posterity, and I will kill of Ahab him that pisseth against the wall' (3 Reges 21:21–22), Yahweh eventually decides to show him mercy because the king humbles himself. Ahab rent his garments, put on sackcloth and fasted. Yahweh is more-or-less satisfied. Speaking to Elijah, he says:

> Hast thou not seen Ahab humbled before me? Therefore, because he hath humbled himself for my sake, I will not bring the evil in his days, but in his son's days will I bring the evil upon his house. (3 Reges 21:29)

Patrick's unhistorical prophecy about the lack of kings in Loiguire's line is thus perhaps most plausibly explained on the basis that Muirchú is overburdened with too many comparanda, some of them already conflicted at the source. Because he is deeply committed to the Elijah narrative, he is forced to juggle with too many balls in the air – with the behaviours of Patrick and Elijah, Benignus and Elisha, Loiguire and Ahab, Baalites and druids in addition to two divine prophecies, in the first of which all royal progeny are to die, and in the second of which they are to suffer evil after their father's death. The scriptural situation may have allowed Muirchú to compromise; Loiguire's sons will live, but will not be kings. It is more probable, however, that he was quoting from memory and simply ran the two prophecies together in a way that falsified each. Secure in the knowledge that a negative prophecy had indeed occurred in his model, he did not pause to think. His desire to follow the biblical model wherever he could was overarching. He also follows it in some other cases where, for example, he famously compares Loiguire at Tara with Nebuchadnezzar at Babylon. In some ways, however, the Elijah/Elisha saga is more orchestrational and important.

These findings allow one to say something more about the nature of dispute in the later seventh century because they reduce the danger of reading what one wishes into the text and enable a sharper focus on issues that Muirchú sought to settle or even exclude. Clearest is this: Armagh's claims to jurisdiction were founded on Patrick's status and mission, but any connection between Patrick and Armagh could be questioned on the basis of an apparent lack of evidence for Patrician transmission of power to Benignus, whom both Armagh and Muirchú wished to regard as the saint's *successor*. Reverence for Patrick the Apostle could perfectly well co-exist with a refusal to recognize bishops of Armagh as his heirs. The weight of such attitudes is also indicated elsewhere in the *VP*, where much effort is expended to show Patrick accepting and royally establishing Armagh (see below) and again when Muirchú almost painfully seeks to show that it is only God's implacable will that can transgress Patrick's dearest wish to be buried at Armagh.[14] Ergo: neither clear episcopal continuity nor a holy body to prove otherwise. Muirchú saw a chance to refute the first of these issues by focusing on the status of Benignus in the *vita*. We can be sure of its precise contemporary significance because his chosen vehicle for argument is the Elijah/Elisha likeness, that place in the Bible where the procedure for succession from prophetic 'father' to his prophetic 'son' is most clearly detailed. It is thus ideal for Muirchú's purpose, and easily identifiable to all biblically trained clergy because of the perception test in conjunction with the mantle transfer. But note especially the nature of the liberties taken with the story. When Elisha acclaims Elijah as his 'father' (his double portion in law depends upon that relationship being expressed), he is apparently a mature enough man to be able to inherit the insignia of the mantle; Benignus is not! No one can doubt that Muirchú would have changed that awkward fact if he could; it would have solved all of his problems. Hence, we can be sure that it was widely known, either in text or tradition, that Benignus was too young to have been ordained as bishop by Patrick (and hence also that Patrick was held to have died before he could have accomplished that task). Muirchú thus had no choice but to invent a *designation* scenario instead – one that was based upon the saga, and in which the boy was shown to be so astoundingly precocious and sanctified that he could see into heaven like his far older and more experienced master. He was eminently worthy to receive the mantle even if he could not yet legally do so. Muirchú then seeks to diminish any questioning about the boyhood issue itself with the intertextual river miracle recalling the fact that Elisha too required time to become as powerful as his 'father'. It is a clever addition.

Two types of inheritance and the pagan option

It is clear from Muirchú's efforts that the idea of a *personal* transmission of power from the founder to his successor was important for the legitimacy of the successor in seventh-century Ireland. Even more notable, so was the view that a saintly figure (whether bishop or abbot, as we shall see) should also be a

14 See especially Sharpe, 'Patrick and the see of Armagh'.

prophetic leader in the OT sense. As for the career of Benignus, however, there is practically nothing that history (as opposed to propaganda) can do for us, since no dates are secure and mentions of Benignus (in Tirechán or elsewhere) do not advance the matter.[15] Perhaps the most interesting of those occurs in the *Liber Angeli* (probably pre-dating Tirechán and Muirchú by a generation or more), which notes that its primatial decrees were made by 'Auxilius, Patricius, Secundinus, Benignus'.[16] This indicates that the name of Benignus had played a significant role in earlier Armagh legal polemic. Particularly interesting in this list is the fact that the name of Auxilius is placed before Patrick and that of Secundinus occurs between Patrick and Benignus. It suggests that an earlier tradition, in which neither Patrick nor Benignus was viewed as the foremost leader, is now being manipulated. Assuming that the names indicate the known existence of an earlier tradition of seniority – a fair supposition since it is very difficult to imagine the emphatically pro-Patrician author of the *Liber Angeli* not otherwise placing Patricius first – then it seems probable that part of Muirchú's task was to counter this known earlier view by placing Patricius first and Benignus second.

In Muirchú's estimation, this theme of Benignus' worthiness to inherit required another miracle. That is the true reason for the burning house episode since it is here that Muirchú lodges his own version of the mantle motif in order to suggest its passing from father to son. That has not hitherto been recognized, however, and requires further analysis. As noted earlier, the fiery house incident stands out because of the very illogicality of Benignus taking Patrick's place in the contest. If one assumes with Muirchú that Benignus is Patrick's successor, however, then one might be inclined to view it in a more favourable light on the grounds that Patrick's heir, even though a small boy, can properly act as his representative when Patrick *deliberately chooses him to act in his place*. And when the fire is burning, Muirchú further shows that Benignus can do what Patrick could have done. He is Patrick's capable surrogate in this testing sphere, just as he was in regards to the other test of seeing into heaven. That must have been Muirchú's purpose because it is the only sufficient explanation for his trick of substitution.

From this perspective, the matter of inheritance is *again* the one being highlighted and one might thus expect that theme to continue in the rest of the episode if the view is correct. In fact, it does, but with the difference that

15 His scant biography is discussed by David Dumville, 'Auxilius, Iserninus, Secundinus and Benignus' in David Dumville (ed.), *Saint Patrick, AD493–1993* (Woodbridge, 1993), pp 89–105. 16 Text in Bieler, '*Liber Angeli*' in *Patrician texts*, pp 184–91. See also Hughes, *Church*, pp 276–81; David Dumville, 'The Armagh list of "coarbs of St Patrick"' in Dumville (ed.), *Saint Patrick*, pp 273–8. An overview of problems appears in James Carney, 'Patrick and the kings' in *Studies in Irish literature and history* (Dublin, 1979), pp 324–74; Binchy, 'Patrick and his biographers'; R.P.C. Hanson, *Saint Patrick: his origins and his career* (Oxford, 1968); E.A. Thompson, *Who was Saint Patrick?* (Woodbridge, 1999).

Muirchú now insinuates the pattern of Uí Néill inheritance ritual rather than one from the Bible. This native ritual is well known, with its earliest witness in the genealogies of the Laud 610 manuscript dating to the mid-eighth century.[17] It too features a house, a smithy in fact, which is burnt down with *royal* sons inside. Like Patrick, the ritual director in the Uí Néill case must remain *outside* the house because his status is established and not in question and he is the one who orders the sons to enter. A reminiscence of the secular pattern thus serves Muirchú's interests while also helping to explain the manner of his narrative; it amounts to a *tanaiste ríg* designation for Benignus. The scenario highlights the point that Patrick is not just a bishop with an honour-price equal to a king; he is an archbishop, the 'king' of bishops, and thus the only full equal of the storied king of Tara. His heir must, therefore, also succeed by the Tara test if that equality argument is to be sustained. The mistake of commentators has always been to suppose that truth and conversion are the main concerns of this episode; in fact, although these are certainly stressed, especially in the earlier chapters of the *vita*, status and primacy are determinative and the rest are secondary. In the secular ritual, the building is then set afire with the sons passing through while their suitability to rule is determined by the symbolic nature of the tools that they retrieve from the building as they exit. Of course, in the *vita* case, only Benignus can survive in order to exit. As he does, he would naturally carry out his father's Christian 'tool', his chasuble, 'which the fire did not touch'. This garment is clearly symbolically important because Muirchú states that it was the only thing left intact in the house except Benignus himself. Although the boy's exit with the chasuble is not mentioned in *VP*, it is a natural consequence of the facts that the prophet's garment was unharmed in the fire – someone had to bring it out – and that Benignus was Patrick's specially chosen servant who would normally care for and carry the items of his master's craft. Because of Patrick's designation, we know that he is the one who will eventually wear the chasuble. The prophet's 'mantle' has thus now been transmitted from one prophet who can witness heaven to another, and it has been done through fire as in the Elijah/Elisha model, even though the carrier is as yet too young to wear it. That too is a reason for Muirchú to turn to the Uí Néill ritual. As opposed to the biblical case, it is the symbolism of retrieval that is important and not any immediate wearing or using.

Although scholars have not previously examined the burning house chapter in terms of a secular ritual that links it to the prophetic succession episode of the *vita*, that procedure actually better explains the scenario as Muirchú presents it. It makes Patrick into a kingly figure who can determine the succession to his

---

17 Kuno Meyer (ed.), 'The Laud genealogies and tribal histories', *Zeitschrift für celtische Philologie*, 8 (1911), 291–338 at 304; Gerard Murphy, *Saga and myth in ancient Ireland* (Cork, 1955), pp 58–9. It is generally assumed in the scholarly literature that the Laud reference is based upon the Patrician ordeal, but there is actually no supportive evidence and it is conjecture only.

throne (as in the Uí Néill tradition) by ordering the testing in fire of his 'son'. At the same time, it reinforces Muirchú's own emphasis in his other chapter on Benignus, where he makes him a prophetic successor according to the Bible. In narrative terms, on the other hand, it explains without strain the illogical switch in the text that inserts the contestant's *heir* into the burning house rather than the contestant. In the present reading, that is a design rather than a puzzle. It also offers one reason (there is another) why Muirchú does not include the mantle motif with the perception test where it belongs; by dividing the two motifs he can double the source legitimation, making it native as well as biblical.

If this interpretation is correct, however, then why does Muirchú not announce it clearly and avoid the ambiguity? Why does he not explicitly treat the episode as a passed burning house test as he does with the perception criterion? And why not have Benignus emerge from the ashes proudly waving the prophet's chasuble? Muirchú cannot afford to do any of this because the burning house test is a purely secular one redolent of paganism and the *druí goba* of profane tales.[18] Indeed, it is a measure of Armagh's desire to change (or create) perceptions about Benignus' relationship to Patrick that Muirchú is willing to include it and let ends justify his means. In order to do so unassailably, in order to provide 'deniability' in modern jargon, he applies an appropriate citation from the Book of Daniel, where we find other young men unharmed in a fiery furnace (Daniel 3:21, 91–94). Benignus is thus like 'the three young men: the fire did not even touch him, and brought him neither pain nor discomfort'. Seen in conjunction with an earlier reference to Babylon and Nebuchadnezzar, these allusions seem fitting. While the passage from Daniel can help prove Patrick's truth against the druids, however, it is useless in proving Benignus' right to succeed him as prophet and bishop. This is now the more important issue since the perception test *requires* a mantle transfer in order to be biblically complete. Perception alone is only half the matter. Not to include the mantle half somewhere – one notes that a chasuble is the near perfect Christian substitute – having already drawn heavily on Elijah/Elisha materials, is to raise a grave question that is then left unanswered. Nor can Muirchú easily allow Patrick to otherwise formally pass the mantle himself because, again following biblical logic, that would mean that Patrick's prophetic reign was over, that he now had to die or otherwise ascend to heaven like Elijah. But that would leave Armagh once more without a body, and with a boy still too young to be a bishop. To all eventualities then, the fiery furnace allusion provides a cover beneath which the significance of an entirely unrelated ritual can be *silently* inserted to serve a godly purpose. It is also tolerable in this guise because, after all, it is part of a demonstration by which Patrick defeats the druidry to which it relates. Patrick's previous contests with

---

18 The legal ritual of *tellach* is described in T.M. Charles-Edwards, *Early Irish and Welsh kinship* (Oxford, 1993), pp 259–73.

the druids are fitting camouflage, but the substitution of Benignus breaks the symmetry and signals the creation of an ambiguity that Muirchú views as necessary to his purpose.

Muirchú is thus an extremely clever, and exceedingly slippery, defender of his community's claims. I would go even further to suggest that a technique of studied ambiguity is a hallmark of his methodology in the VP. It is his chosen forté, one that he is perfectly willing to exploit on those occasions when a mixture of secular and Christian motifs can serve his larger intent of Armagh's aggrandizement. An analysis of some examples of his technique can serve a twofold purpose in the present investigation: first, by demonstrating a pursuit of that methodology itself, and second, by way of vindicating the present interpretation of the burning house episode.

Consider, for example, the long chapter in which Patrick founds his community at Armagh and then gains the hilltop site that he wants. The original grantor, a wealthy man named Dáire, sought to reclaim his lands through the legal process of *tellach*, which begins with an animal grazing the land in question (and, if carried to its end, would conclude with a fire-lighting in the homestead).[19] These events are depicted in detail with description of the landowner's deceptions, attacks and final grant of the hill that Patrick had desired.

> And they went out together, holy Patrick and Dáire, to inspect the marvelous and pleasing gift that he had offered, and they climbed to the top of that hill, and found there a doe with its little fawn lying in the place where there is now the altar of the northern church at Armagh, and the companions of Patrick wanted to catch the fawn and kill it, but the holy man objected and forbade them to do so. He even took up the fawn himself and carried it on his shoulders, and the doe followed him like a meek and loving lamb until he let the fawn go in another glen, to the north of Armagh where, as knowledgeable men tell us, there persist to the present day signs of his miraculous power.

As it stands, the passage can be interpreted as describing a loving shepherd who cares for and protects all animals, wild or tame. The doe and fawn lying in the place where the altar now stands is an especially nice touch which may also show

19 Maud Joynt, 'Echtra mac Echdach Mugmedóin', *Ériu*, 4 (1908), 91–111; Whitley Stokes, 'The death of Crimthann son of Fidach and the adventures of the son of Eochaid Muigmedón', *Revue Celtique*, 24 (1903), 172–207 at 191–203; John O'Donovan, *Miscellany of the Celtic Society* (Dublin, 1849), pp 67–79. In *The sacred isle: belief and religion in pre-Christian Ireland* (Cork, 1999), pp 185–90, Dáithí Ó hÓgain argues strongly that Dáire of Armagh is an echo of the deity known as the Dagda. There is much in his argument that parallels my own, except that I am maintaining that Muirchú deliberately creates the ambivalence. Ó hÓgain also points out that the change to deer-shape in the story is an example of the druid trick called *féth fiadha*, here represented as performed by Patrick. I do not understand why this would be considered a 'cheap folkloric miracle' any more than, say, the miracles performed by Elisha in the OT that are sometimes compared to medieval hagiography. See Howlett, *Muirchú*, p. 175. For the enormous amount of folklore in the OT, see Theodore Gaster, *Myth, legend and custom in the Old Testament* (New York, 1969).

that a mystical meaning akin to the scriptural 'feed my lambs, feed my sheep' theme is present. Equally present, however, is the purely secular theme of kingship over land because deer in Irish story often lead to both. Indeed, the Uí Néill kingship myths just mentioned can also include a hunt for wild animals such as boar or deer that leads to the fertility goddess who bestows sovereignty.[20] We can be sure that this motif is being obliquely recalled because the deer/altar relationship is being established in the explicit course of a *land-claiming* inspection by which Patrick becomes the founding bishop of Armagh whereas his earlier episcopacy had been of a missionary type. Armagh is thus made into the capital of a Christian kingdom.

We know that Muirchú is well versed in this deer/human symbolism of secular story because he again alludes to it as a transformational device in the course of the conflict with Loiguire. It occurred just after the unwilling king was forced to bend his knees and adore the saint. Recognizing that Loiguire actually wished to kill him, Patrick 'blessed his companions, eight men with a boy', who then disappeared so that 'the pagans merely saw eight deer with a fawn going, as it were, into the wilds'. Loiguire beheld this with 'great shame' and returned to Tara with the 'few' of his men who had escaped death. The symbolic deer depart from a defeated Loiguire only to return thereafter to the company of the victorious Patrick. It is thus clear that the deer are playing an emblematic role. In both cases, Muirchú is manipulating the idea of sovereignty, its departure and its beginning. An additional important point in these stories seems to have escaped the attention of scholars, however. Note the unusually precise reference to the number and type of Patrick's companions as *octo viris cum puero*. The *puer* in question is surely an identification of Benignus, who is now described as a fawn in the eight *cervos cum hynulo* who run from Loiguire. He is thus already linked to a deer shape. This complements the doe with its fawn (*cervuam cum vitulo suo*) that Patrick finds on the Hill of Armagh. This extra creature – the fawn – is a divergence from secular story, since the future king finds, and needs only to find, a single transformed animal; two animals are one too many. But not in the designation paradigm that Muirchú has constructed! Read in conjunction with the altar reference and land grant, therefore, Muirchú is not just portraying a new and more sacred extended kingship for a royal bishop, he is actually hinting at the founding of an ecclesiastical *dynasty* in which continuity from older to younger is an important part of the message. The *second* bishop of Armagh (if that is what Benignus historically is) is thereby being forecast. Muirchú's studied ambiguity thus tends to confirm again that the theme of inheritance is vital to him because it is being contested by opponents of Armagh. Although subtly, indeed equivocally, presented, the female deer and her fawn

---

20 For this theme in relation to animal transformation, see Josef Weisweiler, *Heimat und Herrschaft: Wirkung und Ursprung eines irischen Mythos* (Halle, 1943).

99

that is lovingly carried by Patrick constitute a third reference to the inheritance theme, and a second reference to the same native inheritance mythos.

The incident of the departing deer is the final event of a series that began on the night preceding Easter when Patrick lit the vigil fire. This was lit before a coinciding festal fire of pagans said to be the only permissible one to illuminate the plain of Brega on that night. Historically, however, no such pagan ceremony would have existed at that time of the year. It is thus again clear that Muirchú is creating the situations and results that he wishes. And while the vigil fire is certainly a religious one, Muirchú quickly acts to incline it in a political direction because he has the druids tell Loiguire that unless Patrick's fire be extinguished, 'it will rise over all the fires of our customs, and he who has kindled it and the *kingdom* [my emphasis] that has been brought upon us by him who has kindled it on this night will overpower us all and you'. (In his account, Tírechán confirms this direction of argument by having Patrick declare that Benignus 'is the heir of my kingdom'.)[21] In case that broad hint is missed, the druids quickly add that the king should not approach the place of the fire, 'lest perhaps you afterwards adore him who lit it'. Loiguire should stay outside 'so that he [Patrick] may adore you and you be his lord'. The fire explanation is thus being deliberately constructed to bear a political implication as well as a religious one, and hence, after the victorious Patrick creates an earthquake that destroys most of Loiguire's forces gathered in the area before the tent, the defeated king's kneeling to Patrick immediately thereafter has political significance. The fire lit on the Hill of Slane possessed a certain legal potential also. It burned at the apparent border of a territory at the graves of ancestors that, probably, protected it (and Patrick will apparently cross over them next morning on his way to Tara).[22] Both fire and movement are thus again reminiscent of the process of *tellach* – a reclaiming of rightful inheritance – and should be interpreted in that light because Muirchú makes a special point of declaring that a lighting of the first fire on that night is a strictly royal prerogative belonging to the Uí Néill king. By his usurpation of the fire ritual, Patrick becomes the symbolic ruler over Tara and 'the great plain of Brega' just as his 'son' will then follow him as *tanaiste ríg* after a second usurpation in the burning house test.[23] The running sub-text is consistent; Muirchú is thus *systematically* writing on the margins of secular saga against a

21 Bieler, *Patrician texts*, pp 126–7. 22 If he had not already done so in celebrating the first Easter at the site. Bieler, *Patrician texts*, pp 84–5. See further Cathy Swift, 'Pagan monuments and Christian legal centres in early Meath', *Ríocht na Midhe*, 9 (1996), 1–26 at 13–26; eadem, 'St Patrick, Skerries and the earliest evidence for local church organization in Ireland' in Ailbhe MacShamhrain (ed.), *The island of St Patrick: church and ruling dynasties in Fingal and Meath, 400–1148* (Dublin, 2004), pp 61–79. 23 The full meaning of the term is still in dispute. For analysis, see D.A. Binchy (ed.), *Crith Gablach* (Dublin, 1979), pp 107–8; Donnchadh Ó Corráin, 'Irish regnal succession: a reappraisal', *Studia Hibernica*, 11 (1971), 7–39; McGowan, 'Royal succession in earlier medieval Ireland: the fiction of tanistry', *Peritia*, 17–18 (2003–4), 357–81. It is here argued that the term refers to a second in command or to a leader's representative.

background of Patrician conquest in which each element is constituted to resonate in both a secular and religious sphere. It is, moreover, at this time of the night, that is just after the earthquake and royal submission, that the deer and Patrick's 'son' in fawn shape are depicted as departing from Loiguire 'going, as it were, into the wilds'. It is a night-time denouement that, possibly, is meant to balance and correspond to the end of the next sequence of contests after which Loiguire again submits, and is told that 'none of your offspring shall ever be king'. The saint's 'son' will rule but the king's son will not. Patrick's taking of Armagh may thus be seen as a parallel to his symbolic taking of Tara, since *each* occasion features comparable elements of deer symbolism, *tellach*, and lordly submission over territory. Another such secular/Christian mixture will be discussed below.

Excepting the lordship reference and the designation of Benignus, none of these political or quasi-political aspects are clearly raised in the *vita* and all could be plausibly analysed on the basis of a solely religious agenda. Yet, no element ever slants in any direction except that which favours Patrick's domination against a background that functions to bolster Armagh's status and jurisdictional claims. They constitute a repetitive constellational matrix that cannot be accidental since each episode is coded to activate the recall of a traditional set of linked symbols that fit the occasion. Muirchú's ambiguity is thus a honed instrument of literary art designed to flexibly accommodate secular/pagan themes in such a manner that they can be silently expressed or denied at will. He turns the normal criteria of kingship against the king, the ritual of royal succession and prophecy against his offspring, while showing that the supreme authority of Patrick has been passed to his 'son' and hence to all bishops of Armagh. It is a dazzling tour de force that would have been impossible for any rival community to ignore. Had Muirchú been able to sustain this level of artistry, he would have been unbeatable. After the half of the *vita* that contains the Tara confrontations, however (these must have been re-thought many times in order to get pieces and allusions rightly meshed), his intensity flags although it recovers somewhat for the Dáire/Armagh episode and there are fine turns and touches elsewhere.

Patrick's extended dying, on the other hand, is not really well handled. Employing the biblical citations that he knew so well, Muirchú was perfectly capable of making a reader believe that Patrick yearned for Armagh like the face of God in the heavenly Jerusalem; he could have made the shock of its loss seem unbearable, whereas, instead, it is a sore but supportable disappointment. Adomnán did far better with Columba's last day. For sheer genius, however, there is nothing in any text to match the request granted to Patrick in exchange for giving up a burial in Armagh at the angel Victor's will: 'All the Irish on the day of judgment shall be judged by you ... so that you may judge those whose apostle you have been'. Over thirteen centuries, there has never been a time when that promise has not moved hearts, and for all we know may have moved many in the generation after its writing.

As for Patrick's dealings with kings, some commentators have neglected a major lesson of the *VP*, namely that Muirchú did not respect them and may well have despised the entire institution. Perhaps he took seriously those passages in the OT where kingship is denigrated, where it is presented as a creation due to the 'evil' will of the people, and where Yahweh regrets that he had allowed his prophet to give them a king.[24] This is supported by the fact that, as noted earlier, even when drawing extensively on the Elijah/Elisha materials, Muirchú is much harder on Loiguire than Elijah is on the murderously feckless Ahab. Loiguire is repeatedly threatened, browbeaten, humiliated and defeated in public as he watches his followers die around him while on his knees. In fact, his actions are basically defensive ones in the face of politico-religious attack by an aggressive holy man. Muirchú describes this superlatively. As he intended, one is at first willing to suppose that it is all for the greater good, but the fact is that he fine-tunes the cruelty too much. Because he seems happy to do so, one is left with the suspicion of a more personal element in his antagonism. This sense of a personal grievance or dissatisfaction appears to surface when Muirchú has Patrick confront the memory of a 'king', Miliucc, whose slave he had been for some six to seven years. Upon landing in Ireland after a long absence, Patrick thought that

> nothing was more fitting than first of all to redeem himself. Hence he made for the northern parts and went to see that pagan, Miliucc, whose slave he once had been, bringing him a double price to buy himself free from slavery, an earthly and a heavenly one, to free from captivity the man whom he had formerly served as a captive.

Muirchú repeats the point in the same chapter, I 11 (10), where Patrick 'was anxious to go without delay to visit the said man, Miliucc, and bring the price (of his freedom) and in this way, after all, to convert him to the faith of Christ'. When Miliucc heard of his coming, however, when he heard that his slave was

> about to come and see him in order to make him accept, forcibly as it were, a way of life against his will at the end of his days, for fear that he might be subject to his slave and the latter might become his master, the devil put it into his mind to seek death of his own free will in fire. He gathered all his wealth together in the palace where until then he had lived as king, and burnt himself along with it.

Patrick was stunned by this self-destruction when, as Muirchú wrote, he was standing in the right flank of Slíab Miss, and 'he had the first view of the district where he had lived as a slave'. Having expressed his grief at this 'king who chose to burn himself in fire rather than believe', Patrick proceeded to curse Miliucc

24 1 Reges 12:12–25. This becomes the *locus classicus* for much subsequent argument.

and his line: 'none of his sons shall sit on his throne as king of his kingdom in generations to come; what is more, his line shall be subordinate forever'.

The Miliucc episode can be interpreted as the sad suicide of a man driven to madness by anxiety and shame. This is a legitimate reading, but it is superficial and unconvincing if it excludes other significances in Irish thought about kingship. A self-instituted *royal* death in fire is too symbolic and outré a style of demise to be interpreted casually. Muirchú is also recalling the traditional ending of that kingship mythos whose beginning he raised in the fire for 'sons' at Tara. In its theoretical origins that fire functions to preserve justice but it can also lead to a royal pyre if, as with Miliucc, the ruler behaves unjustly. The 'devil' who moved Miliucc to seek death in fire comes from the pagan past: Muirchú is again exploiting the gaps in his chosen terrain of ambiguity just as he has done with the vigil fire, the departing deer, the discovered deer at Armagh and the burning house at Tara. It is even clearer in this instance because, as with the burning house where he had to abruptly subvert the rules of engagement in order to insinuate Benignus into the fire, he now actually invents a king where none existed before. In Patrick's *Confessio*, which Muirchú had read carefully, Miliucc does not appear as a king but simply as a banal landowner for whom Patrick had worked. That merits repudiation for two reasons. One possibility is that, if Patrick were going to be a slave to anyone, then in Muirchú's estimation it should be a king. Second, and more probable in the context, Muirchú needed Miliucc to be a king so that he could suffer a hard death *yoked to the idea of injustice* in order to underscore the idea that Patrick's slavery had occurred despite his virtues and not because of any possible failings on his part; it was a result of a violent crime committed against him in which Miliucc shared in the blame. Only at this point can the bizarre invention of a self-ignited royal burning make genuine narrative sense because only now does it serve a purpose in the text. It acts to help refute any perception that Patrick's six years of servitude might have unfitted him to be considered the most powerful of bishops or, perhaps, even a bishop at all. The utility of Muirchú's two-pronged strategy of ambiguity is especially clear at this juncture. From it one may deduce that the question of Patrick's fitness for the highest office because of the degrading character of his past slavery must have been perceived as one element in the attitude of those opposed to Armagh's claims.[25] Mystic ritual immolation, a purging in fire of an

25 One could also interpret the matter in terms of the illegally absconding slave, and that readily accounts for the references to payments for redemption. See McCone, 'An introduction to early Irish saint's lives', *Maynooth Review*, 11 (1984), 58–9. It seems to me, however, that it is the utterly shameful and dishonorable condition of the slave of six years that would most have worried Armagh, because it could easily be seen as a permanent stain incompatible with the sacred status of a bishop, especially perhaps for one whose community was claiming primatial rights. A money payment alone could not solve this. Armagh's much-censored copy of Patrick's *Confessio* (see below, n. 30) shows it to have been concerned with precisely this topic of humiliation in Patrick's past. Patrick's slavery could not be struck from memory, however, because it was an essential part of his story and thus had to be confronted and combated. Muirchú actually faced a legal and ideological

unjust ruler, is a well-crafted, efficient answer. In these two consecutive chapters (I 11 [10], I 12 [11]), covering Patrick's decision to go to Miliucc, and his witness of the death pyre thereafter, there are four references to slavery and two to a payment for redemption. It is further significant that both slavery and kingship are mentioned when Patrick is portrayed as meditating upon the ashes of Miliucc's house. A king's suicide is thereby turned into requital for an injustice committed against Patrick as a boy. While any reference to the enormity of the offence as such would require the raising of an unwanted troublesome and complicated issue, the entire matter could be dealt with quickly and then permanently dismissed through another instalment of the pagan mythos whereby an unjust 'king' dies in the fire through which he had become sovereign in the first place. While the meaning of one, or even both, of these motifs could be challenged if they answered to unrelated purposes, the fact that they appear rightly in the context of moral crime, invented royalty and retribution through fire can only signify that the Tara paradigm is being manipulated to service an agenda.

The portrayal of a socially risen escaped slave visiting a former master is a device that is designed to call to mind questions about the legitimacy of status and the nature of true lordship. Its mode is curiously presented in the *vita* since Muirchú depicts Miliucc as thinking that his former slave was coming to be his master rather than simply to be legally freed. Thus is the world turned upside down. The reader tends to make up his own explanation for the surprising incongruity, but there is no warrant for it in any previous material. Patrick had only recently landed in the country, and the narrative emphasis until then had been on redemption and on a brief episode of beneficial preaching. That detail about Patrick's mastery over Miliucc is thus a wholly prodigal and unnecessary addition; it says more about Muirchú's desire to create such a linkage than it does about anything that one might rationally expect from Miliucc. Muirchú has elevated his status, made him a king, precisely so that he may die as a bad king does in myth. His self-murder would be interpreted as grotesquely disproportionate by anyone except a proponent of Patrick's immutably regal character. Only to such a viewer might the drastic narrative invention seem called for. Significantly, one finds the same turning to issues of lordship when Patrick

quagmire in dealing with this. In actual fact, negotiations would surely have been necessary before Patrick could have ventured onto Miliucc's lands, for example, the lands of the *dominus* he had illegally fled. He would have been seen as, in some sense, a petitioner and a supplicant, and thus probably subject to an interrogation by Miliucc, who might have required an expression of abject penitence as well as monetary compensation before a deal could be struck. Patrick – still technically a criminal slave – might thus have been required to kneel before being offered or refused a seat. While it is hard to say what might have happened in a genuine case of this kind, the odds are that Patrick's prestige would have suffered in the procedure, and Muirchú's readers would have understood the transaction in this light. It is a propagandist's nightmare, but it can all be turned to advantage, brilliantly so, if Miliucc be treated as an unjust king punished according to tradition. The pagan twist is thus a necessary one. For interesting material touching on some less extreme but comparable procedures in the *VC*, see Brian Lambkin, '"Emigrants" and "exiles": migration in the Irish and Scottish church', *Innes Review*, 58 (2007), 133–55 at 142–7.

approaches Tara. Loiguire's druids advise him to stay away from Patrick's fire 'lest perhaps you afterwards adore him who lit it'. Matters should instead be arranged 'so that he may adore you and you be his lord'. Shortly after, so as to conclude the lesson, Loiguire is to be found kneeling before Patrick. Unlike Miliucc, whose kingship is invented purely so that it can be destroyed as a sign of cosmic sin, the continuity of Loiguire's rule is too well known to kill him off. His gesture of absolute subordination is thus necessary, and so is the comparable cursing of his descendents. In both cases, these references to status are depicted as arising from unjust pagans who are then shown as, in effect, submitting their authority to the saint. In fact, this turning of the question is always Muirchú's intent. All the events and patterns cited have been deliberately constructed to be ambiguous and readable in multiple ways; the evidence here is convincing. Analysis has repeatedly shown that such ambiguities suit the authorial purpose. They are ploys calculated to demonstrate the superiority of Patrick and his heir by every available standard together with the sheer irrelevance of any questions about his past slavery. Patrick is manifestly the lord and judge of all who oppose him; he is the only 'king' who truly behaves as a king. In order to display that lesson in reference to the question of slavery (that had helped to create a need for it), the Tara mythos was raided. Because the justice of a king began in his succession through fire, because his injustice is destroyed in it, the dual issues of a wrongly imposed inferiority and a rightfully claimed truth/superiority/ succession could all be settled by it. Indeed, the claim of Patrick's successors to govern the entire country could also be suggested through the Easter fire that ended in humbling the leader of the family 'that held the kingship of almost the entire island'.

Authenticating the full authority of the 'king' of Armagh whose plenitude has been rightfully passed to his successors is thus the principal issue in *VP*. Muirchú's development of a strategy of ambiguity is calculated to make the best cause of this to the greatest number, and his emphasis on Patrick's aggressive behaviour is linked to a worried insistence that the saint's own affirmations of human weakness in the *Confessio* have to be definitively countered. Armagh's drive to national primacy requires an all-conquering founding bishop whose right to rule through his heirs must be unquestioned and whose past must be untarnished by any sign interpretable as weakness or deficiency. It is this militant urge to power that gives the *vita* an important part of its tone, unity and interest. Far from being the only theme present, it is nonetheless the one that elicits the greatest artistic effort from the author.

Choosing ambiguity and training successors

On one level, Adomnán's attitude towards kings is in radical opposition to all that we have seen in the *VP*. There is no sense of breathless intensity in a desire to humiliate rulers, trounce them or prophesy failure for their sons. On the contrary, Adomnán has certainly thought deeply about presenting Columba as a faithful ally and patron in need. Kings can freely make requests of him, seek his advice, find protection for their lives and vengeance for their deaths while receiving victory in battle, favourable treatment for sons, help in constructing alliances, and refuge on Iona. Through miraculous power, Columba can see them near and far, when they are young or old, suffering or dismayed, and will then go to them with caring words of encouragement and a strengthening blessing. Even when warning them in the knowledge of future wrongdoing, he can offer good counsel, and even when rejecting them, no common thing, he expresses no joy in their loss or death that loyalty to him could have prevented. Whether in life on earth or after death in heaven, he will guard and tutor them throughout their careers.[26]

In the *VC*, neither pagan kings nor druids are treated harshly. When Columba climbs the steep path to the fortress of King Bridei of the Picts overlooking the valley of the Ness, he is visiting a king 'puffed up with royal pride' who bars the gates of his fortress to the holy man (II 35). At a blessing, the doors are thrust open and the king and his followers are alarmed just as on Easter Day when Loiguire sat at table with his princes and druids and 'holy Patrick with only five companions entered through closed doors' (I 19[18]). Anxious to attack Patrick, Lucet Máel, the druid, placed a drop of poison in his cup. Suspecting trickery, Patrick froze the liquor in the cup into ice so that only the drop of poison trickled out.[27] At Bridei's court, Adomnán presents his own cup miracle that begins when Columba asks Broichan, the druid, to free his Irish slave girl. On being refused, he prophesies that Broichan will have little time to live unless he changes his mind. After he has left, Broichan's glass cup shatters in his hands as he is drinking from it. As he begins to die, a message of compliance is dispatched to Columba who sends back a companion with instructions for a cure. Even an enemy is given a choice! Not long thereafter, Broichan and his fellow druids seek to harm the holy man at sea. Columba defeats them by calling on Christ's name 'in the sight of a heathen people' (II 34). No mention is made of retaliation against the druids. There are no mass killings and no scenes of royal humiliation. Rather, Columba seeks to show God's mercy and Columba's forbearance through example. After the door miracle, Adomnán depicts King Bridei greeting the holy man 'with due respect' and welcoming him 'with words of peace'. 'From

---

26 All of the actions and themes mentioned in this paragraph occur in what I have called the 'princely' chapters: see *VC* II, 7–15, 36, III 1–5. The importance of kings to Adomnán has recently been shown again by Barbara Yorke, who finds circumstantial but suggestive evidence of the abbot's involvement in king Aldfrith of Northumbria's accession: 'Adomnán at the court of King Aldfrith' in Wooding et al. (eds), *Adomnán of Iona*, pp 36–50. 27 Further background in Thomas O'Loughlin, 'Muirchú's poisoned cup: a note on its sources', *Ériu*, 56 (2006), 157–62; Aideen O'Leary, 'An Irish apocryphal apostle: Muirchú's portrayal of St Patrick', *Harvard Theological Review*, 89 (1996), 287–301.

that day forward for as long as he lived, the ruler treated the holy and venerable man with great honour as was fitting'.

The presence of a contest with druids and king and the complementary miracles of door and cup at a royal court are important items because they indicate a pattern of loose allusion to Muirchú's description of Patrick's contest with Loiguire and his druids at Tara.[28] But Adomnán has switched Muirchú's emphasis to one of reconciliation and respect between saint and king, and even in the case of the druids who continue to oppose the saint, Columba leaves them chastened but unharmed. Adomnán thinks at least as much of the Elijah saga as Muirchú, but his contests with pagan priests are bloodless, squalls instead of tempests. Indeed, his struggles are deliberately, almost palpably, underplayed, and are designed so as to make that point understood. He is reaching to and beyond Muirchú's audience. In the VC, Adomnán had all the dramatic ingredients at hand to create a powerful chariot-and-bugles spectacle à la Muirchú. He could easily have portrayed Columba as the Christian terror of the Picts. Rejecting that handsome opportunity, he shows his patron as working to free an unfortunate slave girl, as treating a king who had insulted him with even-tempered restraint, and even holding his hand against druids who had sought his death. The messages at this juncture are very clearly drawn, something that is not always the case in VC. Adomnán had almost certainly read Muirchú and – by including two parallel miracles while showing Columba behaving in a sharply contrasting manner to Patrick – wished to display his rejection of that author's entire approach to kingship and conversion. Here, he appears to be saying of his chapter, is the way that you, Muirchú, should have done it at Tara. Here is how a powerful holy man should deal with a ruler and his religious advisors in order to achieve a genuine respect that goes below the surface; the approach that works is one that avoids open challenge and allows a king to maintain honour and reputation. Like diplomacy, Christianity is best advanced by persuasion and not the sword. Unlike Patrick, Columba is the friend of kings and not their subjugator: would you, O king of today, not wish Columba as a friend also? Compare him to your druids or advisors who constantly make demands of you. Is not his king-friendly patronage demonstrably the kind that you would want if you had to make a choice among heavenly powers? Given the suggestive contrasts conveyed through the parallels, this appeal is intrinsic in the events themselves and blunt confrontational statements are unnecessary.

---

28 In such a context, the two authors' contrasting treatments of kings and druids become significant statements of attitude to be reflected in policy. As Thomas Owen Clancy remarks, 'Adomnán writing about Columba is, to an extent, Adomnán writing autobiographically, in the sense that the role he creates for Columba is one which he will have to live up to ... Without doubt some of Columba's actions, whatever their historicity, mirror Adomnán's own concerns': 'Personal, political, pastoral: the multiple agenda of Adomnán's Life of St Columba' in E.J. Cowan and D. Gifford (eds), *The polar twins: Scottish history and Scottish literature* (Edinburgh, 1999), pp 38–60.

Reading Adomnán after Muirchú is like coming to a warm fireside after a cold winter's walk. You are welcomed and can rely on the saint's hospitality. This compassionate persona could easily have developed otherwise, since, just as Muirchú had to combat the fretful and harried Patrick of the $Confessio$, so did Adomnán need to undermine the picture of the incendiary militant, more prideful aristocrat than humble monk, who had incited his relatives to war against Diarmait mac Cerbaill.[29] The contrast between the appeals of Muirchú and Adomnán is thus so blatant that it becomes notable in itself. Between threat and enticement, the latter is probably a more effective tactic against kings who have to be warlike anyway, and whose first reaction to challenge is aggression. Seduction tends to win over intimidation. That is how one achieves so spectacular a triumph as a Synod of Birr for example. And so, except when he is defending a king – it is noteworthy that the king is none other than Diarmait mac Cerbaill (I 36) – the pugnacious Columba of the annals is silently removed from memory. I suggest, therefore, although this is not the only rationale, that one saint's clement and impressively aristophilic persona was deliberately crafted to oppose the harshness of the other, that the VC is, in certain aspects, a quiet but steady argument about the readiness of Columba to support well-disposed rulers and dynasties.

In assessing this question, one should always remember that it is not the saints themselves being compared, but rather the portraits painted of them by their two followers at later dates. In reading the VP, one can always find the essential historical core of Patrick by reading his own letters, and that enables one to judge the alterations and reshapings contrived by Muirchú.[30] For the VC, we lack the authentic first-person voice. The most trustworthy early (and scant) facts about Columba must be gleaned from the annals and the $Amra\ Choluimb\ Chille$.[31] These suggest that he was a zealous soul, one who loved learning, the study of the law of scripture, but one who was a proud and defiant man in no

---

29 See Byrne, $Irish\ kings\ and\ high-kings$, pp 94–7; Michael Meckler, 'The assassination of Diarmait mac Cerbaill', $CSANA\ Yearbook$, 7 (Dublin, 2010), pp 46–57.   30 For the $Confessio$, see A.B.E. Hood (ed.), $St\ Patrick:\ his\ writings\ and\ Muirchú's\ life$ (Totowa, NJ, 1978), pp 23–54. The full text of the saint's $Confessio$ is contained only in Continental manuscripts. The Armagh copy has been 'drastically censored' to remove all passages interpretable as showing Patrick humble or humiliated. These include parts 26–8 that show Patrick censured by his superior; 45–6 that show him as derided by many; 27, 32, in which he is betrayed by a friend who reveals his youthful sin; 37, 50, in which he is accused of conduct comparable to simony; 42, in which his mission is shown to be opposed; 51, 52, in which he is shown as buying his safety from tribal rulers and officials and being placed in chains. See Binchy, 'Patrick and his biographers', 41–2. Armagh's worries about the humble or subordinate Patrick are here demonstrable, and these make it more probable that Muirchú's portrait is at least partly inspired by the wish to compensate, which then becomes overcompensation. 31 Even that is no longer certain if Jacopo Bisagni is correct in his linguistic arguments: see 'The language and date of $Amrae\ Coluimb\ Cille$' in Stefan Zimmer (ed.), $Keltem\ am\ Rhein.\ Akten\ des\ dreizehnten\ Internationalen\ Keltologiekongress$ (Bonn, 2010), II, pp 1–11. See further Whitley Stokes, 'The Bodleian $Amra\ Choluimb\ Chille$', $Revue\ Celtique$, 20 (1899), 31–55, 132–83, 248–89, 400–37. A convenient edition based on Stokes is Clancy and Márkus, $Iona$, pp 96–128.

wise averse to inciting to warfare where he judged it necessary. In this combination of traits, he is actually closer to the picture of an OT prophet than is Patrick, who has also undergone his own process of OT modelling as understood in Irish culture. In his presentation of Columba, therefore, Adomnán is closer to a biblically authentic portrait than is Muirchú, but the emphasis on Columba's compassionate and merciful side appears to have been magnified or embellished. It is a picture of the saint that seems to reflect a solicitous filtering through Adomnán's own sensibility developed during his long experience of leadership by means of persuasion and diplomacy.

If Adomnán is kinder towards kings, and more desirous to aid in the severity of the crises they must often suffer and overcome, it does not mean that he differs in theory with Muirchú about their inferiority when compared to the higher clergy. His ideal society is one in which the king is guided by the prophet who had created him in accord with OT ritual, and who reacts to events in accordance with an OT paradigm in which the prophet/judge is the guide whose admonishments a king must follow. In practice, this means that the prophet would play a deciding role in choosing the ruler, and if necessary, would also exercise the divinely given right – because he is a prophet – to replace him if later found wanting. As shown by the grandeur and proclamation of law at the Synod of Birr, Adomnán thought in these larger and socially transformative terms. His radical view turns on the conception of a heavily Old Testamentary-tinged Christian form of government. Muirchú's vision of kingship would have been anathema to him because Muirchú thought more about Armagh's primatial claims than he did about the right ordering of this newly Christian society. In order to gain recognition of these, Muirchú was willing, despite all Patrick's smashing of idols and breaking of kings, to compromise with the conditions of pagan kingship, to tolerate, however obliquely, traditional rituals of designation and hierarchy even when affecting the foundation of Armagh. Contrariwise for Adomnán, who, probably ostentatiously, never refers to Tara itself, despite the remarkable fact that he mentions by name ten of the fourteen kings of Tara between 560 and 640.[32] His fixation is clear, but his hostility is framed in his omission. To him, of course, the transparency of Muirchú's methodology would have been obvious. How much it influenced him to present his own solution to pagan ritual structure is hard to say. Although he may have pondered the question for a long time, the appearance of the *VP* could well have been the prompt that he needed in order to write. Although one would not wish to argue *post hoc propter hoc*, the odds tend to favour the view that he would not have wished Muirchú's approach to prosper for want of a better alternative. For all of

---

32 Immo Warntjes, 'The role of the church in early Irish regnal succession – the case of Iona' in *L'Irlanda e gli Irlandese nell'Alto Medioevo* (Spoleto, 2010), pp 155–214 at p. 174, where names and reign dates are cited. = *Settimane di studio della fondazione centro Italiano di studi sull'alto medioeveo* LVII.

his apparent exuberance in destructive miracles, therefore, Muirchú appears as the author most willing to compromise with things as they are. His vision is narrowed by a drive for ecclesiastical aggrandizement, whereas Adomnán seeks wider transformation to be achieved through applying OT norms to the governance of Irish society. Adomnán is a pragmatic idealist, however, and does not ignore his own political situation. The prophet who gives impetus to this new conception of right order is Columba, not Patrick, and thus it is the abbots of Iona who will be the licensed guides of future kings. Like a trained debater, Adomnán does not argue on his opponent's grounds; he probably views those as best countered at another venue. Instead, he presents a plan of Christian reform through diplomacy and the management of rulers that, if achieved, would have powerfully strengthened his community, and enabled an efficient neutralization of Armagh's efforts when that became necessary.

Comparison of the two *vitae* is further encouraged by the surprising findings that each author draws substantially on the same OT texts for highly significant aspects of his message and presentation of detail. I have analysed the Columban side of this intertextual approach in the previous chapter and hence will only summarize some results where necessary. As shown above, a key narrative for Muirchú is the Elijah/Elisha saga. He uses it to shape Patrick's battles with the druids, especially the burning house test, part of the treatment of Loiguire and his line, and the vision test for Benignus, where, however, the mantle motif of the saga is transferred to the burning house episode, where it can serve the inheritance theme by another route. Adomnán draws upon the same motifs of mantle and prophetic perception, but his treatment differs markedly. The contrast is instructive because the various nuances of usage inform us more clearly than heretofore of the purposes of the authors and of those fields of dispute where the authors *themselves* believed that their arguments needed to be fortified. We thus have an unusual opportunity to get closer to contemporary meaning.

For Adomnán, it is the mantle motif of the Elijah story that is crucial. He introduces it in III 1 of the *VC*, where it is a 'robe of marvelous beauty' that is given in her dream to Columba's just pregnant mother in order to show that her child is a prophet 'from the womb' like the towering figures of Isaiah and Jeremiah. The cloak grows ever larger, 'so that it seemed to be broader than the plains and to exceed in measure the mountains and the forests'. It is this mantle that appears in I 1, where Columba 'seemed so tall that his head touched the clouds' and where, standing in the middle of an army's camp, it covered nearly all perimeters. The angel, who allowed the saint's mother to hold the robe for a short time, told her not to be upset when he took it away because her son 'shall be reckoned as one of the prophets'. In the following four chapters of this sequence leading up to III 5 – it is important to remark that it is a sequence – this 'becoming' of the prophet is indicated in various ways: by the child's foster-father, who witnesses the Holy Ghost in 'a fiery ball of light' pouring grace over him; by saints Brendan and Uinniau, who call other monks to witness that angels accompany Columba (as an angel accompanied Elijah and as 'sons of the prophet' witnessed Elisha with Elijah's robe); and in III 5, where an angel carries the 'call' of the prophet to Columba, which shows him to be the prophet who is divinely commissioned to anoint kings and to supervise them thereafter.

Seen from Muirchú's vantage point of biblical adjustment in favour of Patrick and Benignus, Adomnán's adaptation of the Elijah saga must have seemed like a perverse Columban exaggeration, if not worse. In the mid-seventh century, Columba must have been viewed by many as a come-lately Cenél Conaill saint. His career had been troublesome for the country and he had left it after excommunication to go into an exile of some kind.[33] If his prestige was now rising, it was mainly due to his powerful relations in the north and at Tara and, most recently, to the great skill and fame of Adomnán, another relative and successor. That same Adomnán was now trying to take a regional saint and exalt him to the level of national rank held uniquely (in Armagh's opinion, at least) by Patrick. He too was being depicted as a missionary apostle, but one who actually surpassed the elder figure because his paruchia was an international organization that included Britain as well as Ireland, all the islands of the ocean in fact. It is the divine bestowal of the mantle on Columba that best expresses this institutional claim to the territory. Its spreading immensity is a statement of absolute independence. It is the perfect geographic complement to *snádud* and *turtugud* in Irish law, those terms signifying the legal level of protection that one man of rank might confer on another of equal of lesser rank.[34] Sent by God expressly for his *chief* prophet, worn by Elijah, Elisha and Samuel of the OT, mystically covering plains, mountains and forests, the wearer of this inherited garment clearly holds a rank beyond what anyone else can hope to match. Like a *termonn* around a monastic sanctuary, the mantle's fringes establish an inviolable border. Such an area would normally be consecrated by king, bishop and people, but that has already been accomplished in monumental scale by the Creator of all.[35] We know that Adomnán thought in exactly these terms because, in the *VC* I 1 incident already mentioned, he provides an example of the breadth of Columba's protection granted to king Oswald's army. It is established by the extent of the giant saint's robe that covers nearly all the army camp. Those few not covered were destined to die on the morrow's Battle of Denisesburn, by which Oswald the prince became the ordained emperor of all of Britain. This is the worth of Columba's protection. Its compass is suggested by the broad territories and nations won by those who nestle beneath it.[36] The measure of

33 *VC* III 3. Sharpe, *Adomnán*, pp 12–15; Smyth, *Warlords*, pp 90–3.   34 Binchy, *Críth Gablach*, pp 106–7; Fergus Kelly, *A guide to early Irish law* (Dublin, 1988), p. 140.   35 Hughes, *Church*, p. 148; Lisa M. Bitel, *Isle of the saints: monastic settlement and Christian community in early Ireland* (Ithaca, NY, 1990), p. 73.   36 Clare Stancliffe, 'Oswald, "most holy and most victorious king of the Northumbrians"' in Stancliffe and Cambridge (eds), *Oswald*, pp 33–83.

Iona's jurisdiction was thus greater than Armagh's and that will have been preached before it was written. As Adomnán had St Brendan proclaim, God had predestined Columba 'to lead the nations to life', and he had made Mochta, Patrick's disciple, declare that Columba 'will become famous through all the provinces of the ocean's islands'.[37] Whether or not these grandiose claims were expressed in eirenic terms, they must have seemed like a daring challenge to the longer-standing fame of Patrick, whom Muirchú and Tirechán had compared to the founder Moses, the first prophet/judge of Israel. And Muirchú was right, it was a challenge! One recognizes this in the very reaching for OT renown in which Adomnán likens Columba to Isaiah, Elijah and Jeremiah, as well as explicitly to Peter, the head of the apostles, Paul, the greatest theologian and missionary, and John, the author of a gospel and beloved disciple, among all of whom Columba takes his place as he sits before the Trinity (II 32). The Armagh saint has no seat at this gathering; he is back in the ranks somewhere. As Tara is silently disdained in not being mentioned, neither is Patrick except, pointedly, in reference to his follower's praise of Columba.

Patrick's rank among saints seems to have been rising through the course of the seventh century. Muirchú's portrait of him as national apostle may not have been widely held at its beginning. When Columbanus was writing in Milan to Pope Boniface IV in 613, he stated that the Irish were bound to St Peter's chair because they had received the faith from the pope at Rome.[38] This is surely a reference to Palladius, sent as first bishop by Pope Celestine in 431, who laboured in the southern part of the country, and whom Muirchú mentions only to say, probably wrongly, that he quickly set about returning home. But Muirchú is not much worried by this earlier tradition in the 690s; he would have spent more time on it if it had been required. What he wishes to recall is the sentiment uttered by Cummian, who wrote to Abbot Ségéne of Iona about the Easter question in 632 or 633 and referred to Patrick as *sanctus Patricius papa noster*.[39] While Patrick's work and rank above kings are certainly crucial foci in Muirchú's estimation, his status as national apostle, as opposed to apostolic ruler, *almost* seems to be taken for granted. Muirchú's demonstration in this regard does not quite match the intense effort that Adomnán devotes to Columba's legitimation. Whereas Adomnán is most anxious to document Columba's status as apostolic prophet to the islands, Muirchú appears overly worried about the status of Benignus. The revised Patrick legend had probably been heavily promoted in recent generations and Columba's fame had lagged behind. Whereas Adomnán uses the device of Elijah's mantle to cover Columba, Muirchú employs it in a subsidiary way to point to Patrick's successor; Patrick himself doesn't seem to

---

37 *VC* III 3, Second Preface; Richard Sharpe, 'Saint Mauchteus, *discipulus Patricii*' in A. Bammesberger and A. Wollmann (eds), *Britain, 400–800: language and history* (Heidelberg, 1990), pp 85–93. 38 G.S.M. Walker (ed.), *Sancti Columbani Opera* (Dublin, 1970), pp 38–9. 39 Maura Walsh and Dáibhí Ó Cróinín (eds), *Cummian's letter 'De controversia paschali' together with a related*

need it. It is quite otherwise in regard of earthly rank, which, apparently, contained a taint never forgotten. Muirchú works hard to demonstrate Patrick's overcoming of his earlier servile condition, and his exercise of miraculous power is thus not only directed at defeating kings, but at showing that his control of them is so complete that any questioning of his background or nature becomes preposterous. Adomnán needs none of this for Columba's assured aristocracy can be casually displayed in his unaffected dealings with kings, his ability to grant protection to them and his guidance of princes as well as exiles. Neither does he forget the common people as a number of chapters show Columba dealing kindly and thoughtfully with ordinary men and women. In the final analysis, however, Adomnán's greater appeal is to the elite, while Muirchú's is broader. Unlike Columba, Patrick is only incidentally the judge of princes; his final goal is to be the judge of all those in the nation whose apostle he has been. Certainly an imperial desire, it is also all-embracing.

A comparison of the Lives, partial as it is, thus uncovers several foci worth considering in a new light and with a refined attention to authorial emphasis. Most notable is Muirchú's strategy of studied ambiguity that enables him to construct an outwardly Christian condition or context that can nonetheless appeal to traditionalists because it is deliberately reminiscent of secular or pagan custom. That approach can serve multiple purposes, but the emphases in the *vita* seem to make these most important: first, Muirchú aims at fortifying Patrick's character as a lordly personage whose foundation at Armagh reflects his political equivalence but miracle-based superiority to all kings; and second, he wishes to exhibit Patrick as choosing Benignus to succeed him and doing so explicitly through tests of prophetic capacity that follow both biblical and secular precedent. There is a puzzle in the second case that we do not have enough information to decipher but which indicates that either something was amiss with episcopal continuity at Armagh or else something was amiss with Benignus' career that reflected on the issue. At Iona, on the other hand, succession is treated more subtly within a monastic framework, but its enormous importance to Adomnán is signaled by the fact that it both opens and closes the *VC*. I 2 of *VC*, which follows the summary first chapter, depicts a group of holy men who, like 'sons of the prophet' at the Elijah/Elisha transition, agree that Baithéne, Columba's 'disciple' at his death, is also his fitting successor. He is 'holy and wise' and an easy man to talk to and friendly towards strangers. He is shown as Columba's intimate to whom he reveals secret foreknowledge. In III 18 and the closing chapter III 23, he is chosen as the saint's heir. Along the way, however, his progress towards abbacy is seen to develop through a good monk's learning curve in which he can also make mistakes and be scolded. As Jennifer O'Reilly has shown,[40] this is part of a

---

Irish computistical tract, 'De ratione computandi' (Toronto, 1988), pp 92–5. **40** Jennifer O'Reilly, 'The wisdom of the scribe', pp 159–211; eadem, 'Adomnán and the art of teaching spiritual sons' in Wooding et al. (eds), *Adomnán of Iona,* pp 69–95.

process of long-term internal search and refinement that is meant to produce an heir who has graduated through a series of mental stages in which he has learned 'the fear of the Lord', and then gone beyond it to become a sage of spiritual wisdom. Even more notably, I would argue, Adomnán sees this developmental process as one that produces a mystically gifted scribal *prophet*. It is a goal especially suited to the monastic life, to years of copying scripture (which means that scribal monks know God's word better than anyone), and then to further years of deep meditation that brings them ever closer to the mind of God. It is this mind-to-mind connection that enabled Columba, even 'as a young man', to enjoy 'the spirit of prophecy, to predict the future and to tell those with him about things happening elsewhere' (I 1). It enabled 'a miraculous enlarging of the grasp of the mind'. In keeping with these conceptions, Adomnán shows Columba as copying the Psalms when he foresees his death, and stating 'here at the end of the page I must stop. Let Baithéne write what follows'.

> The verse that follows is: 'Come my sons, hear me; I shall teach you the fear of the Lord'. This is appropriate for Baithéne his successor, a father and teacher of spiritual sons, who, as his predecessor enjoined, followed him not only as a teacher but also as a scribe. (III 23)

This conspicuous allusion to a teacher and scribe is meant to recall Matthew 23, where Jesus scorns the scribes and pharisees but promises to send true scribes, prophets and wise men to the world: *Ecco ego mitte ad vos prophetas, et sapientes, et scribas* (23:34). It is an important theme in what follows. In a few cases, all three characteristics can be found in one individual, and it is this mixture, with an emphasis on prophetic character, that Adomnán wishes to reproduce in his monks.

Adomnán wishes to institutionalize this biblical goal by training successors who are prophets in their own right and wise men *because* they are scribes. His idea of the authority of the scribe is a magnified one that goes far beyond what one might expect. His succeeding scribe is not, I suggest, a spiritual visionary only; he is also the teacher of God's law for those outside the monastery. This naturally follows from the certain practice of Columba himself, as Adomnán presents and interprets it. It also follows from the behaviour of the very OT models that Adomnán has selected. Both Elijah and Elisha are thoroughly involved in the politics of their times through their dealings with kings and aristocrats. This is in addition to their teaching of large numbers of trainee prophets among their followers who will be seen as the ancestors of monks in the West. If Elijah curses, chastises and kills the followers of the Omride dynasty, Elisha plots, spies, slaughters and miraculously blinds their allied soldiers. Like Columba, he determines winners and losers in battle. In the end, the new ruler of Israel whom Elisha has supported simply asks him: 'My father, shall I kill them?' (4 Reges 6:8–33). To be a prophet according to this model does not simply require one to participate in the worldly affairs of rulers, it actually requires that one directs them according to God's will. This is a much larger vision than biblical study and the ascetic headship of a monastery – although that is how the preparation for leadership begins – because it seeks to replicate the OT category of a prophet who guides the people both directly and indirectly because he also creates, instructs and monitors their kings. That is what the prophet with the mantle normally does!

In his picture of Columba's interactions, Adomnán is also sketching the socio-political approach that his successors must imitate. And if the successor must be capable of a special divine perception, as Muirchú also believed, it looks as if Adomnán thought it possible to regularize, routinize and teach important elements of this charism through an intense emphasis on scriptural copying and meditation for those most spiritually advanced. Here too he is following the general pattern of Elijah and Elisha, whose disciples, whom they direct and sometimes live with, are also presented as possessing true prophetic skill (for example, 4 Reges 2:3, 5). Of course, such a prophet would not enjoy the same rank as the founder whom God had chosen from the womb, but he could achieve a measure of his 'father's' mystic inheritance. Like a prince who can always call on the dead Columba in battle, the successor will always have access to the founder's heavenly spirit. Part of this thinking is traditional since at least the time of Gregory the Great, but Adomnán's interpretation is more radical because it seeks to revive and rejuvenate an OT paradigm for a new age of prophets. Indeed, there is some reason to think that it may have had a certain quasi-theocratic dimension.

As I read the evidence, Adomnán's programme for prophetic (and not solely scribal) succession is outlined in *VC* III 17–21, a series in which apparitions of divine light and reaction to their effects are key elements. These chapters highlight firstly Columba's prophetic gifts and extraordinary receptivity to mystic knowledge, but they are also crafted to show that a measure of that gift was teachable and could thus be passed on to others. That teachability and heritability, through a preparation of the mind of selected followers who are thus made receptive to God's special grace, is a feature of the biblical model and texts that Adomnán makes Columba adhere to. Chapter one of the series demonstrates that Columba's holiness is attuned to the fire and light of the Holy Spirit and this makes Columba the leader of Ireland's saints. The following four chapters reinforce and expand the theme by suggesting that the scribal study of scripture develops a visionary power that leads to wisdom, leadership and abbatial succession. They also provide an instructive parallel to Muirchú's attention to Benignus, and it may well be that the comparison was deliberate and intended. This five-chapter sequence begins with the statement that four 'famous' monastic founders once came to visit Columba on Iona. 'With one accord', they chose Columba to act as celebrant of the Mass:

There, while the sacrament of the Mass was celebrated, St Brendan moccu Altae saw a radiant ball of fire shining very brightly from St Columba's head as he stood in front of the altar and consecrated the sacred oblation. It shone upwards like a column of light and lasted until the mysteries were completed. Afterward, St Brendan disclosed what he had seen to St Congall and St Cainnech.

This radiant 'ball of fire' (*igneum globum*), also called a 'column of light' (*columna luminosa*), is clearly a sign of God's presence and powerful regard for Columba as his enlightened representative.[41] Amid the five founders, it confirms a judgment and a choice. It signified Columba's special status and marks him also as a divinely sent *guide* (as such fiery columns also behave in the OT) for the peoples of his islands. It thus echoes Isaiah 51:4: 'Hearken unto me, O my people, and give ear to me, O my tribes: for a law shall go forth from me, and my judgment shall rest to be a light of the nations'. It recalls two other prophecies of the *VC* (III 3 and Second Preface). In the first, Brendan of Birr, another founder, reports that 'I saw a very bright column of fiery light going in front of the man [Columba]' and he read this as 'visible proof' that Columba had been 'predestined to lead the nations to life'. In the second, 'a holy disciple of the holy bishop Patrick' makes a 'marvelous prophecy' through 'revelation of the Holy Spirit'. He declares that 'Columba will become famous through all the provinces of the ocean's islands, and he will be a bright light in the last days of the world'. The theme of the extent of Columba's dominion as a prophet had already been broached in *VC* III 1, where the vast magnitude of his influence is suggested by his prophet's cloak that exceeded in measure the mountains and the forests. Behind the easily misleading simplicity of the *vita* descriptions lies a wealth of theological analysis that is frequently constructed, although more subtly so than in Muirchú, to bear a strong political meaning. One might wish to argue that such communication need have no relation to Armagh's claims as expressed in *VP* and elsewhere, but one is entitled to doubt that so much effort would have been expended on showing the agreement of monastic founders on precedence, and on the symbolism of dominion, destiny and heavenly approval of Columba's status, if Adomnán had not seen it as his duty to respond to the postulate of Patrick's hegemony. As warmly generous in tone as it usually is, the *VC* is not wholly lacking in signs of its origin in clerical conflict. Something that goes far beyond a simple witness to holiness is driving the rhetoric of these chapters.

A further sign of the importance of these points to Adomnán is the grandiose conception of the following chapter in the sequence which contains the most vaulting magnification of Columba that one finds in *VC*. It also contains a notable reference to his relative and successor Baithéne:

---

41 Stephen Sharman, 'Visions of divine light in the writings of Adomnán and Bede' in Wooding et al. (eds), *Adomnán*, pp 289–303; James Bruce, *Prophecy, miracles, angels and heavenly light?* (Eugene, OR, 2004), pp 140–7.

On another occasion when St Columba was living in Hinba, the grace of the Holy Spirit was poured upon him in incomparable abundance and miraculously remained over him for three days. During that time he remained day and night locked in his house, which was filled with heavenly light. No one was allowed to go near him and he neither ate nor drank. But from the house rays of brilliant light could be seen at night, escaping through the chinks of the doors and through the keyholes. He was also heard singing spiritual chants of a kind never heard before. And, as he afterwards admitted to a few people, he was able to see openly revealed many secrets that had been hidden since the world began, while all that was most dark and difficult in the sacred Scriptures lay open, plain and clearer than light in the sight of his most pure heart. St Columba regretted that his foster-son Baithéne was not there. If he had been present for those three days, he could have recorded from the saint's lips a great number of mysteries, both in ages past and future, unknown to other men, together with some interpretations of the sacred books. However, Baithéne was held up by adverse winds in Eigg, and could not be present until those three days and three nights of unique and glorious visitation had come to an end.

This chapter seeks to portray Columba as the closest possible intimate of the Holy Spirit. His enlightenment is conducted in a manner public to all ('no one was allowed to go near him') in the locked house where it occurs. It goes beyond anything in the OT (even the exotic descriptions in the 'call' of Ezekiel), because it describes a divine ecstatic experience of unheard of duration accompanied by brilliant light and most miraculous continuous revelations of truth. It is intended to demonstrate that Columba is the next great prophet after the apostles, that he is a leader of such consummate virtue and wisdom that any questioning of him is beyond lèse-majesté – an affront to the Holy Spirit himself, who has consecrated him as a *unique* vessel of revelation in the islands. His credentials for judgment are overwhelming, since anyone who could survive such an experience must be a walking avatar of the Spirit himself. In such a case, one hardly needs to descend to trivial sublunary detail in order to declare that Columba's will must always be supreme in Ireland; this world-shaking epiphany itself constitutes that argument and that warrant.

The name of Baithéne in this fabulous context captures one's attention. Why is he mentioned? As Columba's *successor* referred to in a house permeated with the *light*, if not fire, of the Holy Spirit, one might well expect a reference to inheritance. And it is there in the allusion to Baithéne who would then have recorded the words of the prophet in the same way that, in III 23, Columba directs him to continue to copy the psalm book that he himself had left unfinished. Such was appropriate because Baithéne was 'a father and teacher of spiritual sons', and Baithéne followed him as abbot 'not only as a teacher but also as a scribe'. Hence, this matter of scribal competence is strongly emphasized in the *VC* and is linked to inspired enlightenment of mind. *VC* I 23 is entitled 'Of the Letter I'. It refers to Baithéne's request of Columba to loan him one of the brethren 'to help me go through the text of the psalter I have copied and correct any mistakes'. The saint replies 'Why do you bring this trouble on us when there is no need? For in your copy of the psalter there is no mistake – neither one letter too many nor one too few – except that in one place the letter I is missing'. And so, when the entire psalter was examined, it was found to be as the saint had predicted. This small letter, formed by a single stroke of the pen, was of interest to theologians because it could point to the Greek *iota* and thus to Christ whose name in Greek begins with *iota*; it could 'mysteriously express the wholeness and perfection of scripture' divinely inspired.[42] The implication is thus that Baithéne is near to, but has not yet reached, the perfect harmony of whole wisdom. That is confirmed in the luminous house chapter, which notes Baithéne's shortcoming as well as his wondrous ability to copy in heavenly light. The conceptual trajectory thereby runs from scribal copying to knowledge gained of God's word, to 'fear of the Lord' that is the beginning of wisdom, and then to an indwelling of the Holy Spirit in the purified mind. As in III 17, with its fiery globe 'shining very brightly from St Columba's head' like a 'column of light', it is here that the ultimate talent is expressed, for the Holy Spirit can now communicate easily with that mind and his illumination transforms and encircles it. It is the light of knowledge and fire of inspiration that are seen as the spiritual gifts that the heir of Columba should possess. To name Baithéne, alone of all the Iona community, as that scribe who could have recorded the founder's answers in the luminous house, to regret, in addition, his absence causing the loss of those expositions, is to effectively isolate him from other brethren and to underline by inherent comparison his greater degree of worthy competence to act amid the light of the Holy Spirit. He and Columba share this ability but of all monks only Columba is more able. A slightly veiled announcement about inheritance, about abbatial succession, is thus stated here in III 18 and only confirmed by a further symbolic reference to Baithéne's scribal task of continuance in III 23.[43] Conceivably, these allusions to an absent Baithéne in a house bathed in light rather than fire might also have had an additional purpose; they may have been intended to scorn the Uí Neill inheritance ritual in the biblical guise given it by Muirchú in the *VP*. The existence of a small hint of satire on Adomnán's part is not entirely to be excluded. In both *vitae*, a brightly lit house activates a concern with succession.

An examination of spiritual capacity – it actually amounts to an evaluation of the prophetic capacity that enables one to act as an Iona abbot – is thus underway in the first two chapters of the sequence, although it is a coded progression according to a theological conception whose full significance can now only be

---

42 O'Reilly, 'The wisdom of the scribe', pp 179–82. 43 I must thus oppose O'Reilly's interpretation in 'The wisdom of the scribe', pp 192–9, an essay which I admire and from which I have learned a great deal. Because she excludes III 17, with its inherent judgment of Columba's leadership by a group of recognized monastic saints, she diminishes the connection with hierarchy and abbatial inheritance in what follows and can find it only in the continuity of copying in III 23.

recognized through analysis. Reaction to the illuminating light of the Spirit is the key criterion. That is further indicated by the three chapters that follow. Each fixes on the appearance of fire/light set in III 17 and continuing in III 18 until the thematic instruction is ended in III 21. These anecdotes illustrate how a pattern of gradual enlightenment learned through stages of growth in the 'fear of the Lord' that brings wisdom and inspiration comes to be present among the brethren of Iona. Each concerns a spiritual 'son' of Columba's. First is Fergnae (Virgno), who 'was so moved by the love of God burning within him that he entered the church alone to pray while the others slept'. He knelt in a side-chapel with a door ajar. After an hour or so, Columba entered the main building and 'with his arrival, the whole church was filled with a golden light shining from the heights of heaven'. Even though a partly closed door intervened, Fergnae was thrown into fright 'so that his strength failed him utterly'. Columba was supernaturally aware of all that transpired and the next day called Fergnae to him in order to comfort the still fearful monk: '"O my dear son", the saint said, "what you did last night was well pleasing in the sight of God, lowering your eyes to the ground for fear of his brightness"' (III 19). A similar thing happened on another night to one of the brethren named Colgu. He happened to be standing at the door of the church for a brief prayer when suddenly the church was filled with light, 'instantaneously as if it were lightening', as Columba was praying within. Afraid, Colgu immediately returned to his lodging. Next day, Columba called him and 'reprimanded him somewhat harshly' (III 20). In the future, he should not attempt to see surreptitiously the light from heaven that was not given to him. In the third case, Columba earnestly warns his foster-son Berchán not to come to his lodgings that night for his tutoring. Berchán disobeyed and contrived to spy on the saint through a keyhole as a heavenly vision was unfolding in a radiance of light. Unable to endure the light, Berchán ran away. Next day, he was reprimanded 'very severely' and told that the only reason he survived was because the saint had prayed for him at the moment of his spying. Columba prophesied an evil life for him but his soul would be saved in the end by the saint's intercession (III 21).

It is not clear that the lights of these chapters are always of the same kind or that they match those of other chapters. The light of III 18 is certainly the most significant, for it accompanies the descent of the Holy Ghost himself and is thus unlike, say, the lights of III 23, which accompany Columba's passing. These are apparently commemorative, meant to 'proclaim how much honour' God had conferred on the holy man. The light of III 18 has a more sharply defined focus, however, in that it transforms a specific intellect; it effects a change in that Columba now sings chants never heard before as his eyes are being opened to secret revelations hidden since the world began. All the puzzles of scripture are now made plain to him in a special grace that is being poured out in incomparable abundance. It is the grace appropriate to a great prophet, the highest level of light so to speak, while those that follow are perhaps less in dignity because they are simply 'angelic' lights or 'divine' lights, which, however, are still extremely difficult to bear even for the virtuous and pure of heart. They too bring unusual access to the mind of God even if they are not of the intensity that Baithéne could have worked in. The relation of light to a conception of hierarchy is already established by III 17. Nonetheless, all the lights of III 17–21 form a didactic unity, and that is especially the case for III 18–21, because each depicts Columba either referring to or actively instructing his monks. They belong to a teaching scenario that is designed to prepare the heart for God's inspiration manifested in the form of light.

In these chapters, a monastic scale of virtue is being explained, although Adomnán's form of didacticism teaches by example and makes no allowance for those ignorant of the theology on which it is built. Berchán is both disobedient and crafty, a youth who will not obey and inclines to wrong. His fear is that of the surprised thief. Colgu, by contrast, is already on the ladder of wisdom, teachable because he is earnest, but one who requires steady supervision because, apparently, his fear is still not of the right quality.[44] Columba, although probably not others, is able to discern this. Fergnae has a better character and his fear is of a superior kind. Three allusions are made to it in the chapter. He is 'moved by the love of God burning within him' and comprehends something of the depth of marvel that he partially witnesses. His lowering of eyes signifies a right devotion within his dread, a fearful reverence rather than fear alone. It is this that pleases God and Columba. It shows that he is on the right path to spiritual perfection – the same path that one must tread in order to become the abbot. Adomnán makes us aware of this important connection in his lengthy heading to III 19, where he described Fergnae as 'a young man of natural goodness, who by the will of God later was the head of this church that I too, though unworthy, serve'. He is the fourth abbot of Iona, dying in 623.[45]

Considering the relationship between wisdom, mystic development and leadership potential, the spiritual perfection or near perfection that creates prophetic skill is the same quality that creates a successful abbatial governor, one who, in the words of an early ninth-century rule, acts to preserve 'the rights of the church from the small to the great'.[46] Adomnán views both sides of this talent as established by the monk's ability to commune rightly with the supernatural that is demonstrable through the presence and tolerance of apparitions of light. Consider, however: reactions to apparitions of light do not tell us much about a scribe, *as scribe*, although they do say something about prophetic talent since the appearance of light is not the symbolism for the rising skill of a copyist, but rather for the coming of divine inspiration that brings a new order of comprehension to one who has been prepared to accept it through the continual

---

44 Ibid., pp 206–9.   45 Sharpe, *Adomnán*, p. 370, n. 389.   46 From the Rule of St Carthage cited in Hughes, *Church*, p. 157.

practice of copying. It is therefore a related mixture of talent – that of scribe, wise man and prophet as promised by Christ in Matthew 23:34 – that Columba wishes to develop, and of these, prophecy is the highest spiritual stage.[47] It is also the one that best fits the abbot to maintain his monastery amid the problems of the world outside; it is this spiritual mastery that is the source of a community's strength. To appreciate the unspoken advantage that Adomnán expects from these talented 'sons', like Baithéne and Fergnae, one need only look to the nature of the impact that he ascribes to their 'father'. In some sixteen or more chapters dealing prominently with princes, Columba constantly deploys his prophetic skill to advise, warn, designate, create and manipulate.[48] His hard-won sanctity gains him the power to choose victors and survivors in battle and he will fight against heaven to defend his judgment. Columba is perfectly willing to be repeatedly flogged by an angel rather than change his mind about whom he prefers as king (III 5). Taking sides, defending his own, is part of his OT prophetic persona. When worldly politics are the business of a heavenly angel, how can an Iona abbot not play a role in the business? Flourishing in the light is not simply an intramural teaching tool that eventually produces advanced holiness, it bestows the power to discern God's intentions, and that is also the

---

47 One must remember that Elijah's test is one of the perception of what occurs rather than of any ability to write about it, even though Adomnán's description means that Baithéne could have done both. The three elements of scribal skill, wisdom and prophecy in the abbatial successor each has its own reference in *VC* (I 2, III 18, and III 23), although a combination is actually present in III 18. The quality that may seem to have been underplayed, namely Baithéne's character as wise man, is part of his portrait near the beginning of the work. This vignette depicts the colloquy of a future saint, a wise old priest, and two of Columba's monks. At the death of Columba, all are encouraged by the news that his *alumnus* Baithéne had been left to succeed him: 'And all cried out, "It is meet and right"'. Baithéne is then described as *virum sanctum et sapientum*. He is an easy man to talk to and friendly to strangers. It is also added that Columba had entrusted him with at least one secret prophecy so that he continues his 'father's' task in that regard. In sum, therefore, the gospel promise of Christ is being fulfiled at Iona in the persons of abbots like Baithéne and Fergnae who have been trained by Columba. Since these demonstrations seem to have been carefully planned to harmonize around Christ's words, however, it is also instructive to remark their context in Matthew 23. It is part of Christ's repetitive scorning of the hypocritical 'scribes and Pharisees' who oppose him, who seek the first places at feasts and wish to be exalted (VV. 2, 6, 12 etc.). They are, it is silently suggested, not true 'sons of the prophets', but rather 'the sons of them that killed the prophets' and their house shall be left desolate; they are the 'generation of vipers' (VV. 31, 33, 37–8). To follow Christ's promise, therefore, perhaps inevitably, is to be opposed as Christ had been: 'Therefore, behold I send to you prophets, and wise men, and scribes: and some of them you will put to death and crucify, and some you will scourge in your synagogues, and persecute from city to city' (Mt 23:34). Adomnán's enemies at Armagh, and in Northumbria and Pictland, are the likely targets of this circuitous message. He had employed a similar code earlier. In *VC* III 3, we are meant to link Columba's excommunication at the Synod of Tailtiu with the false believer's driving of Christ from the synagogue at the beginning of his ministry (Lk 4:16–30). Note also that the approval of Baithéne's status by a group of monks in I 2 corresponds to the approval of Columba in III 2–4 and III 17, although as with Baithéne's copying, all aspects are slightly less imposing than in Columba's case. The Elisha theme of 'a little bit less' or 'a little bit lacking' is constantly present and so is that of the approval by 'sons of the prophets'.　48 As shown in chapter one. It is part of Columba's commission from God to be an 'assayer' of princes as was that other 'prophet from the womb', Jeremiah.

power to shape and coerce; it is a righteous means of furthering Iona's safety, independence and worldly influence. In the chapter sequence under discussion, where Adomnán's topic is the ladder of virtue beginning with 'fear of the Lord', its techniques and effects are purely spiritual, but its impact *extra muros* can be quite a different matter. Ultimately, spiritual achievement can make a scribe into a statesman of compelling grace, an Ezra for modern times who is guided by God. Add the support of a great king impressed by Columba's ability to grant power, and one comes closer to Adomnán's chosen biblical model for the reproduction of right order in Ireland and Britain.

Adomnán's demonstration of the degrees of enlightenment is not something that begins with anecdotes about Baithéne, Fergnae, Colgu and Berchán;[49] it is a consistent theme in all five chapters of the sequence where cosmic rightness is stressed first in the choosing of Columba, who then celebrates a Mass distinguished by a 'radiant ball of fire' and then receives a spectacularly sanctifying set of revelations from the Holy Spirit. It is in this time of supreme inspiration or just afterwards that the coming advancement of Baithéne is declared (even if indirectly) by the vigorous affirmation of his awesome capability as a scribe. Columba is even more aware of his progress than that of the others whose scrutiny follows, since he is quite certain that Baithéne could not only endure the light, he could continue to work accurately in the midst of it. But the truly peculiar fact about the saint's confidence in Baithéne is that it is actually expressed in a manner and context that subtly, simultaneously, suggests the 'son's' shortcoming. Adverse winds prevent his crossing from Eigg to Hinba. Unlike his master, whose power over wind and water is highlighted in several chapters, he cannot command them. It is this strikingly paradoxical swing between certitude of virtue and subtle notice of deficit that is so bizarre and requiring of an explanation for it is too pointed a juxtaposition to escape notice.[50] The text appears to have been deliberately structured in this manner, but its oscillation cannot be explained by supposing that the mysteries revealed to Columba on Hinba through manifestation of the Holy Spirit's power actually 'transcended the kind of knowledge which could be dictated to a scribe, even to a future abbot of Iona'.[51] Such evaluation cannot be correct, since Adomnán affirms the precise opposite: 'If he [Baithéne] had been present for these days, he could have recorded from the saint's lips a great number of mysteries, both of ages past and future, unknown to other men, together with some interpretations of the sacred books'.

It is the apparent paradox that creates a space for doubt. It is removable, however, if one accepts that Columba's opinion of Baithéne's superior ability is an expression of his preference for Baithéne as heir. Succession (with an

---

49 As in Jennifer O'Reilly's interpretation.   50 Especially so because Columba also advises Baithéne on sea-crossing in I 19.   51 O'Reilly, 'The wisdom of the scribe', pp 198–9.

emphasis on *prophetic* succession) would then be a matter at issue and, in such a case, Adomnán is again following the pattern of the Elijah/Elisha saga that he had introduced for Columba in *VC* III 1 with the appearance of the mantle that miraculously covers the saint's great territory and indicates his inherited status of chief prophet of the islands. Except that Adomnán now wishes to adapt this pattern to another theme of a pupil's prophetic ability achieved through an inner growth in spiritual nearness to God that is produced in the talented by intense extended attention to scribal copying and a close compatibility with the master. Recall that the Bible's way of showing that Elisha was less great a prophet than Elijah was by the fact that he could not easily perform the wonder of the crossing through the water that his spiritual 'father' had done. In a similar vein, Adomnán is stating that Baithéne cannot cross the waters between Hinba and Eigg and by that difference in power falls short of Columba's stature. Like Elisha, this does not make Baithéne any less a successor or any less a prophet; he is, rather, an eminently worthy heir of a lesser rank. How could it be otherwise, since the very meaning of the three-day enlightenment of Columba by the Holy Spirit is the proclamation of his extraordinary uniqueness in the world? Because this interpretation explains the seeming paradox of the chapter while also fitting the prophetic context in which it is set, it also establishes that abbatial succession (that Adomnán makes similar to prophetic succession) is indeed an issue in *VC* III 18. The chapter on Fergnae (who becomes the fourth abbot of Iona right after the short tenures of Baithéne and Lasrén) is logically placed next in line.

If one now looks to the entire chapter from this vantage point, it is clear that Adomnán's original concept derives from the OT's prophetic model for inheritance. Columba's reference to Baithene's ability to understand and write amid the light of the Holy Spirit reflects the influence of the perception test that is set for Elisha in the biblical narrative, and it is thus probable that the coming to earth of the bright Holy Spirit to Columba must also be related to the similar descent of the fiery chariot from heaven in order to raise up Elijah, who then drops his symbolic mantle to his notable but less powerful 'son'. The fire from heaven, the perception test and the effort to cross water are all present in varied form. OT ideas of perceptive capacity, heirship, descending chariot and descending spirit are all joined to perform according to Adomnán's vision of useful adaptation. It is thus precisely the concept of the transmission of *prophetic* power from the Holy Spirit to Columba to succeeding Iona abbots that is central to Adomnán's intent in the sequence, and its existence as a programme is demonstrated by the testing for spiritual capacity carried out by the chief prophet. The torch is thereby shown to be righteously passed in the light of the Holy Spirit. The heavenly grant of the great paruchia to Columba in III 1 is now being joined to a heavenly ratification of his transmission of power over it to his chosen successors. As further testimony to the source, notice that the scriptural parallel of the prophet's departure at the juncture of inheritance is being adumbrated as well. It is thus at the end of this apparition-of-light sequence that the heading to III 22 announces 'How Columba had a vision of angels setting out to meet his holy soul as though it were soon to leave his body', and III 23 then proclaims 'How our patron St Columba passed to the Lord'. Adomnán is seeking to maintain a thread of continuity through his device of highly abstract allusions to the Elijah/Elisha saga. Apparently, he viewed this context as so well established by his earlier sequence of III 1–5 that he expected an easy recognition of III 17–21. In his own time, that was probably the case.

Although the analysis now becomes tighter, some questions remain. If all Adomnán had wanted was to show Baithéne as Columba's rightful and talented successor according to the Elijah/Elisha precedent, then that had been accomplished in III 18. After all, it had been enough for Muirchú's Patrick at a similar juncture who had then said to Benignus, 'I see now that you are worthy to be my successor'. And even if one (reasonably) supposes that Adomnán had wished to suggest a stouter measure of continuity by going further, that had been done through the Fergnae chapter. Why then the Colgu and Berchán episodes? And how should they be related to the rest of the sequence that began with a visit to Columba of four famous saints? Understanding the mix of materials here is a more complex task than it seems, and a multiplicity of more-or-less related motives and models may be involved.

A large part of the answer seems to lie in Adomnán's view of the OT groups called 'sons of the prophets'. One begins with the observation that Adomnán had made an intense study of prophecy and the creation of prophets – as is shown by the *VC* III 1–5 sequence based on the OT 'call' of the prophet – and had reached the conclusion that (with the exception of Isaiah and Jeremiah, who were prophets 'from the womb' and had been important for that reason in III 1) most prophets were made and not born. Ancient Israel may have possessed too many of them. They formed guilds of apprentices, who must have been of various ages and accomplishments, around leaders like Samuel, Elijah and Elisha.[52] King Ahab once assembled some four-hundred prophets (3 Reges 22:6) and colonies of them lived in Gibeah, Ramah, Bethel, Jericho, Gilgal, Samaria and elsewhere.[53] They seem to have lived in *coenobia*, taken their meals as a group and performed in music-accompanied trance before the 'father' (1 Reges 10:6; 4 Reges 3:13–15). Under such conditions, even laymen might be inspired upon coming among them. So it was when Samuel was protecting David at Najoth and Saul sent officers to capture his rival: 'And when they saw a company of prophets prophesying, and Samuel presiding over them, the spirit of the Lord came upon them, and they likewise began to prophesy' (1 Reges 19–20). This happened twice more until a frustrated Saul also went to Najoth and then he too 'prophesied with the rest before Samuel' (19:23–24). These bands are important

52 Lindblom, *Prophecy*, p. 69f.   53 Ibid., p. 65.

to Adomnán. One reason is because they are pictured as accompanying major OT figures and so, in his typologically influenced estimation, that means that they should also accompany Columba. By his time, it was a truism that 'sons of the prophets' were the revered ancestors of the communities of monks.[54] A second reason is because the 'sons' are shown to be important in witnessing and recognizing the transition from one chief prophet to another in the OT. Adomnán almost certainly had them in mind in III 17–21, since chapter 18 appeals directly to the Elijah/Elisha model for transition and it is just there that he has been shown to imitate the precedents. Although the precise meaning of the 'sons' behaviour during the biblical transition is never explained, the scenario presented has a pronounced ritual feel to it and seems to require a questioning of the likely successor who then answers until, upon the death of the 'father', he must perform miraculously in his place. That is what happens to Elisha, who, in a brief span of narrative, is twice approached by 'sons' (from Bethel and Jericho) who set the same question and receive the same answer:

> The sons of the prophets, that were at Bethel, came forth to Elisha, and said unto him: Dost thou know that this day the Lord will take away thy master from thee? And he answered: I also know it: hold your peace. (4 Reges 2:3)

The crossing of the water, fiery chariot and perception notice follow. Elisha then takes up Elijah's mantle, crosses back on his second try, and is greeted by the 'sons' who declare 'The spirit of Elijah hath rested upon Elisha'. And coming to meet him, they worshipped him, falling to the ground. Immediately thereafter, they are depicted as requiring Elisha's consent in order to act. In Adomnán's sequence, however, it is the chief prophet himself who directs the process, based perhaps on the view that Elijah had done so (although that is not mentioned) or perhaps the view that Elisha had already assumed some kind of special status through Elijah's original casting of his mantle upon him. This would have made him the prophet-in-waiting and his special status seems to be indicated by his dismissive 'hold your peace' replies to his questioners, some of whom were probably his seniors. Adomnán's two references to Baithéne's status as successor in Book III – one in chapter 18 to his ability to record mysteries in divine light, and the other in chapter 23 to his continuance of Columba's scribal task – may, perhaps, follow this dual pattern of designation, although one would then have expected the second reference to appear earlier. While Columba's comments to his 'sons' are more cautionary than interrogatory, a similarly probing atmosphere is created by the question of future leadership itself. Adomnán is seeking to achieve the same results as the OT, namely a selection of the most talented heir.

---

54 As in the *Regula Monarchorum* IV of Columbanus: ... *scientes lepram esse cupitatem monarchis imitatioribus filioruim prophetarum* ... Walker, *Sancti Columbani Opera*, p. 126.

Just as in 4 Reges 2, where reference to Elijah's passing calls forth an interplay among his company of 'sons', so too Adomnán feels constrained to create his own parade of 'sons' when he begins to picture the departure of Columba and the succession of Baithéne. He had drawn upon the same pattern in VC III 2–4 when other holy men were portrayed as witnessing Columba's new status as mantle bearer. The difference now is that, unlike the Bible, the Iona prophet demonstrates how his 'sons' are actually trained to their precognitive task. This is necessary because Adomnán is committed to reviving the biblical governance template for his own time and must thus persuasively demonstrate how Columba's line of successors qualify to fit the true OT mould. It is an important part of his strategy. Together with III 18, it amounts to a wonderfully subtle series of insinuations, whose significance can easily escape even the attentive reader because he is expecting only a series of glorifying miracle stories. But if such as Saul's officers can be inspired to prophecy, then surely Columba's own wisdom-loving God-fearers can reach an even higher plateau because of their capacity to perceive and think in heaven's light. VC III 1–5 and 17–21 are thus mutually reinforcing companion pieces. They seem to take for granted that leading holy men will possess prophetic powers, and perhaps indicate that training in vatic techniques was not unusual for Columba's time or for Adomnán's own. Portrayal of Columba's biblically mindful prophetic succession 'from the womb' in III 1 is complemented by the choosing of Baithéne in III 18, and, with variable emphasis and reference, both elevations have been devised to recall the Elijah/Elisha milieu of 4 Reges 2. The aspect of extended continuity is then made manifest in the person of Fergnae, another abbot-to-be, while the exclusion of some in the scribal and education-by-light cycle attests to the rigour of the process for those who remain, hence the lessoning of Colgu and Berchán. A new community of true prophets is thereby *re*created to flourish in the living spirit of its master, Columba and of his forerunners Elijah, Elisha and Samuel, all of them bearers of the mantle.

The matter of training 'sons' to be prophetic successors in terms of worldly affairs outside the monastery also finds confirmation in the OT, a point that would have been of special interest to Adomnán's readers. As a matter of principle, it is contained in the very nature of the biblical institution where headship over spiritual disciples intervening in politics is shown to continue from Elijah to Elisha. Two instances depict how it functions in practice. In 3 Reges 20:29–43, the chapter that follows Elijah's casting of his mantle over a successor, we read that 'a certain man of the sons of the prophets' perceived that King Ahab of Israel had done wrong in the eyes of the Lord by showing an unjust mercy to the defeated king of Syria, even though another prophet had informed Ahab before the battle that Yahweh would deliver that army of enemies into his hands in order that 'you shall know that I am the Lord'. This 'son' approached Ahab in disguise and tricked him into pronouncing a judgment upon his own guilty behaviour. Now simply called a 'prophet' with no modification, the 'son' declares:

> Thus saith the Lord: 'Because thou hast let go out of thy hand a man worthy of death thy life shall be for his life, and thy people for his people'. And the king of Israel returned to his house, slighting to hear, and raging came into Samaria. (3 Reges 20:42–3)

Exactly this unjust pardoning of an enemy ruler is part of the behaviour that causes Samuel to revoke Saul's kingship over Israel. It is one of two such precedents that Adomnán had in mind in describing Columba's gift of victory to Oswald over the pagan Cadwallon,[55] and his bestowal of an ordained rule over an empire thereafter in VC I 1. A second instructive example appears in 4 Reges 9:1–13. Now Elisha, who has recently become the prophet with the mantle, sends one of the 'sons of the prophets' to anoint another king of Israel:

> And Elisha the prophet called one of the sons of the prophets, and said to him: 'Gird up thy loins and take this little bottle of oil in thy hand, and go to Ramoth Galaad. And when thou art come thither, thou shalt see Jehu the son of Josephat … Then taking the little bottle of oil, thou shalt pour it on his head, and shalt say: "Thus saith the Lord: I have anointed thee king over Israel"'.

Doing so, the young man also conveyed the order that Jehu should work to destroy the house of Ahab and revenge the blood of the prophets that he and Jezebel had shed.

The prophetic 'sons' thus continue the same work of political intervention that their 'fathers' Elijah and Elisha performed and are indeed explicitly delegated to do so. Given the fact that the 'sons' are not widely mentioned in the OT, it is telling that they are involved in those worldly areas of victory bringing, admonishing and creating kings that are precisely the concerns expressed in VC. In showing Columba's training of his 'sons', therefore, Adomnán is again following precedents, essentially the same ones that prompted his design and formation of Columba's persona in the first place. Except for his usage of light symbolism, there are few ad hoc elements in his presentation; rather, a systematic pattern of biblical spiritual and political relationships – prophet with the mantle, sons of the prophets, and anointed kings – is being deliberately recreated. Although that is the fundamental picture, a number of details and additional perspectives remain to be introduced and elucidated before our analysis can be complete.

One is the possibility that Adomnán had cast a wider net in his review of Elijah precedents and that more of them exist than has been noticed. It may be

---

55 See also 1 Reges 13:13–14 and 15:23–26 and chapter one of the present work.

that III 17, for example, and the chapter that precedes it, each owe something to the biblical narrative of Elijah's later career, and so too with III 22. Consider the parallels. In 3 Reges 19, Elijah is depicted as fleeing the wrath of Ahab and Jezebel. He left a settlement and 'went forward one day's journey into the desert'. Weary and dejected, he lay down and requested of the Lord that 'he might die'. As he slept, an angel of the Lord came and bade him to rise up. The angel came a second time with food because he must travel 'unto the mount of God, Horeb'. The Lord now honoured Elijah with a personal appearance. In effect, his request to die was refused and he was given a series of tasks to perform, one of which was the choosing of Elisha, which he accomplished by casting his mantle upon him. Adomnán does not use all of this material, he selects what he wants and modifies it, but the general shape of the typology appears to be present. Thus in *VC* III 22, Adomnán reveals that Columba 'desired with all my strength' to die near the end of his career but that the Lord had indicated his refusal through the agency of his sent angels. Both the refusal of his death wish and the presence of angels appear to be prompted by Elijah's journey in 3 Reges 19. Elijah's journey to the mountain may also have prompted an episode in miniature from *VC* III 16 where Columba states his intention to an assembly of the brethren of going to the machair on the west coast of the island. Once there, angels flew to him to hold conference as he stood 'on a knoll among the fields'. The monks called it *Cnoc nan Aingel*, the 'Angel's Knoll'. It was the site where they would read from Columba's books in order to repair a drought. It was the islands' equivalent to Mount Horeb where God had told Elijah to 'stand upon the mount'. Adomnán's following chapter (17) begins the sequence of light apparitions investigated above. It shows Columba's precedence among monastic founders but also contains the miracle of 'a radiant ball of fire shining very brightly from St Columba's head as he stood in front of the altar and consecrated the sacred oblation'. In the course of the Mass, the consecration is designed to bring about the presence of God, which, in this case, occurs in special relation to Columba, the celebrant of the ritual. The fiery light shone upwards until the mysteries were completed. In terms of the Elijah model, therefore, *VC* chapters 16 and 17 loosely follow the motif pattern of his journey, where the angelic appearances are followed by the enormous honour of God's personal manifestation. The choice of Columba's leadership by four saints is thus spectacularly ratified in relation to the story of Elijah, the prophet who, among other things, apparently symbolizes rightful selection. The divine epiphany in light is then spectacularly expanded in chapter 18 as the glory of Columba's honouring continues in the selection that also recalls the heavenly fiery chariot that precedes the inauguration of Elisha. A dual process is thus underway – on one hand a portrayal of the choosing of heirs in chapters 18–19, and, on the other, its encapsulation within the larger typology of Elijah's life in the flanking chapters of 16–17 and 22 that are designed to illustrate the depth of

Columba's connection to Elijah in that both prophets encounter God and his angels in similar ways. The sequences here are flexible, but their intricate multiple connections are not just created to depict Columba as a prophet, but rather to demonstrate that, like Elijah, he is the great chief of prophets who endows his sons with an incontestable legitimacy.

Significantly, I think, this emphasis on 'greatness and specialness' is further emphasized on the last page of *VC*:

> Every conscientious reader who has finished reading this three-part book should mark well how great and special is the merit of our reverend abbot; how great and special is his honour in God's sight; how great and special were his experiences of angelic visits and heavenly light; how great was the grace of prophecy in him; how great and how frequent was the brilliant light of heaven which shone on him as he dwelt in mortal flesh and which, after his most gentle soul had left the tabernacle of the body, does not cease even today. For the place where his bones rest is still visited by the light of heaven and by numbers of angels, as is known from those of the elect who have themselves seen this.

Angelic visitations and the brilliant lights that shone on Columba are thus linked to his 'grace of prophecy' so that whatever other authors might think of them, Adomnán holds these three items to be the functional package that demonstrates uniqueness. Nor did the visitations and lights cease after Columba's death. They are known to continue. Here, and in the following final paragraph, where Adomnán refers to the 'great and special' renown of Iona, Adomnán is echoing his statements in *VC* I 1, where he repeatedly asserts that Columba's power to grant victory in battle is a 'special privilege' and 'special honour' and where he maintains it to be 'as true after he quit the flesh as it had been in this present life'. One is thus viewing bookend statements meant to indicate a mature continuity of judgment. No matter what else Columba may have done, he is most distinguished as prophet and victory-bringer.

The additional remark on the presence of lights and angels at Columba's grave is worth a pause. Richard Sharpe observed that 'the continuance of such manifestations at the grave of the saint is something not mentioned of other Irish saints'.[56] One wonders if Adomnán was not also thinking of the death of Patrick, which had required a number of contrivances from Muirchú because Patrick was not buried at Armagh – highly unusual if his primacy was there – and because his final resting place was hidden.[57] Muirchú related (II 10 [8]) that during the first night of Patrick's exequies, angels kept a vigil over his body but men were later warned away from his resting place by fire bursting forth from his tomb (II 12 [10]). Angels and fire (if not light) are thus important to Muirchú also, but the angels do not continue to visit, and the fire is meant to frighten away anyone

---

56 Sharpe, *Adomnán*, p. 377, n. 421. 57 Sharpe, 'Patrick and the see of Armagh', 40–5.

seeking the body. Patrick's passing is thus unorthodox and is in marked contrast to Columba's known burial site and to Adomnán's celebratory remarks about it. In other statements in the same chapter, we learn that Columba's funeral ceremonies were 'performed in accordance with the good custom of the church', that they befitted 'one of his honour and status' and that his grave was a chosen spot that was visited by his community. Although one cannot be sure, it may also be significant that, after taking leave of his island home, Columba had blessed a horse who wept at knowledge of his coming departure, whereas Patrick had angrily killed a horse during his founding of Armagh (although he later revived him). It is impossible to say if the contrast in animal treatment is deliberately constructed, but it is an odd detail that does create a polarity that reminds one again of the antithetical treatments of kings and druids in the two works.

One chord of our broader theme may be struck anew. The essence of Adomnán's statement concerning Baithéne is similar to Patrick's about Benignus after both had witnessed heaven: 'I see now that you are worthy to be my successor'. Although the nature and sequence of the miracles are not parallel, and although Columba's statement is about what could have happened rather than what did, each scenario involves succession to office that is linked to a hut and includes a manifestation of heaven followed by a problem with water. Variations on the theme of inheritance, of Elijah's fiery chariot from heaven, of Elisha's perception test and the crossing of the Jordan River are present in some form in each *vita* but are filtered through the author's own spectrum of attitudes. Once again, although in faint, quick and elusive manner, Adomnán may be slighting Muirchú's depiction of Patrick and Benignus in the *VP*. In fulfiling the perception test, Adomnán declares that Baithéne could have worked within the light of the Holy Spirit (as Benignus had viewed heaven with Patrick), but shies from an actual depiction. Indeed, his whole concept of the training of the scribe through 'fear of the Lord' would seem to cast doubt on the *VP*'s facile description of the untrained servant boy said to possess the astounding ability to see heaven alongside a mature saint. Of course, the point is complicated and made uncertain by the very fact that each writer is adjusting the same biblical story in his own way. On the other hand, Adomnán may have been thinking almost as much about Muirchú's narrative as that of the Bible. There is nothing about a hut in the Elijah/Elisha story, but one appears prominently in both *VP* and *VC*, in the first case containing fire and in the second light. Because both huts are linked to succession, however, one might wish, as in the case of *VP* although here to a lesser extent, to allow for the possible influence of vernacular culture even though any direct link to a kingship mythos is absent in *VC*.[58]

---

58 In the Irish procedure of *tellach*, 'entry' (Welsh *dadannudd* is similar), hereditary land could be claimed through a process that culminates in a lighting of a fire in a house. The practices involved are pre–Christian, and it seems probable that the Uí Neill ritual that establishes a coming kingship

The importance of these contrasts centring on graves and successors becomes clearer when it is realized that holy bodies in graves existed in a dimension that enabled them to continue to aid their friends,[59] and that bishops, abbots, saints and other devouts working in Ireland were all viewed as being organized in a hierarchy of status from the top to the bottom that, theoretically at least, depended upon the spiritual rank of these 'dead' holy founders.[60] Bishop Tírechán, a contemporary of Muirchú and a strong supporter of the familia of Patrick, assumes these points when he relates that Patrick climbed Cruachán Aigli and stayed there forty days and nights. He intended to fast according to the example of 'Moses, Elijah and Christ'. God favoured Patrick and 'the choir of all the holy men of the Irish came to visit their father'.[61] The desire to honour the founder is clear. In 'notes supplementary to Tírechán', which probably belongs to the eighth century, we are told that Patrick was similar to Moses in four ways, one of them being that 'nobody knows where his bones rest'.[62] That was actually a serious problem for Armagh since possession of the mystically vigorous bones of the holy man was a key way of demonstrating the power of his heirs to call for his aid.[63] According to this text, Columba was available to find an answer.

> Columb Cille, moved by the Holy Spirit, showed where Patrick's grave was and confirms this, that is, in Saulpatrick, in the church near the sea, where there is the coming together of the martyrs, that is, of the bones of Columb Cille from Britain and of all the saints of Ireland on the day of Judgment.[64]

Columba is thus shown to belong to that 'choir' that follows Patrick regardless of Adomnán's desire for an independent paruchia, and his bones will be drawn from Britain to that church near the sea where Patrick is buried when the choir leader arises to judge the Irish. Columba's special powers as a prophetic diviner

over land draws in part on this symbolism of fire. The elements of fire and hut are again linked to a kingship claim over Cashel in the 'Story of the finding of Cashel'. The two swineherds for whom a hut was made also 'saw a cleric in his white chasuble', that symbolized 'the coming of Patrick'. Here, as in *VP*, the hut and Patrick's chasuble again are related. Although the part of the text mentioning this probably dates to the tenth century, the coincidence of hut, fire, chasuble and rule over land remains notable. For discussion of the Old Irish tract *Din Techtugad*, 'on legal entry' (CIH 205.22–213.37 = ALI IV 3.1–33.32), see Kelly, *A guide to early Irish law*, pp 186–8; Charles-Edwards, *Irish and Welsh kinship*, pp 259–73; Myles Dillon, 'The Story of the finding of Cashel', *Ériu*, 16 (1952), 61–73. 59 See, for example, Thomas O'Laughlin, 'The tombs of the saints: their significance for Adomnán' in John Carey, Máire Herbert and Pádraig Ó Riain (eds), *Studies in Irish hagiography: saints and scholars* (Dublin, 2001), pp 1–14. 60 Thomas Charles-Edwards, 'Saints' cults and the early Irish church', *Clogher Record*, 19 (2008), 173–84. 61 Bieler, *Patrician texts*, pp 153–4: *Et perrexit Patricius ad montem Egli, ut ieiunaret in illo quadraginta diebus et quadraginta noctibus, Moysaicam tenens disciplinam et Heliacam et Christianem … quia corus sanctorum omnium Hibernensium ad eum uenit ad patrem eorum uissitandum….* 62 Ibid., p. 164: *iiii Ubi sunt ossa eius nemo nouit.* 63 Sharpe, 'Patrick and the See of Armagh', 35–59. 64 Bieler, *Patrician texts*, pp 164–5: *Colomb Cille Spirito Sancto instigante ostendit sepulturam Patricii, ubi est confirmat, id est in Sabul Patricii, id est in aeclessia iuxta mare proxima, ubi est conductio martirum, id est ossuum Coluimb Cillae de Brittannia et conductio omnium sanctorum Hiberniae in die iudicii.*

seem to be recognized here, but one can also see why Adomnán placed so much effort into firmly planting Columba into his own place with God's angels approving, with His lights defining (and not just sanctifying) the ground, and with all of Columba's Iona familia in attendance. It was a grand array of combined spiritual witnesses (far more witnesses than were called for in Deuteronomy) to Columba's sovereign status as ruler of his own monastic empire.

Honouring Patrick and obeying Patrick, or obeying the bishop of Armagh who claimed to speak in binding fashion in Patrick's name, are all different matters. In Irish practice, a great deal depended upon whom one regarded as founder, or,[65] to state it otherwise, whom one regarded as 'father'. When Tírechán wrote of Patrick on Cruachán Aigli, for example, he described him as the 'father' of all the holy men of the Irish. Cummian sapiens said much the same in his Paschal letter of 632/3 to Abbot Ségéne of Iona and the hermit Béccán in an attempt to answer their criticisms on the 'Roman' Easter; he called Patrick sanctus Patricius papa noster.[66] After waiting a full year, he wrote:

> in accordance with Deuteronomy, I asked my fathers to make known to me, my elders (that is to say, the successors of our first fathers; of Bishop Ailbe, of Ciaran of Clonmacnoise, of Brendan, of Nessan, and of Lugid) to tell me what they thought about our excommunication by the aforementioned Apostolic Sees. Having gathered in Mag Léne ...[67]

The passage of Deuteronomy referred to is a command by Moses telling the Hebrews to remember the law: 'Remember the days of old, think upon every generation: ask thy father and he will declare to thee: thy elders and they will tell thee' (32:7). Thomas Charles-Edwards writes: 'For early Irish law that is the one and only reference to succession you will get, the standard scheme for succession to the abbot's see'.[68] Remarkably, although all these men are successor abbots to monasteries, they are not referred to in these terms, but rather as the heirs of founders. Because a monastery gave first place in authority to the kindred of the founding patron, all his successors who ruled as abbots were probably cousins if not 'sons' of the founder. The significance of a biological and spiritual fatherhood could thus easily become mixed. In referring to Patrick as papa noster, however, Cummian was probably thinking in a general way of Patrick's authority, framing it in terms of his preaching of the faith and his bringing of the first Easter. He cannot have been thinking in institutional monastic terms, nor in his citation of Deuteronomy can he have been thinking of the early patriarchs like

---

65 Charles-Edwards, 'Saints' cults', pp 173–8.   66 Walsh and Ó Cróinín, Cummian's letter, p. 84.
67 Ibid., p. 90: Anno igitur, ut praedixi, emenso, iuxta Deuteronomium, interrogaui patres meos ut annuntiarent michi, maiores meos, ut dicerent michi, successores uidelicet nostrorum patrum priorum Ailbei episcopi, Quera(ni C)oloniensis, Brendini, Nessani, Lugidi (quid sentirent de excommunicatione nostra, a supradictis sedibus apostolicis facta. At) illi congregati in unum, alius per se, (aliu)s per (legatum suum uice suo) missum, in Campo Lene sancxerunt.   68 Charles-Edwards, 'Saints' cults', pp 173–4.

Abraham, Isaac and Jacob. All involved at Mag Léne were monastics, and, as we have seen, their spiritual fathers were the prophets who ruled the proto-monks, the 'sons of the prophets'. Even Tírechán shares this attitude, since his Patrick on the mountain is there in imitation of Moses, Elijah and Christ; he has established a trio of prophets (to which Patrick will be added) in which Christ figures as the third person of the genealogy. All three are exemplars, but Elijah bears special meaning for monks, since, as Cassian and Columbanus held, he and Elisha were the founders and patrons of monasticism. As we have seen, their biblical conception of the rightful transmission of authority is the one followed by Adomnán and Muirchú. Competitors though they were, they appealed for guidance to the same desert fathers of scripture.

Cummian was writing in 632 or 633 and, at that time, the followers of Columba probably had little to complain about. It is the later joining of Patrick's honoured status to the jurisdictional claims of Armagh's bishops that caused, and had to cause, a reaction. When it happened, Adomnán simply bypassed Patrick by claiming Elijah's mantle of chief prophet from heaven and adding, in the case of his appointed task of judging and creating kings, the support of heaven's angel, who carried, and left with him, a holy book on ordinations. He will continue to honour Patrick the great holy man, but with his own 'sons' at hand, now trained to become prophets after him, he has created the weapons to protect his community and confederation. All he requires is that kings continue to support Columba.

Scribal prophets: Ben Sirach and Ezra

Adomnán found the details and context of all of these themes to be directly relevant to his own situation as leader of a great extended community. But he also found providential guidance elsewhere. As interested as he was in the testing and functioning of scribes, he would probably have looked to the famous scribes of scripture for inspiration, and we may profit by doing the same in our search for the components of his design. In Jennifer O'Reilly's perceptive analysis of the scribal 'fear of God' theme for 'spiritual sons' in VC, she suggests that the testing episodes about Fergnae, Colgu and Berchán derive from *Aipgitir Chrábaid*, the 'Alphabet of Devotion' ascribed to Colman mac Beognai, nephew of Columba, and dated to *c.*600. She also sees the influence of OT wisdom literature.[69] Although a significant connection to the former work does exist as we shall see below, this material in the 'Alphabet of Devotion' can only be relevant in part since the individuals of unequal talent or character whom it briefly compares are only just coming to Christianity from paganism and are not

69 Convenient translations will be found in John Carey (ed.), *King of mysteries: early Irish religious writings* (Dublin, 1998), pp 231–45; Clancy and Márkus, *Iona*, pp 193–207; O'Reilly, 'The wisdom of the scribe', pp 207–8.

like those described in VC III 18–21 who are already convinced believers or monks. Searching further leads to a more important source (on which the Alphabet itself draws) because it centres on the relationship between wisdom, scribal activity and divine inspiration. This is the OT book Ecclesiasticus. Its author, Jesus Ben Sirach of Jerusalem, is himself a scribe who makes the fear of the Lord into a dominating motif of the first half of his work.[70] The same basic conception as in the VC is present. Here one also finds again the motif of testing sons. Ben Sirach's book opens by declaring that 'All wisdom is from the Lord' and has always been so. He pictures wisdom as a woman created in the Holy Spirit and poured out (*effudit*) on those who loved God.[71] To those who fear the Lord, wisdom distributes blessings, knowledge, gladness and length of days. In chapter two, the opening line addresses the reader as 'son', so that it is clear that (as in Proverbs 4:1–3) an instructional teacher–pupil relationship is envisaged. The 'son' is told to be of humble heart, patient and enduring. He must survive the test of temptation and keep patience 'for gold and silver are tried in the fire, but acceptable men in the furnace of humiliation' (2:5). One who can endure in these preparations will achieve mercy, delight and enlightenment. Others will be forsaken when the Lord begins to examine them (2:17). They are the faint-hearted and impatient, apparently comparable to Colgu when Columba reprimands him 'somewhat harshly', and those who are of double heart and turn to evil, apparently like Berchán, who was disobedient and whom Columba reprimanded 'very severely'.

While these testing verses point to our context, Ben Sirach is especially notable because of his intimate linkage of wisdom with the art of the scribe (which he practices himself). In chapter 24, he describes wisdom as being like the great rivers (as in Gen 2:11–14) that carry knowledge throughout the world. He then switches his rhetoric to the first person and compares himself to a brook or channel or aqueduct that will 'make doctrine to shine forth to all as the morning light' that penetrates even to the lower parts of the earth and 'will enlighten all that hope in the Lord'. The scribe now becomes a true prophet: 'I will yet pour out doctrine as prophecy, and will leave it to them that seek wisdom, and will not cease to instruct their offspring even to the holy age' (23:40–47). In chapter 38, Ben Sirach contrasts the man of wisdom with labourers and artisans who, although skilful in their own crafts, lack the leisure to study. His ideal wise man is the scribe: 'The wisdom of a scribe cometh by his time of leisure: and he that is less in action shall receive wisdom'. Ben Sirach goes on to provide the most famous description of the scribe, whom he calls the 'wise man', in biblical literature:

---

70 On Ben Sirach and the various texts and versions of his book, see Alexander A. Di Lella, 'Wisdom of Ben-Sira' in Gary A. Herion et al. (eds), *Anchor Bible dictionary* (New York, 1992), VI, pp 931–45. 71 As in I:9–10.

The wise man will seek out the wisdom of all the ancients, and will be occupied in the prophets. He will keep the sayings of renowned men, and will enter withal into the subtleties of parables. He will search out the hidden meaning of proverbs, and will be conversant in the secrets of parables. He shall serve among great men, and appear before governors. He shall pass into strange countries: for he shall try good and evil among men. ... For if it shall please the great Lord, he will fill him with the spirit of understanding: And he will pour forth the words of his wisdom as showers. ... And he shall direct his council, and his knowledge, and in his secrets shall he meditate. He shall show forth the discipline he hath learned and he shall glory in the law of the covenant of the Lord. Many shall praise his wisdom and it shall never be forgotten. ... Nations shall declare his wisdom, and the church shall show forth his praise. If he continue, he shall leave a name above a thousand. ... I will yet meditate that I may declare: for I am filled as with a *holy* transport. (39:1–16)

Ben Sirach moves to conclude his meditations with his own scribal note: 'Therefore from the beginning I was resolved, and I have meditated, and thought on these things and left them in writing' (39:38).

In Ecclesiasticus, the gaining of wisdom, inspiration and 'fear of the Lord' is an ongoing set of motifs firmly anchored in scripture. Citation of its elements is thus endowed with permanent authority. Its description of the wise scribe who is also a prophet glorying in the Law recalls Columba himself in the sequence III 17–21, but especially in the luminous house of III 18. Ben Sirach's wisdom that fills the scribe with understanding is a creation of the Holy Spirit (I:9), and its knowledge of secrets, meanings and subtleties in scripture resonates closely with Adomnán's description of the Holy Spirit's imparting of secrets and knowledge of difficulties in the holy books. *VC* III 18's reference to the involvement of a scribe as a recorder of mysteries thus seems more appropriate if the source is Ben Sirach's own splendid eulogy of the scribe who is conversant in secrets. In what follows in the rest of the sequence, however, Adomnán takes the idea of the 'sons' who are tested and follows a method that is suggested by the Alphabet. In both works, reference to the evaluation of worthiness is preceded by a figure of speech to indicate the methodology of proof. In Ecclesiasticus, it is to the 'son' who is like gold and silver because he is 'tried in fire' (2:5). In the *Alphabet of Devotion*, the metaphor is based on light: 'as a lantern raises its light in a dark house, so truth rises in the midst of faith in a person's heart'.[72] Although the Holy Spirit can appear as either fire or light, it is the latter aspect that Adomnán prefers in this case, as he applies it to the luminous house of III 18 and to the testing episodes of III 19–21. Ben Sirach's book may thus have contributed something to Adomnán's strategy for scribal inspiration and abbatial succession while the Alphabet may have helped influence his means of presentation with regard to light rather than fire.

72 Clancy and Márkus, *Iona*, p. 203.

Adomnán was attracted to biblical materials on scribes and prophets, especially to those texts where the vocation in each sphere is explicitly combined in one individual, one hero of God's design. This is confirmed by the VC III 18 sequence, but also by Adomnán's interest in Ben Sirach's Ecclesiasticus. In attempting to further our understanding of VC, however, it becomes notable that another even more remarkable example of the scribe-prophet-wise man combination exists. Given Adomnán's demonstrable interest in OT based modelling, a brief discussion of his activities holds some promise of further instruction, and may also be justified by the fact that this scribe is cited at length in the *Hibernensis* book *De regno*, which, arguably, reflects some aspects of Adomnán's reform programme for insular society (indicated by his prophetic call and his innovations in the fields of ritual and imperial rule theory). The OT figure in question is Ezra (or Esdras), the author in tradition of I and II Ezra (with the second book also called the Book of Nehemiah). Many modern Jews view Ezra as a key founder of their religion, but for our purposes he is significant as a possible model, as a figure whose example may have helped to inspire Adomnán's conception of state reform.

Ezra was the appointed leader of a band of Jewish exiles returning to Jerusalem some time after the Persians had conquered Babylon. The chronology of his mission is uncertain, but, for present purposes, unnecessary to seek to unravel.[73] Ezra returns with the full support of the Persian king Artaxerxes, who appears to act according to his wishes and provides him with plenipotentiary power. Ezra is introduced in 7:1–6, where he is identified as a priest whose exalted pedigree reaches back to Aaron. Not only is he the leader of the exiles, he is also a 'ready scribe in the law of Moses' (*scriba velox in lege Mosi*), who acts 'according to the hand of the Lord his God upon him'. This is the source of his authority.

> *Ezras enim paravit cor suum ut investigerat legem Domini et faceret et doceret in Israhel praeceptum et iudicium.*
>
> For Ezra had prepared his heart to seek the law of the Lord, and to do and to teach in Israel the commandments and judgment. (7:10)

Ezra is thus the scribe who had learned 'fear of the Lord' and had become a prophet, as well as being the author of his own scriptural book. At the same time, he is a priest and teacher of the law. The next verse states that Ezra is the priest and scribe 'instructed in the words and commandments of the Lord, and his ceremonies in Israel'. Artaxerxes proclaims that the people of Jerusalem should grant all that Ezra requires including 'all that belongeth to the rites of the God of heaven' lest his wrath be enkindled 'against the realm of the king and of his sons' (7:23). Furthermore:

---

73 A useful guide is Jacob M. Myers, *I and II Esdras: introduction, translation and commentary* (Garden City, NY, 1980). This is a volume in the Anchor Bible series.

And thou Ezra, according to the wisdom of thy God which is in thy hand, appoint judges and magistrates, that may judge all the people ... yea and the ignorant teach ye freely. (7:25)

In himself, Ezra is a precursor of the prophets, wise men and scribes referred to by Christ in Matthew 23:34. He is charged with rebuilding the temple, reforming the rites, teaching the people and appointing judges 'according to the wisdom of thy God'. His interpretation of the law of his God is paramount and whoever will not obey it is to be executed, banished, deprived of his goods or imprisoned (7:26). On his way to Jerusalem, Ezra proclaims a fast which the people obey. When he reaches the city, however, he is shocked to find that the people there have become lax and ignorant of right order. Even the priests and Levites have taken foreign wives, and have produced children of mixed blood, some of them unable to speak Hebrew. He thus calls 'an exceedingly great assembly' of the people and compels them amid tears and lamentations to separate from their strange wives and children (9:1–15; 10:1–19). All their princes, priests and Levites are similarly bound. In his second year of rebuilding the temple and social reformation, Ezra reaches the high point of his career. The people request him to bring out the book of the law of Moses: then Ezra the scribe and priest 'brought the law before the multitude of men and women, and all those that could understand'. The people rose as he opened the book and made silence to hear it. On the following day, he interpreted to them the words of the law. And for seven days, 'he read in the book of the law of God day by day, from the first day till the last' (II Ezra 8:1–18).

In reading of a scribe's lawgiving at the 'exceedingly great assembly', it is hard not to think of Adomnán at the Synod of Birr, especially since it too dealt with clerics, women and children. The difference is that Adomnán there draws on the spirit of the NT as well as the OT. It is from the law, modified by this spirit, that Adomnán derives his confidence. It exceeds the power of bishops and emperors because it binds and overshadows them. Instead, it favours monks because they spend their virtuous lives copying law as scribes and studying it as scripture. It makes them see more clearly than others, and thus can make the best of them into true prophets. Such is all but impossible for laymen and even for other clerics because they live in the world and suffer from its distractions and anxieties. Set apart from the world, however, as Gregory the Great explained in Book III of his *Dialogues*, hermits and monks are strangers to its disturbances. They 'win a hearing from God sooner than others, for by the purity and simplicity of their thoughts they resemble God to a degree, becoming of one mind with Him as far as that is possible'.[74] Monasticism is thus the royal road to understanding and teaching God's intentions. As it did for Ezra, the law of scripture prepares any scribal heart that is grown in wisdom – 'the fear of the

---

74 Umberto Moricco (ed.), *Gregorii Magni dialogi libri IV* (Rome, 1924), p. 174.

137

Lord is the beginning of wisdom' according to Psalm 110 – to teach, command and judge. Unlike the more famous prophets who must often oppose kings, even when they have created them, Ezra works through an emperor who, apparently, has been inspired by God like King Cyrus. As Ezra had the power to appoint officials, control rituals and reform Jewish society, so might the Iona scribal prophet who perceives God's will choose the best of kings and anoint them and their successors. While there are several sources for Adomnán's intended reforms of royal inauguration and princely guidance (the example of Samuel the prophet/judge is the most important), the model of Ezra in his specific role as *reformer of a kingdom* would have been part of his intellectual arsenal as well, since it provides an extra element of justification for scribal/abbatial control over princes, land and people. While the right to anoint kings, for example, naturally devolves from Columba to his heirs, that legacy can also be cogently supported theologically through a theory of monastic prophet creation that finds an OT foundation in the nearly perfect pattern of the reforming *scriba velox*, who can bind an entire nation through his exposition of the law.

The run-up to the Synod of Birr could be perceivable in this light also, since the Ezra material might provide a guide as to how Adomnán would have theorized/legitimated his law-making task at that assembly. This suggestive pattern is something aside from and in addition to the power to make rulers. If the similarities be taken as indicative, they may well constitute an indirect clue as to the scope of Adomnán's plans after his own reform through royal anointing project had taken root. Adomnán's reliance on OT precedent has now been shown to be formative and that in itself offers a path forward. Although the speculative element cannot be eliminated, since we are dealing largely with sets of suggestive parallels, it seems significant that Ezra is given prominence in the *Hibernensis* book *De regno*, where he is cited on that same power-granting directive of Artaxerxes that has been noted above.[75] Ultimately, some sort of extensive practical relationship between king and prophet seems to have been envisioned in which societal oversight may have been part of the mix. This is the apparent logic of both the Ezra and Samuel/Elijah models, although, as has been suggested, several OT figures have contributed to the full theoretical reform scheme. It seems likely that Adomnán did not think only in terms of the imitation of exemplary individual prophets, he may have perceived a biblical *office* of the (Iona) prophet in relation to an office of the *ordained* island ruler. While the prophet is to be chosen by his Iona brethren, the ruler is (as with Saul and Samuel) to be chosen by God, who then informs the prophet, who in turn ensures that Columba backs the new king for the course of the succession

---

75 Chapters 13 and 14 of Book XXV *De regno* are largely extended citations from I Ezra 7:21, 25, 26; 10:7, 8; II Ezra (=Nehemiah) 5:1–12. These last citations from II Ezra in Cap. 14 are more heavily condensed. Chapter 13 stresses the association of the great king with the 'speedy scribe', the authority Ezra wields, his power to punish, power to call to assembly and compel attendance.

warfare that is, in the nature of things, likely to ensue. Adomnán's law of the Synod of Birr in 697 admirably complements this conception, since, unusually and perhaps exceptionally for the time, it covers all of Ireland.[76] It does so under the administrative leadership of Iona, which has thus successfully brought together an array of churches and states in a common policy that benefits both spheres. The Pictish kingdom is also included so that the Iona stamp is sharply defined. A common unifying intellectual conception thus seems to underlie all of Adomnán's major political innovations, textual or otherwise, and these are best comprehended as the features of a single man's reform plan.

The concept of the priestly prophetic scribe of aristocratic genealogy is thus one that has important ramifications because he is also the figure whom the Bible presents as the builder of the city with the power to bind its inhabitants to the traditional law of God. He does so with the support and consent of a powerful king of kings, who grants him carte blanche. But he does not really impose; in tune with the spirit and direction of Adomnán's reform plan, he *reimposes* the law on a people that had largely forgotten it. Therein lies a significant feature of his paradigmatic importance. The exile now returns to his homeland to become the transformer of state and society. There is an interesting possible foreshadowing here of Columba the exile building the new monastic Jerusalem on Iona that spreads its light to the islands of the West, and then produces an heir in Adomnán, who binds the princes of the islands to a new law that is inherent in the old. Adomnán would never have been unaware of these prophetic likenesses. In conjunction with the developmental scheme of monastic theology exemplified in the 'fear of God' maxim, the model of Ezra the scribal prophet adds a strong element of charismatic authority to leaders like Baithéne or Adomnán if or when they seek a reform affecting society or protecting their prerogatives. Such Iona leaders have been especially sanctified to their tasks because they are the successors of a powerful *prophet* who had in effect trained his monks to be holy seers and diviners.

The Ezra model adds further ideological components to a monastic scribal theology because it relates to a programme of politico-theological reform once carried out by an emperor and his prophetic scribe on the apparent basis of divine decree, and because it links closely with the Matthew theme of scribes, prophets and wise men that is heavily present in Adomnán. It is capable of providing a strong defence against claims of jurisdictional superiority made by bishops or advanced by writers like Muirchú. It is nowhere *specifically* advanced in the *VC*. Like much else in that work – like the inherent power of an ordaining abbot to reject a royal candidate, for example – it is only hinted at in the idea of heirs who can be trained to learn the will of God because of the cumulatively enhancing effects of acute scribal introspection that leads to inspired insight.

76 For the distinction between types of *cánai*, see T.M. Charles-Edwards, 'Early Irish Law' in Ó Cróinín, *A new history*, pp 334–7.

The step to action is not a great one, however, because the founder himself had taken it so many times. One might add that a subtle measure of the same kind of thinking, even more gingerly expressed, may also have influenced Northumbrian Bede in the generation after Adomnán. He is the author of *In Ezram et Neemiam*, a commentary penned between 725 and 730, and rather surprisingly, apparently the only complete such work of the entire Middle Ages.[77] One reason for his exposition was his worry and indignation at the outlook of ambitious bishops. Ezra is thus a useful model for monastic authors who seek to draw contrasts between worldliness, ecclesiastical authority and commitment to scriptural law. Concern with him may well have been an undercurrent in monastic thinking in the generations on either side of 700 when the episcopate was becoming more assertive of its powers. In Ireland, it may well have been a significant aspect in an appeal to prophetic charisma as one postulate in a theory that Adomnán developed in order to protect the *paruchia Columbae* from any attack by an evolving monarchic episcopate. He may have been looking ahead and thinking in purely prophylactic terms based upon his observation of events in Northumbria after 664, but the prophetic scribe approach is useful to abbots no matter what the conditions. Any principle of asserted hierarchical jurisdiction can always be countered by an appeal to a charismatically based prophetic leadership![78] As we shall see, however, certain cultural conditions played a role in this conception as well.

It should be noted, on the other hand, that Muirchú also applies a prophetic paradigm to add to Patrick's credentials. In I 28 (27) of *VP*, where he uses Patrick's visionary ability to legitimate Benignus as his episcopal successor, he tells us that Patrick witnessed heaven open and beheld the Son of God and his angels in a type of miracle hitherto vouchsafed only to St Stephen. For Patrick, it was a 'familiar' experience, *consueta caeli vidit miracula*. But this miracle is unique only in the sense that Patrick witnessed specifically the 'Son of God', since the witnessing of God or heaven was otherwise not that unusual for prophets receiving their 'call' and 'commission' in the OT, although it was most often confined to them.[79] Muirchú would have been well aware of these conditions and thus he is not only claiming a special distinction for the saint (who had earlier been summoned to his task by the angel Victoricus in a vision), he is also claiming something else quite remarkable – that Patrick's *puer* is *already* a prophet as well. Although a demonstration of such visionary capacity is important to Muirchú, his interest declines after the Benignus chapter. Thereafter, he seems to rely more on a theory of archiepiscopal power that may

77 D. Hurst (ed.), *In Ezram et Neemiam* (Turnhout, 1969), 119A; Scott de Gregorio (ed.), *Bede: on Ezra and Nehemiah* (Liverpool, 2006).　78 Lindblom, *Prophecy*, pp 108–37, 148–65, 182–97. 79 Ibid., pp 122–37.　80 Charles-Edwards, *Early Christian Ireland*, pp 429–40; Howlett, *Muirchú*, p. 181ff. This development could well have been internal but, because we cannot clearly know, the temporal coincidence assumes significance.

have been acquired through knowledge of events in Britain under Theodore since 669.[80] Nor does Muirchú worry much about mystic illumination elsewhere in the *vita*, even though the historical Patrick had been deeply concerned with matters of dream and vision in chapters 23 to 25 of his *Confessio*. Rather, Patrick's power in the *VP* is shown by miracles of other kinds, in his raising of the dead, for example, or in winning special favours from God. He is thus a powerful intercessor and authoritative bishop, but his prophetic ability is only one arrow, if also an important one, in his quiver. It is quite otherwise for Adomnán, who emphatically presents Columba as the greatest of visionary prophets. He too can raise the dead (like Elisha) and aid his followers – he is especially good at military help and protecting the souls of the recently dead – but his strength lies in his extraordinary ability to win comprehensive knowledge, wisdom and enlightenment through mystical communion, in his talent of 'achieving a miraculous enlarging of the grasp of the mind' (I 1) or the gift of seeing 'brightly and more clearly, with a mental grasp miraculously enlarged' the 'whole earth and the sea and sky around it' (I 43). Since boyhood, he had devoted himself 'to the study of wisdom' with a joyful heart, because 'his heart was full of the joy of the Holy Spirit' (Second Preface). He may not, in later legend, have been the darling of poets simply because he protected them, but because, as these and other lines in the *VC* indicate, he emblemized a poet-like dedication to an inspired inward search for the mystic essence of awareness.[81] He is thus the saint that is closest to the *filid* in their technique of inspiration.

A related point demands attention. This is Adomnán's emphasis on the extent of Columba's personal and prolonged enlightenment by the Holy Spirit in *VC* III 18. It is remarkable in itself. And so is the emphasis on techniques by which this extraordinarily intense outflow and indwelling is transmitted to those who take up Columba's mantle. The logic of this forceful underscoring suggests the existence of some concern with the status of Columba in relation to his paruchia and/or in further relation to the power of succeeding abbots, perhaps even of Adomnán himself. One cannot escape the sense that the duration of the Holy Spirit's extended epiphany in III 18, far beyond anything one finds elsewhere in the literature, is simply *too* spectacular a device. Its origin in the story of the descent of a fiery chariot to Elijah is obscured and transformed to make it a ringing proclamation of the most exalted theophany in all of post-biblical history. Like Patrick's fireworks at Tara, it is a kind of hagiographical overkill that suggests the existence of a concern or a sore spot, and is not incomparable with Armagh's concern to demonstrate the legitimacy of the succession of Benignus. It may indicate, in some quarters, at least, an indeterminate concern with the doctrinal purity of Columba and the abbots of Iona. A report of the Holy Spirit's choosing of Columba as a unique vessel of divine knowledge, of his dramatically

81 Perhaps to be associated with changes of visage, for example, *VC* I 28.

extended stay and outpouring of scriptural secrets, would then constitute a telling retort to critics, and the theme of a rightly chosen prophetic succession could easily fit into such a context as well. Adomnán did something similar in III 3, where he has St Brendan see a vision (of 'fiery light' and holy angels) that vindicates Columba against accusations of enemies at the Synod of Teiltiu. If such an interpretation be applicable, then it would also point to the continuing difficulties faced by Adomnán in dealing with the Easter question and its fallout,[82] a topic that would have provided ammunition to Armagh and to opponents in Northumbria.

Adomnán shows a special attachment to the most notable OT scribes. He views them as models especially suited to monastic endeavour, but also as prophets whose supernatural ability is tied to their occupation. Ezra the prophetic scribe easily flows into Ezra the prophetic commander and lawgiver, while Ben Sirach the prophetic scribe can easily oversee the testing of any and all candidates according to established scriptural principles. When Adomnán contemplates them, *it is always a means of thinking about his own community and his own island nations*. As prophets, they can function both within and without a monastic environment; they have been endowed with the right and power to set the world in order as Adomnán had done at Birr. The means by which they achieve that power to intervene, reform and test can be learned. It can be routinized by a process of selection among the talented, who are then examined in their abilities as they grow in sanctity. In the direct and indirect testing of III 17–21, Adomnán suggests that this was Columba's favoured mode of choosing a successor during his lifetime. Each Iona abbot is thus meant to become a powerhouse of spiritual energy in his own person, in the imprint passed on through the founder's training, and in the direct inspiration that he will be granted by the Holy Spirit. This is a pronounced version of a continual renewal ideology. Its home is the charismatic group that seeks to maintain, defend and propagate itself. All authority comes from within the group, and is sanctioned by a direct link to God that no one, bishop, king or otherwise, may gainsay. No human decree can affect it. As developed by Adomnán, it is a biblically sanctioned search technique designed as a long-term protective corollary to the divine grant of an independent paruchia to Columba in III 1 of *VC*.

Once this matter of succession is expounded, Adomnán can then proceed to the topic of Columba's passing, and to the protection and sanctification of the most sacred of his islands (III 23). In this exposition, where the prophet blesses, and thereby claims as his, Iona, its inhabitants, its monastery, its barns, grains and animals, where he promises that in heaven he will intercede with God for his followers, one finds the natural culmination to the issues of independence,

82 See now Clare Stancliffe, '"Charity with peace": Adomnán and the Easter question' in Wooding et al. (eds), *Adomnán of Iona*, pp 51–68.

inheritance and communal territorial protection that are fundamental currents in the chapter sets that have been discussed.

Assumptions, strategies and a syncretistic intellectual milieu

While much more could be said about the ways in which Muirchú and Adomnán develop their respective cases, the exemplary topics chosen for comparison have yielded enough evidence and nuances of insight to present some conclusions. Both writers belong to a devout, educated elite. Each is a superb propagandist who thoroughly distrusts the other, but is fully committed to the worldly advancement and security of his own organization. Although sharing much in common, it is their opposing allegiances that give a sharp edge to their views that can be read in the emphases and turns of their arguments. That edge is better masked and finessed in *VC* because Adomnán's style is not confrontational but seeks to persuade by a presentation of sometimes episodic vignettes that seem to follow their own particular route of elucidation. In looking at Adomnán's invention of a package of ruler-friendly offerings, for example, one tends to forget that they are the precise opposites of the forceful threats and humiliations that Muirchú invents for his portraits of kings. One writer offers generous support, while omitting any reference to its cost in royal independence, while the other demands immediate submission and allegiance thereafter for fear of retaliation. Although Patrick sometimes grants miraculous favours to his supporters, Muirchú says relatively little about them, whereas Adomnán goes out of his way to indicate that benefits ensue when one is loyal to Columba. The goals of each are not wholly different – neither biographer has any high opinion of kings – but one allows a measure of dignity for the ruler and his family while the other cares most about prompt obedience and curses both the living and the dead (Loiguire, Miliucc and their sons). For his part, Columba simply withholds his favour from those who offer no sign of sympathy (see also I 12, 14). Adomnán thus deliberately seeks out his royals – they are to be his most valuable clients – while Muirchú tends to see them as potential enemies. He could have imagined a dozen different ways of Patrick approaching Loiguire, for example, but settled on the one that began with an insult to royal prerogative and then opted thereafter for the route that created the most havoc. It is easiest to imagine Muirchú as a monk rather indifferent to the world whose ideas about suitable politics come from reading the harsher lessons of the OT, whereas Adomnán has been tempered by heavy responsibilities, cross-cultural travels and spirited interaction with the worldly powers. He is the successful diplomat and consensus-builder who seeks measures to avoid dispute.

Up to a point! For Adomnán is actually a revolutionary and Muirchú will accept compromise. That too is clear from their works. The latter is a highly talented but conventional religious and social thinker who supposes the greatest

143

favour to be that of Patrick who will judge all of the Irish, all of his clients, in a way that aids them. He sees the most powerful in society as the greatest obstacles, and thus does not stress the winning of that class as supporters; he thinks of the (arch)bishops of Armagh as the only rightful 'kings'. He has no patience with the secular variety and tends to view them in opposition to the Irish people as a whole. He is totally committed to Armagh's claim of jurisdiction over all, whereas Adomnán is equally committed to avoiding that possible future and wishes loyal kings accustomed to Columba's patronage as bulwarks of autonomy. In his own lifetime, he has perhaps been traumatized by witnessing the manner in which kings and hostile bishops had turned against Columba and caused the loss of Northumbria to the Iona confederacy. It was not the sentiments of the people that had produced this catastrophe; it was the fickle opinions of their leaders egged on by ecclesiastics seeking their own advantage.[83] As much as he admired Cassian, he might have recalled that author's remark that monks should avoid bishops by any means possible.[84] Muirchú, on the other hand, can afford a lack of concern with questionable secular custom, whether it be a burning smithy or a guiding deer. He will not overly interfere with popular tradition because it does not affect his aims of advancing his church, and diminishing the autonomy of the churches of others. Overt paganism is no longer a serious threat; its lingering echo is a secondary issue deserving benign neglect so as to avoid damaging sensibilities of possible use in a more serious contest. Muirchú can thus luxuriate in ambiguity. He can employ it as a signal of Patrick's universal dominance, but also as a means of indicating his lack of interest in upsetting a rooted routine. Adomnán lacks the option. He must bind his international crew of leading kings to follow a precise biblical model, since that is the only one that offers a practical motivational lever by joining the ruler and his anointer in a sacramental or sacramental-like act.[85] He must oppose any lingering paganism or pagan mythos expressed in royal ritual – hence his silence on Tara – because these reflect Armagh's contemporary tolerance of a certain politico-religious ambiguity and hence belong to a potentially damaging mindset of use to his opponents. Given his deep allegiance to the OT, he would probably have actively opposed them anyway, but the point being made here is that neither plan nor principle was in conflict; each reinforced the other as a means of protecting the *familia Iae*, and that aim was surely God's aim.

More precise and direct, however, are the questions as to the purpose of the *VC* testing sequence from Baithéne to Berchán, and how this relates to the

---

83 For some background discussion, see Clare Stancliffe, *Bede, Wilfrid and the Irish* (Jarrow, 2003); Charles-Edwards, *Early Christian Ireland*, pp 429–38. 84 *De institutis coenobiorum*, 40:18: *Omnimodis monachum fugere debere mulieres et episcopos.* M. Petschenig, *Corpus Scriptorum Ecclesiasticorum Latinorum*, 17 (Vienna, 1888), p. 203. 85 Ideas about baptism, ritual fatherhood and OT anointing precedents are here mixed. For some background, see Arnold Angenendt, 'Bonifatius und das Sacramentum initiationis', *Römische Quartalschrift für christliche Altertumskunde und Kirchengeschichte* (1977), 133–83; idem, *Kaiserherrschaft und Königstaufe*, pp 91–165.

earlier 'call of the prophet' sequence of III 1–5. As remarked earlier, Adomnán had learned that most biblical prophets were not born but made, and he took seriously the tradition that held the 'sons of the prophets' to be the original model for contemporary monastic communities. If, as John Cassian had written, Elijah and Elisha were the founders of the monastic life,[86] and if Adomnán's other models of John, Peter and Paul (cited in II 32) had also 'walked in the same manner' in chastity and in the girdles and skins of the desert, then surely, he seems to have reasoned, nothing could be more perfect but that Columba's own monks should be trained to the same level of discernment as the followers of Elijah and Elisha. They should be taught to ascend a ladder that begins with the Psalmist's 'fear of the Lord' and ends with the best of them achieving that closeness to the mind of God that permits one to work in His light and to perceive His intentions. Along with prayers and the practice of the monastic virtues, a learning of scripture accompanied by its constant scribal copying seems to have been Adomnán's chosen device for the winning of this goal. As a pattern, it dovetails exactly with the prophetic call to reform kingship expressed in *VC* III 1–5, since, if kings were once again to be anointed according to ancient biblical ritual, then the prophets doing so ought to have also recapitulated the past; they ought to have undergone a training by the 'father' in the 'desert' of the new mantle-bearer's ascetic brotherhood. Future kings to be made and advised would then always be matched by prophets of the Iona familia fit to guide and correct them.

Nor is an alternative hypothesis easily available. It has been shown that *VC* III 18 draws upon the Elijah/Elisha pattern of *prophetic* succession and the pattern continues in III 19 with Fergnae, who also succeeds. (The additions of apparitions of light in a building depend upon a combining of motifs taken from *Ecclesiasticus* and *Apgiter Chrábaid*.) And since other monks are shown to be excluded from advancement by the same procedure, then leadership in a hierarchy is clearly the point at issue. The purpose of that leadership, moreover, includes the exercise of policies that go far beyond the boundaries of the monastery. Elijah and Elisha steered the course of kingdoms and dynasties. So did the Iona oracle, who conducted the apparition tests, and who otherwise employed his abilities to prophesy for kings and to grant his favourites victory in battle. Adomnán, the kinsman who wrote of him, would also walk the halls of the mighty, and would crown his expertise in their outlook by persuading an extraordinary number of them to come and do his will at the Synod of Birr. A limiting or self-denying ordinance for a practically non-existent 'secular' sphere is hardly to be expected from Adomnán, whose work can depict an angel as divinely sent to whip the prophet into choosing to support one king rather than another. By the nature of their office, almost all abbots are, or find that they must

---

86 See John Cassian, 'Institutes' in Philip Schaff and Henry Wace (eds), *A select library of Nicene and post-Nicene fathers of the Christian Church* (Grand Rapids, MI, 1998 repr.), p. 201.

become, passable politicians, and the abbot of a confederacy of monasteries ends up bound to his expedients like a hostage to his good behaviour. He has no choice but to participate in society and no option but to seek the advancement of his community. Hence, any spiritual device for selecting an abbot must also be one that selects for a projector of power beyond the spiritual. A non-political Columba is a mirage. Adomnán's reform plan draws on both of these dimensions, however, and both the sequences that have been examined exploit it. In these, he actually devises a way to reproduce the prophet–king relationship of his most revered source, while also inventing a means to overcome the plan's main defect, a prophetic power that dies with its wielder. In his second sequence, Adomnán makes the prophetic actor a part of an institution – actually ties him to abbatial selection within *his* institution – and thereby hopes to guarantee Iona's status and future influence. It is an ingenious answer to a difficult dilemma, in that it marries the theory of OT kingship to the institution of contemporary Iona monasticism.

Unlike Muirchú, Adomnán had to weigh his responsibilities as abbot of an international organization. Poised on a tiny island between Ireland, Dál Riata, Pictland, Northumbria and Britain, every move had to be scrutinized and evaluated in terms of cultures that were related but hardly identical. His monastic theology expressed in the 'fear of the Lord' episodes that lead to an abbacy is another example of the same type and condition as that mentioned above. He believes in it profoundly – it expresses one version of a common vision of all monks – but if it can also be adapted to advance the *familia Iae*, then so much the better. Here is another possible reason why Adomnán would speak in imperial terms of kings of 'all Ireland' and 'all Britain'. The fact is that thinking in lesser terms does his international community no good; he is condemned to a monarchic insular internationalism that is tolerable to him because his creed is what is most important and that crosses all boundaries. His views have been affected by the lasting wound of the loss of Northumbria, by frequent wrangling on the Easter question that has divided his community, by bishops who frequently seek worldly power at Columba's expense, by encounters with princes whose needs are predictable but conflicting, and by success at Birr. His looming problems centring on Iona succession (his new allegiance to the 'Romanist' Easter certainly caused division) and the predictably fluctuating support of kings are large ones that require both offensive and defensive measures. He is quite astute enough to foresee such troubles in Ireland because he had already witnessed them in Northumbria, and he requires large-scale partners to manage them, not a hundred satraps with fluctuating family alliances. No one could be more aware of such factionalism than the man who had organized the international assembly of Birr. His worries are political, theological and multi-cultural all at once; in the *VC*, therefore, he is most concerned to develop a long-term intellectual foundation for succeeding generations of prophet–abbots who can draw on the portrait and instruments that he has provided in order to fortify the Columban order in their own broad territories. That is the essential purpose of VC.[87] He foresees political unifications that may be followed by ecclesiastical encroachments and he offers his biblically honed tools to his heirs, whom, he hopes, will find it easier to negotiate with and influence insular emperors. His own experience with the expanding power of the Uí Néill and his recognition of the power once exercised by Northumbrian Oswald may have suggested to him that such was a workable goal for the future to be advanced where possible. Faith in Columba would always be repaid.

As for the context of writing, VC may be interpreted as a quietly limited retort to VP because of the studied contrasts in such areas as kingship and aristocratic alliance, because of the deliberately elevated status of Columba as God's chosen leader of prophets within his own paruchia that is defined by a heavenly mantle, and because the emphasis on unfettered *prophetic* succession within his own community is a strong message that cannot help but clash with Armagh's claim to insular jurisdiction. These are arguments that assert the independent policies of a governing group within a sphere of complete autonomy and sovereignty. Of course, a good deal of this special pleading might be expected in any *vita* that extols the virtues and policies of its protagonist. When considered in the light of the consciousness of opposition that Adomnán displays by his choosing of the Pictish court incidents and his protective guardianship of loyal kings, however, they effectively indicate an origin within an atmosphere of rivalrous contention. His difference in approach in this small world of contemporary writers not only reflects a personal disposition, it suggests an awareness of opposing forces at work. In the particular area of kingship, Adomnán's policy of friendly 'carrot' contrasts too vividly with Muirchú's policy of admonishing 'stick' to be merely coincidental. Neither author wrote in a climate of neutrality, although Adomnán's fine sense of discretion means that his animosity is subtly conveyed more through contrasting examples rather than contrasting arguments.

Prior to Adomnán, nothing on the Columban side could match the quality of Muirchú's work nor the challenge that it posed in the evolving conditions of the later seventh century. On the other hand, it must be stressed that the need for a reply to Muirchú *in his own person* was not Adomnán's *main* reason for writing. Adomnán never mentions him – indeed he hardly mentions Patrick. His target is what these two figures represent, the power behind the propaganda. Without

---

87 To be joined of course to the intent of depicting the most glorious and powerful of Irish prophets who was especially dear to God and who would respond to appeals by those who loved him and his community. For other approaches, see J.-M. Picard, 'The purpose of Adomnán's *Vita Columbae*', *Peritia*, 1 (1982), 160–77; T.M. Charles Edwards, 'The structure and purpose of Adomnán's *Vita Columbae*' in Wooding et al. (eds), *Adomnán of Iona*, pp 205–19; Herbert, *Iona, Kells and Derry*, pp 145–8.

ever naming her, Adomnán is actually contesting the hierarchical ambitions and jurisdictional claims of Armagh. That is an underlying message of both sequences of VC chapters that have been examined. The first (III 1–5) sets forth his claim to an entirely independent territorial confederacy based on a grant of dominant power to a divinely selected prophet. This grant is seconded by groups of monastic saints, and its secular effects are manifested in Columba's power to choose and anoint kings, to select their successors (for example, I 9), and to ensure their protection by the punishment of opponents who contemptuously overlook his power to protect his own (I 1 and I 36). In these assertions of a miraculously designed prophetic leadership over his own paruchia, and in the advancement of Columba as the patron of temporal rulers, an effective counterweight is created to assertions of any other jurisdiction beyond that of the Iona founder. It is not the episcopal hierarchy of ecclesiastics that is decisive, but the divinely inspired prophetic hierarchy of succeeding abbots. That is what produces the mystic torches of a holy fraternity who benefit all through their communal prayer and sacrifices. The superior power of this prophetic grouping of 'sons' is further underlined in chapters displaying the outstanding favour of the Holy Spirit at work in the hearts of monks who fear God and dwell in His light. This is as much a response to Armagh's rationale as Adomnán's wardship of kings is a rebuke to Muirchú's contented depiction of their humiliation. In his second sequence then (III 17–21), and in chapters related to manuscript copying (for example, I 23, III 23), Adomnán shows how an element of prophetic power can be mustered, enlarged and transmitted in order to produce prophetically gifted successors to the founder. Subsequent abbots can thus point to a theory of education based upon biblical teaching and models that enable them to effectively share in the profound spiritual energy of both Columba and the Holy Spirit. Their decisions are thereby sanctified and require no outside approval. Although the territorial and jurisdictional claims of Armagh are never mentioned in the text of VC, Adomnán has given these his full attention, and has quietly – that is, without direct allusion – laid the groundwork for a set of theologically sophisticated arguments that oppose them. These establish the integrity and territorial sovereignty of his own community; in addition, they define the sanctified nature of Columba's special means of choosing a successor and they fix the permanent power of this successor as sole overseer.

Excepting perhaps the Pictish instances mentioned, these considerations help to explain the highly indirect nature of Adomnán's engagement with Muirchú. While some account is indeed taken of Patrick's behaviour in his *vita*, especially in the area of his dealings with kings, it is the intellectual foundation of Armagh's enterprise that is being most actively challenged through a series of responses that combine monastic spirituality with ideas about saintly intercession, the status of biblical prophets in their responsibility for the direction of kings and people, and the concept of a scribal mode of education as a means of eliciting and perfecting the prophetic talent of the gifted young. It is, I suggest, an amalgam well suited to Iona's circumstances. Iona's needs were far different and went far beyond anything that Muirchú addresses, and Adomnán thinks more of his needs than his antagonisms. While open to all, he most earnestly seeks the support of a particular class, a trans-national aristocracy with armed followers, and not that of any kingdom's populace, although, obviously, he would prefer to have both. Columba's supportive role at Druim Cett in brokering an agreement between kings on either side of the Irish Sea is an early example of this strategy; it is emblematic of the way that any Iona abbot must approach the relational constant between politics and the geography of islands. It is a world-view that Iona must systematically maintain and its existence requires us to clear a wider mental space for princes like Oswald, for the conversion of his soldiers, and for Adomnán's deliberate exegesis of his saint as a battle champion. Scholars have often mentioned (without fully explaining) this dimension of the saint's appeal, although the palpable fact is that his biographer made it a foundational aspect of Columba's persona. Muirchú's hero is a seasoned enactor of violence; it is characteristic of Adomnán that he makes it part of a theory. Adomnán has thus pondered deeply the best way to achieve influence over the military elite of the archipelago and his answer is Columba's patronage of kings in battle.[88] He will also emphasize an OT strain in church law, because that too crosses boundaries and reinforces his web that links prophets, kings, warfare and Iona's independence. Adomnán's intellectual opposition to Muirchú is quite certain, therefore, but his side of the debate emphasizes the positive in a way that is both narrower and more extensive – narrower because his primary (but not exclusive) focus is on the elite, and more extensive because it encompasses northern Britain and the islands as well as Ireland. Both Columba and Patrick are described as travelling, for example, but Adomnán is constantly underway to Ireland, Dál Riata, Pictland, Northumbria and the islands, whereas, as far as we know, Muirchú rarely moves from Ireland's northeast and even his saint's journeys in other regions of the country are probably mostly fictional.[89]

If Adomnán presents Columba as a patron of successful warfare, if he exploits this 'special privilege' from God as a means of influencing armsbearers and their leaders, then how does it relate to the Cáin Adomnáin at Birr, where Adomnán formally proclaims a law for the perpetual protection of women, clerics and boys in both Ireland and north Britain, and where the judges of the law are to be 'the clerics whom the community of Adomnán chooses'.[90] To modern eyes, at least, the special patronage of the saint in both fields may seem incongruous and the

---

88 The politics of Northumbria were deeply important to Adomnán and are discussed in chapter three.   89 Binchy, 'Patrick and his biographers', 58. On Patrick's itinerary in Tírechán, see Bieler, *Patrician texts*, pp 35–43, 122–63. For recent discussion, see Nathalie Stalmans, *Saints d'Irlande: analyse critique des sources hagiographique* (VIIe–IXe siècles) (Rennes, 2003), pp 112–18.   90 Meyer, *Cáin Adamnáin*, pp 26–7.

relationship does not seem to have been much studied. The association deserves a fuller analysis than can be essayed here, but it may be that Augustinian concepts of the 'just war' are present in Adomnán's thinking, and are being invoked in order to protect special classes of persons who are noncombatants. Adomnán is also thinking of classifying those who may attack them, for he speaks of groups up to 300 or 1000 or beyond.[91] He is thus concerned with warbands and warband-like armies. He does not mean Columba to be the patron of warfare in general but rather advances him as the heavenly judge of legitimate violence[92] – it is a divine gift permanently given to him alone – so that armed men must always appeal directly to him and present their case for victory. It is the same for judges of his law who must be chosen by his community alone. Since victory is Columba's to give or deny, and since the frequent victims of warfare are under his protection also, most aspects of legal or illegal military activity come under his supervision across all the isles of ocean, and his patronage of this highly practical politico-military field can counter Armagh's influence, or anyone else's influence for that matter, in the area of episcopal supremacy. Adomnán does not have to reply to his opponents in kind. A threat of another's ecclesiastical jurisdiction does not necessarily require that Iona proclaim herself an equal in ecclesiastical rank, although it probably does require a strong statement of divinely sanctioned independence as in *VC* III 1; the power of prophecy combined with the favour of victory are weapons at least as potent. Such arguments are also directly linked to Adomnán's proposed reform of kingship, since warfare against the enemies of God, who are by definition unjust, is the explicit reason for the anointing and sacral protection of kings and emperors in the OT. The ritual act and the military condition are connected. Adomnán includes Dál Riata, Pictland, and Northumbria in this grand framework, for the messages of III 1 and III 18 cannot be separated from his inventions of the imperial ordination of Oswald in north Britain and Diarmait in Ireland, each involving the powerful intervention of Iona's prophet who sees further than anyone else.[93] Adomnán is certainly seeking to maintain influence and independence in both islands. Ambitious bishops are the real source of his troubles and he expects them to get worse. As in the OT, the prophet has the ultimate right to determine the just war, and to employ princes who will carry it out as he wishes.[94]

---

91 Ibid., pp 24–7.   92 Ní Dhonnchadha, '*Lex Innocentium*', p. 5.   93 It is such connections that demonstrate that a genuine theory of reform lies behind the allusions. The chief kings are meant to be created and advised by the chief prophet. That prophet is also influential in warfare, since, in the *Books of Kings*, it continues to have strong cultic and sacral elements. Prophets like Samuel could give directions to armies and their leaders. They were the 'authorized spokesmen of the whole body of the people': see von Rad, *Old Testament theology*, II, pp 52, 123.   94 What is 'just', however, appears to have had more to do with the armed man's relation to Columba than with any concept of Christian virtue. It is the traditional pattern of clientage that seems most important. See now Fraser, 'Adomnán and the morality of war' in Wooding et al. (eds), *Adomnán of Iona*, pp 95–111.

The theme of Birr is thus not unconnected to the equally innovative theme of royal reform in VC. In terms of OT patrons and judges of law, these topics again link Samuel and Ezra as builders of just societies by different means who follow God's will. Adomnán is thus entirely consequential. His promulgation of the 'Law of the Innocents' at Birr is linked to his programme of advocacy in VC, where Columba appears as battle champion, and is seen again in the emphasis on royal justice and the protection of widows and orphans in chapters 3 and 4 of $De\ regno$ in the $Hibernensis$.[95] Adomnán had probably been considering these topics for a long time. It seems logical to relate them to his freeing of Irish captives in Northumbria in 685, for example, and one also finds them in his attention to aristocratic hostages and exiles in a number of chapters of VC (for example, I 11, 13). It is one more sign of the kinds of motives that made a new $vita$ of Columba necessary in order to clearly enunciate and publicize an innovative conceptualization of the Cenél Conaill holy man. He is now presented as a revived biblical prophet who anoints just kings,[96] selects their heirs, enables their empires and passes these prophetic powers on to his Iona successors, who will do the same after he is gone.

One must, finally, say something more about the striking role of prophecy and prophets in the two $vitae$, but it is especially necessary to do so in the case of VC where the prophetic principle is frequently pressed. Adomnán's conception is not without its own peculiarity. This lies in the fact that his term $profetatio$ not only means the prediction of future events, but also refers to an ability to discern contemporary happenings in distant places.[97] Both abilities appear to draw on

Adomnán seems to have been a 'realist' about warfare in many ways. **95** Wasserschleben, $Kanonensammlung$, pp 77–8. **96** The anointed ruler of the OT is the ordained ruler of Adomnán's terminology, and the OT sees the spirit of the Lord resting upon him through that act. According to von Rad, $Old\ Testament\ theology$, II, pp 169–70, he cares especially for the poor and weak and his commission through the sacramental act consists 'pre-eminently in the establishment of the divine justice on earth'. The anointed one is the 'guarantor of justice' and his 'administration of justice displayed most clearly man's attitude to God' (149). The 'ruler' is not the real 'king', however. Only Yahweh is king, and the prophet is his mouthpiece who thus advises and counsels the ruler in the right usage of the spirit that sits upon him so that blessings follow for the kingdom. This is the pattern that one finds in Adomnán and in the $Hibernensis$. It is what connects ordination to $ordo$ and justice, and both to the prophet. Unction, and its results in just decisions, enable a bridge to native Irish conceptions and that is why one finds the connection between both made in the $Hibernensis$ book $De\ regno$ 1–4. It is essential to remark that the results cited there are attached to the prophetic act of anointing, which joins cap. 1 on Samuel's unction of Saul to cap. 3–4 on the behaviour of kings who do or do not carry out their commission. It is clear, therefore, that cap. 2, $de\ ordinatione\ regis\ cum\ sorte$, does not bear the same meaning as cap. 1. Contrary to what scholars have often supposed, it $does\ not$ present an $alternative$ method of ordination! It is present only because it is a second ritual that can be used during inauguration (and after the first) since that is exactly the way it appears in 1 Reges 10, which both $De\ regno$ chapters cite and appeal to. While kings can be spoken of as 'ordained' in both cases, it is only through a prophet's unction that the spirit of God alights upon a ruler, and in the Irish view of the $Hibernensis$, then joins the king in the cosmos of God's creation. Anointing by the prophet is itself constitutive, and it is that which controls the biblical theory that Adomnán and the $Hibernensis$ compilers follow. Wasserschleben, $Kanonensammlung$, pp 76–8. **97** A recent discussion appears in Charles-Edwards, 'Structure and purpose', pp 207–10.

the same inner power. Thus, in VC I, Adomnán states that, as a young man, Columba began to use the 'spirit of prophecy' so that he could predict the future, but he could also 'see what was done afar off, because he was there in the spirit though not in the body. For as St Paul says, "He that is joined unto the Lord is one spirit"'. Such an approach goes further, since, as the heading to Book II declares, 'miracles of power' are 'often also prophetically foreknown'. The spirit of prophecy is thus joined to the ability to intervene in cases where, for example, the prophet might wish to bless or curse or even, as in I 37, simply refresh weary followers.[98] Adomnán also provides a number of examples of prophetic intervention over distance in order to illustrate both the saint's kindness and his 'terrible vengeance on his opponents' (an intriguing remark because Adomnán is not commonly so forthright about Columba's willingness to inflict damage on his enemies). Especially notable in this pattern, however, a cause of puzzlement to commentators, is the fact that all of these conditions should be subsumed under the single heading of 'spirit of prophecy', and one can hardly avoid asking why prophecy should also include spirit walking and the ability to miraculously transform.

Some of this broad conception of prophecy as a 'mental grasp miraculously enlarged' that brings knowledge of the whole earth (I 43) is drawn from Gregory the Great's *Dialogues*, but scholars appear to have overlooked a source that would have been more important to Adomnán. It is one that Gregory also prized and actually cited to the same effect, so that, for the Iona writer, each source would have reinforced the other. The key texts come from 4 Reges 5, which recounts the story of Naaman, an honorable general of the king of Syria who is also a leper and is cured by the prophet Elisha. Now we know that this story was dear to Adomnán's heart because Naaman is specifically recalled in Luke 4, which refers to him as part of the justification for Christ's statement at the beginning of his mission: 'Amen I say to you, that no prophet is accepted in his own country'. It is through this allusion that Adomnán can hint that Columba's departure (or exile) from Ireland was actually providential, for, like Christ, he had been 'predestined to lead the nations to life' (III 3). Cited by Christ in a way that seemed to foreshadow Columba, Elisha's behaviour is especially noteworthy. What follows after Naaman's healing is a further sign of Adomnán's thinking, however, because it displays Elisha's miraculous knowledge of events elsewhere. After his cure, Naaman wished to reward Elisha, who refused, although pressed, to accept his treasure. But Elisha's greedy servant, Gehazi (or Giezi) saw this as a route to riches. After the general had departed, Gehazi ran after him with a story that some 'sons of the prophets' had just arrived and required money and garments for their support. Naaman gladly gave more than was requested and

'For Adomnán, the general term *profetatio* included both *visio*, perception of distant events, and *praescientia*, knowledge of the future'. Noted also is the prominence of prophecy in the Life.
98 Ibid., p. 209.

Gehazi hid it all from his master. And when Elisha confronted him about where he had been, he lied about it. But Elisha knew all that had transpired: 'was not my heart present, when the man (Naaman) turned back from his chariot to meet thee? (*at ille nonne ait cor meum in praesenti erat quando reversus est homo de curru suo in occursum tui*).' Along with Naaman's treasure, therefore, Elisha also gave his servant Naaman's leprosy (5:19–27).

In this tale, the prophet cures the general but is also mystically aware of what the general does when he is elsewhere. As a further sign of the same kind of power that is his because of his status, Elisha then curses Gehazi by transforming him physically. Actually, 4 Reges provides several other examples of this, what Gerhard von Rad calls 'parapsychic capabilities, such as clairvoyance and seeing from afar'.[99] In 6:12, Elisha is able to hear (and report to the Hebrew king) all the secrets of the Syrian ruler's privy chamber, and in 8:10, he knows the nature of the Syrian king's disease and can predict its outcome. Gregory the Great had studied these texts also and had drawn conclusions that he passes on to Adomnán. In his second dialogue, he ascribes the power to see from afar to St Benedict, who is able to discern when a traveller on his journey listens to a minor devil. In the words of Gregory's interlocutor, 'this proves that the servant of God (Benedict) possessed the spirit of Eliseus. He, too, was present with one of his followers who was far away'.[1] The allusion is most probably to the story of Gehazi. The 'spirit of Eliseus' is thus Adomnán's 'spirit of prophecy', which combines prediction with knowledge from afar and the capability to work 'miracles of power'. When Adomnán thinks of Columba's 'spirit of prophecy', therefore, he is applying the lessons of both Elisha and Gregory. Even the very profusion and variety of his miracles in *VC*, especially notable perhaps in *VC* II, may also owe something to this OT source. As von Rad remarks of Elisha's career, 'nowhere in the OT are so many miracles crowded into so small a space, and nowhere is such open pleasure taken in the miraculous, or such sheer delight shown at the repeated and astonishing proofs of the prophet's *charisma*'.[2] Adomnán's understanding of his prophet's relation to war and its exercise may have been affected also. Much of the warfare of the OT partakes of a 'sacral character' in which Yahweh is directly involved and inspires his prophets to play special roles and to lead, advise or oppose the rulers and peoples caught up in it.[3] They are to guide their peoples whether leaders accept it or not. Like other topics in *VC*, Adomnán's portrait of Columba's patronage of battle should also be analysed in the light of this system. It is part of the OT conception of the prophet's divine office, and hence one need no longer be surprised to find a

---

99 von Rad, *Old Testament theology*, II, p. 27, n. 44.   1 Moricco, *Gregorii Magni dialogi*, p. 100. *Petrus. Ego sancti viri praecordiis Helisei spiritum video inesse, qui absenti discipulo praesens fuit.* See also the incident that follows, in which Totila, the Gothic ruler, puts Benedict's 'prophetic powers' to a test. Odo John Zimmerman (trans.) *Saint Gregory the Great: Dialogues* (New York, 1959), p. 79. 2 von Rad, *Old Testament theology*, II, p. 27.   3 von Rad, *Der heilige Krieg*, provides many examples.

reflection in Adomnán's work. As an angel proclaims in III 1, God has settled Columba's destiny and 'he shall be reckoned as one of the prophets'.

Muirchú and Adomnán constantly think in terms of OT texts, figures and practices linked to the prophets when they refer to clergy, kings, nations and law. Thus Patrick is a prophet like Jonah, Moses, Elijah and Daniel; so too is Columba in a general way, but he is particularly comparable to Samuel, Elisha, Isaiah, Ezra and others. These prophets are cited, modelled and imitated in ways that make them the icons of the socio-political, theological and legal agendas of the authors. Columba's divinely granted authority over Britain and the islands is indicated by means of a dream in which his pregnant mother receives Elijah's mantle, and the task that confronts him is prophesied by St Brendan. When Adomnán wishes to introduce a new king-making ritual by Columba, he justifies it by the transmission of angelic command while the saint is *in extasi mentis*. Similarly, when Muirchú wishes Patrick to indicate an heirship for Benignus, he does it by means of a visionary procedure that follows the precedents set by Elijah and Elisha. It is the idea of *prophetic* succession that appears central. Other ecclesiastical inauguration rituals, election, acclamation and ordination necessarily occur, but they are not the items emphasized or even always mentioned; they are thus culturally downgraded in favour of the mystic trance that provides the essence of true knowledge that leads infallibly to right action. Those who can perform in this way are prophets and their status at certain times and places may well have transcended in effect and prestige the normal church offices of priest, bishop, abbot or monk. A regard for the prophet's charismatic access to divine awareness may often have trumped a respect for the norms of hierarchy, even when the context is that of episcopal succession. If this were indeed the predominant cultural attitude, then the official canonical differences between bishops and abbots may have seemed less significant in the kingdoms around the Irish Sea. It would have been the status and behaviour of the seer-like prophet that counted the most. The term does not simply refer to prognostication; it conveys the impression of a shamanistic worker of miracles.

While hagiographers in other countries occasionally rely on similar thinking or justification, it is clear that their references lack the degree of resonance and continuity that one finds in Irish culture.[4] The explanation for the special reverence given to prophets thus lies in Irish culture also where the prophetic practitioner was already admired before Christianity. Overt paganism did not end in the seventh century, although it probably did not last much beyond it, as far as we can tell. Druids continued to exist in this period, at a time when the church was successfully struggling to occupy the same religious slot that they had filled for so long. In ousting the druids throughout the country, in claiming the respect and privileges that they had once held, the church found it necessary

4 Kottje, *Studien zum Einfluss*, pp 106–9.

to ally with the less offensive poetic order in an epochal compromise that seems to have occurred over several generations from about the mid-seventh century onwards.[5] One price for the order's agreement was toleration of the truth-deriving poetic trance in the practice of *imbas forosna*, the mystically inspired 'great knowledge that illuminates'.[6] Another was toleration of the secular miracle of effective satire. It too required a perfect joining of words to a cosmic order and produced miraculous effects at a distance. Such techniques must have been acquired though a long training in visionary methods that were, apparently, seen as acceptable equivalent to the music, dancing and drumming procedures employed by some OT prophets.[7] Irish culture thus possessed *two* legitimate *learned* groups exercising licit visionary power, one of which constantly drew on pre-Christian tradition (although the church at first insisted that poets should behave in ways comparable to Levite priests).[8] The effect was to endow mystic practice with enormous cultural as well as religious prestige. Prophets of the OT could thereby be seen as the most talented of model-worthy saints. Indeed, one has the sense that in order to be considered 'saintly' in this period, one must first have exhibited the signs or spirit of prophetic power. It may, perhaps, have been seen as a necessary talent comparable to the instructed inspiration of poets. An ideal of transcendent visionary ability would then continue in the culture as a mutually reinforcing occupational package that allowed a notably non-Christian element to survive under ecclesiastical protection. In both cases, moreover, as in the OT, prophecy was a skill that apprentices could be set to learn. The parallels were thus closer than might now appear at first glance and a remarkable measure of harmony within dissonance was thereby achievable in the culture.

The trance of the poets that sought to match flawless speech to cosmic truth that achieved change was not the same thing as the rapture of ecstatic ascetics, but neither was it decidedly different since both trades invoked a talent for perception through concentration. In the common ground that resulted, space could be created for a Gaelicized approach to Christianity comparable in some ways to the Germanization that was occurring on the Continent, except that, in the Irish sphere of influence, it was effected through the consciously harmonizing accommodation of institutions. The works that have been examined reflect this cultural compromise in different measure and nuance. It is what made Muirchú's ambiguities possible. Even Adomnán, the radical transformer

5 Much relevant material will be found in John Carey, 'The two laws in Dubthacht's judgment', *Cambridge Medieval Celtic Studies*, 19 (1990), 1–18; 'An edition of the pseudo-historical prologue to the *Senchas Már*', *Ériu*, 45 (1994), 1–32; Kim McCone, 'Dubthacht maccu Lugair and a matter of life and death in the pseudo-historical prologue to the *Senchas Már*', *Peritia*, 5 (1986), 1–35; *Pagan past and Christian present in early Irish literature* (Naas, 1980), pp 84–103, passim.   6 Nora Chadwick, '*Imbas Forasnaí*', *Scottish Gaelic Studies*, 4 (1934), 98–135.   7 Wilson, 'Prophecy and ecstasy', 321–37; Lindblom, *Prophecy*, pp 29–65, passim.   8 Liam Breatnach (ed.), *Uraicecht na Ríar: the poetic grades in early Irish law* (Dublin, 1987), pp 104–5. In doing so, of course, the church was essentially recognizing a relationship in the sphere of guild holiness that could be made acceptable to Christians through a reliance on selected OT texts.

attached to visionary experience, can draw freely on this dual-sourced culture. Not long after 597, the year of Columba's death, the *Amra Choluimb Chille* was already turning traditional poetic language to praise of the poet-prophet, 'the seer who used to keep fears from us', the teacher 'who would explain the true Word'. It may be that the sixth, seventh and perhaps early eighth century was the dominant age of this 'culture of prophecy' and that subsequent generations saw its force among the elite diminished to some degree by more effective institutionalization and division of the spoils. Those questions, as with the validity of the hypothesis, must await future research.

CHAPTER THREE

A Columban covenant in Northumbria: interpreting *VC* I 1 and II 46

Adomnán was an especially innovative politico-religious thinker whose inspiration derived in considerable part from the prophetic and historical books of the OT. As I tried to show in chapter two, the focus of much of this inspiration in practice was prompted and abetted by the nature of the ecclesiastical power politics coming to a head during his time as abbot of the Iona confederacy. Claims to primacy and jurisdiction over the churches of the entire country made by Armagh propagandists like Muirchú meant that he too had to reply with arguments and miracle stories that countered theirs, while advancing his own interests. In discussing this simmering pot of hormonal ecclesiasticism, I concentrated on Ireland and presented only a brief and partial analysis of Adomnán's material on Oswald and Northumbria. Returning to it now, it is clear that much remains to be unwrapped and examined in a more penetrating light. The powerful role played by OT typology in Adomnán's thinking about the right relationship between prophets and kings is one such topic of interest, but even more so are his ideas about supernatural covenant and island-wide kingship in relation to the Iona abbot's position as leader of an international federation of monasteries. Although a number of scholars have examined aspects of these questions, a considerable advantage in perspective can be gained if we focus on what has been most widely and unfortunately neglected, namely on Adomnán's thinking about Columba as an aristocratic patron of battle. Attention here can expose an additional axial perspective that draws much force from the Oswald episode of *VC* I 1. In contrast to the Andersons' view in their edition of *VC*, Richard Sharpe decided that this Oswald topic was probably covered in the very first chapter of *VC* in order to give it 'special prominence', and in his recent insightful analysis of the composition of *VC*, Mark Stansbury suggested that it represented material written by Adomnán but 'later moved to this prominent place by someone who wanted to emphasize Columba's posthumous power'.[1] In the present chapter, I shall also maintain that the paragraph that follows the Oswald episode in *VC* I is closely related to its message and that both should be seen as linked to *VC* II 46 on Adomnán's trip to a plague-ridden Northumbria.

---

1 Sharpe, *Adomnán*, p. 250, n. 38; Mark Stansbury, 'The composition of Adomnán's *Vita Columbae*', *Peritia*, 17–18 (2003–4), 154–82 at 168.

Since constant allusion will be necessary, it seems best to print all of the relevant material of I 1. Thereafter, because it can be demonstrated that the Oswald episode is essentially a targeted mixture of OT themes, and even of specific OT narrative, I will move to a discussion of OT warfare principles and the specific reason for Adomnán's application of them to Northumbria. The relevant material of I 1 is as follows:

Some kings were conquered in the terrifying crash of battle and others emerged victorious according to what Columba asked of God by the power of prayer. God who honours all saints gave this special privilege to him as to a mighty and triumphant champion, and it remained as true after he quit the flesh as it had been in this present life.

We shall provide one example of this special honour granted by the Almighty from heaven to the honourable man. This was revealed to the English King Oswald on the day before his battle against Cadwallon, the most powerful king of the Britons. While this King Oswald was camped ready for battle, he was asleep on a pillow in his tent one day when he had a vision of St Columba. His appearance shone with angelic beauty, and he seemed so tall that his head touched the clouds and, as he stood in the middle of the camp, he covered all of it except one far corner with his shining robe. The blessed man revealed his name to the king and gave him these words of encouragement, the same the Lord spoke to Joshua, saying, 'Be strong and act manfully. Behold, I will be with thee'. In the king's vision Columba said this, adding: 'This coming night go out from your camp into battle, for the Lord has granted me that at this time your foes shall be put to flight and Cadwallon your enemy shall be delivered into your hands and you shall return victorious after battle and reign happily'.

Hearing these words, the king awoke and described his vision to the assembled council. All were strengthened by this, and the whole people promised that after their return from battle they would accept the faith and receive baptism. For up to that time the whole of England was darkened by the shadow of heathendom and ignorance, except for King Oswald himself and twelve men who had been baptized with him in exile among the Irish. Why say more? That same night, just as he had been told in the vision, he marched out from the camp into battle with a modest force against many thousands. A happy and easy victory was given him by the Lord according to his promise. King Cadwallon was killed, Oswald returned as victor after battle and was afterward ordained by God as emperor of all Britain.

My predecessor, our Abbot Failbe, related all this to me, Adomnán, without question. He swore that he had heard the story of the vision from the lips of King Oswald himself as he was relating it to Abbot Ségéne.

This too is not to be passed over: certain men, wicked and bloodstained from a life as brigands, were protected by songs that they sang in Irish in praise of St Columba and by the commemoration of his name. For on the night they sang these songs, they were delivered from the hands of their enemies, who had surrounded the house of the singers, and escaped unhurt through flames and swords and spears. But a few of them made little of the holy man's commemoration and would not sing these songs. Miraculously, these alone perished in the enemies' attack. It would be possible to produce not just two or three witnesses of this event, enough to satisfy the law, but a hundred or more. For the same occurrence did not just happen at one place or time, but it can be clearly shown to have happened at different places and times in Ireland and Britain, and in the same way with the same reason for the deliverance. We have learnt of it with no room for doubt from informed people in each area where the same miracle took place.[2]

Oswald's authority waxed after the victory of Denisesburn. 'In fact', writes Bede, 'he held under his sway all the peoples and kingdoms of Britain, divided among

---

2 Sharpe, *Adomnán*, pp 110–12. *VC*, pp 198–202: [...] *In bellorumque terrificis fragoribus hoc a deo virtute orationum impetravit, ut alii reges victi et alii regnatores efficerentur victores. Hoc tale praevilegium non tantum in hac praesenti vita conversanti, sed etiam post ejus de carne transitum, quasi cuidam victoriali et fortissimo propugnatori a deo omnium sanctorum condonatum est honorificatore.*

Hujus talis honorificantiae viro honorabili ab omnipotente caelitus conlatae etiam unum proferemus exemplum, quod Ossualdo regnatori saxonico pridie quam contra Catlonem Britonum regem fortissimum proeliaretur ostensum erat. Nam cum idem Ossualdus rex esset in procinctu belli castrametatus quadam die in sua papillione supra pulvillum dormiens sanctum Columbam in visu videt forma coruscantem angelica cujus alta proceritas vertice nubes tangere videbatur. Qui scilicet vir beatus suum regi proprium revelans nomen in medio castrorum stans eadem castra, excepta quadam parva extremitate, sui protegebat fulgida veste. Et haec confirmatoria contulit verba, eadem scilicet quae dominus ad Jesue bén Nun ante transitum Jordanis mortuo Moyse prolocutus est, dicens: 'Confortare et age viriliter. Ecce ero tecum', et cetera. Sanctus itaque Columba haec ad regem in visu loquens addit: 'Hac sequenti nocte de castris ad bellum procede. Hac enim vice mihi dominus donavit ut hostes in fugam vertantur tui, et tuus Catlon inimicus in manus tradatur tuas, et post bellum victor revertaris et feliciter regnes'.

Post haec verba expergitus rex senatui congregato hanc enarrat visionem; qua confortati omnes totus populus promittit sé post reversionem de bello crediturum et baptismum suscepturum. Nam usque in id temporis tota illa Saxonia gentilitatis et ignorantiae tenebrís obscurata erat, excepto ipso rege Ossualdo cum xii. viris qui cum eo Scotos inter exsolante baptizati sunt. Quid plura? Eadem subsequta nocte Ossualdus rex sicuti in visu edoctus fuerat, de castrís ad bellum cum admodum pauciore exercitu contra milia numerosa progreditur. Cui a domino sicut ei promisum est felix et facilis est concessa victoria, et rege trucidato Catlone victor post bellum reversus postea totius Britanniae imperator a deo ordinatus est.

Hanc mihi Adamnano narrationem meus decessor noster abbas Failbeus indubitanter enarravit. Qui sé ab ore ipsius Ossualdi regis Segineo abbati eandem enuntiantis visionem audisse protestatus est.

Sed et hoc etiam non praetereundum videtur, quod ejusdem beati viri per quaedam scoticae lingae laudum ipsius carmina et nominis commemorationem quidam quamlibet scelerati laicae conversationis homines et sanguinarii, ea nocte qua eadem decantaverant cantica, de manibus inimicorum qui eandem eorumdem cantorum domum circumsteterant sint liberati; qui flammas inter et gladios et lanceas incolomes evassere. Mirumque in modum pauci ex ipsis, qui easdem sancti viri commemorationis quasi parvipendentes canere noluerant decantationes, in illo emulorum impetu soli disperierant. Hujus miraculi testes non duo aut tres juxta legem sed etiam centeni aut eo amplius adhiberi potuere. Non enim in uno aut loco aut tempore hoc idem contegisse conprobatur; sed etiam diversís locís et temporibus in Scotia et Brittannia simili tamen et modo et causa liberationis factum fuisse sine ulla ambiguitate exploratum est. Haec ab expertís unius cujusque regionis ubicumque res eadem simili contegit miraculo indubitanter didicimus.

159

the speakers of four languages, British, Pictish, Irish, and English'.[3] He sent to Iona for missionaries and inaugurated an alliance that was to last for the next thirty years, the period of Adomnán's youth and young manhood.[4] Both Bede and Adomnán saw the victory at Denisesburn (or, less correctly, Heavenfield) as crucial, but whereas Bede largely interpreted Oswald as a Constantinian hero beneath the cross as his special sign (*signum sanctae crucis erexit*),[5] Adomnán sought quite carefully to place him within the ranks of OT type rulers. To understand why requires a brief overview of some principles and parameters of OT warfare, for it can be shown that that is the background that influenced Adomnán.

In the early history of Israel from Moses through the early monarchy, two kinds of military conflict appear: ordinary war and holy war.[6] In the first, armies and their leaders may negotiate, reconsider their enmity, exchange captives or craft treaties; in the second, cultic considerations predominate and genocidal annihilation is the only tolerable outcome. Although, as a practical matter, Adomnán was probably far more familiar with the first type of conflict, and hardly wished for any peoples' annihilation, it is to the principles of the second type that he appeals in the *VC* citation above. Biblical scholars have long argued about such conflict's theological significance and refer to it in a variety of ways: as 'holy war', 'Yahweh war' (which is preferred by many), 'covenant warfare', the '*herem*' or 'the ban'.[7] The Hebrew word *herem* is difficult to translate, but essentially refers to a sacrificial slaughter of all enemies (and practically all non-

---

3 B. Colgrave and R.A.B. Mynors (eds), *Bede's Ecclesiastical history of the English people* (Oxford, 1969), pp 230–1: *denique omnes nationes et prouincias Brittaniae, quae in quattor linguas, id est Brittonum Pictorum Scottorum et Anglorum divisae sunt, in dicione accepit.* 4 For the Columban background and Adomnán's abbacy, see Herbert, *Iona, Kells and Derry*, pp 9–57. A recent anthology of relevant articles is Wooding et al. (ed.), *Adomnán of Iona*, and a useful overview of the British context is Yorke, *Conversion of Britain*. 5 Stancliffe, 'Oswald, "most holy and victorious king of the Northumbrians"' in Stancliffe and Cambridge (eds), *Oswald*, pp 33–83 at pp 63–4; J.M. Wallace-Hadrill, *Bede's Ecclesiastical history of the English people: a historical commentary* (Oxford, 1993), pp 88–9. In her fine essay, however, Stancliffe is one of the few scholars who points out (pp 50–1), although only in passing, that Adomnán casts Oswald 'more in an Old Testament guise', and suggests that 'we should accept that Oswald attributed his victory to the intercession of Columba'. 6 The basic work, drawn upon by all scholars in the field, is von Rad, *Die heilige Krieg im alten Israel* (Göttingen, 1958). Equally fundamental is his *Old Testament theology I: the theology of Israel's historical traditions* (New York, 1962), and *Old Testament theology II: the theology of Israel's prophetic traditions* (New York, 1965). Both were translated from the German by D.M.G. Stalker. 7 Amid a large literature, see F. Stolz, *Jahwes und Israels Kriege: Kriegstheorien und Kriegserfahrungen im Glauben des alten Israel* (Zurich, 1972); M.C. Lind, *Yahweh is a warrior: the theology of warfare in ancient Israel* (Scottsdale, PA, 1980); T.R. Hobbs, *A time for war: a study of warfare in the Old Testament* (Wilmington, DE, 1989); P.D. Miller, *The divine warrior in early Israel* (Cambridge, MA, 1973). A useful modern scholarly overview is G.H. Jones, 'The concept of holy war' in R.E. Clements (ed.), *The world of ancient Israel: sociological, anthropological and political perspectives* (Cambridge, 1989), pp 299–323. Also W. Dietrich, 'The "Ban" in the age of the early kings' in V. Fritz and P.R. Davies, *The origins of the ancient Israelite state* (Sheffield, 1996), pp 195–211. The

Hebrews in Canaan were enemies) whose women, children, animals and possessions were all consecrated to Yahweh who expected and demanded their deaths.[8] One famous case, which illustrates the severe consequences to a leader of not carrying out the full severity of the *herem*, deserves citation. It occurs in 1 Reges 15 and focuses on war with the Amalekites:

> And Samuel said to Saul: the Lord sent me to anoint thee king over his people Israel: now therefore hearken thou unto the voice of the Lord: Thus sayeth the Lord of Hosts: I have reckoned up all that Amalec hath done to Israel ... Now therefore go, and smite Amalec, and utterly destroy all that he hath: spare him not, nor covet anything that is his: but slay both man and woman, child and suckling, ox and sheep, camel and ass.

But after defeating the Amalekites, Saul decided to spare their king and the best of his herds. Yahweh was angered:

> And the word of the Lord came to Samuel saying: It repenteth me that I have made Saul king: for he hath forsaken me, and hath not executed my commandments.

Samuel informed Saul that he had 'done evil in the eyes of the Lord'. Such refusal to obey is 'like the crime of idolatry' and it thus severs Saul from his compact with Yahweh and with Yahweh's prophet.

> Forasmuch therefore as thou hast rejected the word of the Lord, the Lord hath also rejected thee from being king ... The Lord hath rent the kingdom of Israel from thee this day, and hath given it to thy neighbor who is better than thee ... And Samuel said: Bring hither to me Agag the king of Amalec ... And Samuel hewed him in pieces before the Lord in Galgal.

Here, the prophet himself carries out the Lord's command by cutting the enemy king into bits. He is not alone in this readiness to spill blood. Elijah, for example, will personally slaughter scores of captive priests of Baal (3 Reges 18:40). These are the same priests that Elijah mocked because they routinely cut themselves with knives and lances so as to gain the attention of their god.

In the early books of the OT, the side that wins will often seek to destroy its opponents. Nor do the prophet/judges who lead the Hebrews think otherwise; they are not modern 'peace-and-conflict' students, they are perfectly willing to

---

world of biblical scholarship is seriously divided on many questions and tendencies. For an urbane introduction by an expert, see James Barr, *History and ideology in the Old Testament: biblical studies at the end of a millennium* (Oxford, 2000). 8 For four different theological viewpoints on 'Yahweh war', see C.S. Cowles, Eugene H. Merrill, Daniel L. Gard and Tremper Longman III, *Show them no mercy: four views on God and Canaanite genocide* (Grand Rapids, MI, 2003). As these are all within a similar tradition, other interpretations are possible.

personally kill large numbers of their opponents, and they have a limited tolerance even for royal dissent. They inhabit a stark landscape in which the behaviour of a people's gods reflects their own desperate need to survive by holding and defending the limited number of productive districts and usable routes available. One must remember that Yahweh is frequently perceived as a 'warrior', as a personally blood-soaked Near Eastern god of war whose battlefield is sacred space. Exodus 15:3 states that 'the Lord is as a man of war, Almighty is his name'. He is routinely held to personally participate in holy war battles; he leads the army and wins victory for his worshippers: 'not with thy sword', he declares, 'nor with thy bow' (Jos 24:12); or further: 'when they [the Amorrhites] fought against you, I delivered them into your hands, and you possessed their lands' (24:8). Yahweh is normally presented as defeating the enemy through miracles but he can also be pictured like a soldier in the ranks. Although not all scholars agree, many believe that he is the 'prince of the host' depicted before Jericho (Jos 5:13–16):

> And when Joshua was in the field of the city of Jericho, he lifted up his eyes, and saw a man standing over against him, holding a drawn sword, and he went to him and said: Art thou one of ours, or of our adversaries? And he answered: No: but I am prince of the host of the Lord, and now I am come. Joshua fell on his face to the ground. And worshipping, said: What saith my Lord to his servant? Loose, saith he, thy shoes from off thy feet: for the place whereon thou standeth is holy. And Joshua did as was commanded him.[9]

The cultic nature of this stage of the war with the Canaanites is clear because of the seven processions around Jericho by priests with the Ark of the Covenant, by the miracle of the falling walls and by the execution of all inhabitants thereafter (except for the family of a single woman who had protected Joshua's spies).

Most of Adomnán's remarks actually refer to these kinds of cultic warfare events and their connections. This cannot be accidental. One thinks of the very fact of Columba's patronage of battle that not only existed in life but extended also to his afterlife so that he is 'a mighty and triumphant champion'. One might suppose, as it seems most scholars have done,[10] that Adomnán was thinking of

---

9 The Douay version contains a note identifying this figure as St Michael, called in Daniel 10:21 'prince of the people of Israel'. In the evangelical tradition, however, there is no doubt that the prince is Yahweh himself: 'After all, before what other person would Joshua fall "facedown to the ground in reverence?"'. Tremper Longman, 'The case for spiritual continuity' in Cowles, *Show them no mercy*, pp 161–87 at p. 164. In general, the appearance of a divine figure before battle is a feature of the war literature of many cultures in the ancient Near East: Miller, *Divine warrior*, pp 128–31. A useful OT commentary is L.D. Hawk, *Joshua* (Collegeville, MN, 2000).   10 For example, see Jennifer O'Reilly, 'Reading the scriptures in the Life of Columba' in Bourke (ed.), *Studies in the cult of St Columba*, pp 80–106 at pp 81–5. She relates the vision element in the Oswald story to

Constantine's experience of divine favour at the Battle of the Milvian Bridge when he wrote about Oswald's vision of Columba. Reference to Columba's 'privilege' of bestowing victories, which has been alluded to previously, would then be an adaptation of this well-known Roman legend, and the material that follows it in VC would be a more-or-less fanciful hagiographical extrapolation.

Such a view is not sustainable, as we shall see. The only plausible part of the assumption is the use of the idea of a vision as an explanatory or legitimating device before a battle and even that need not necessarily be part of a Constantinian scheme. Indeed, Adomnán suggests otherwise since he goes out of his way to highlight the explicitly OT context in which he wishes us to think. He does so by direct reference to Joshua, the famous victor in battles against Cananites ('Be strong and act manfully' etc.). He then reasserts the context with Columba's assurance to Oswald that 'your foes shall be put to flight' and 'your enemy shall be delivered into your hands'. In both cases, we are dealing with parts or slight variations of well-established biblical *holy war* formulas. The first belongs with what specialists call the 'fear not' formula, and the second is the so-called *Übergabeformel*, by which 'Yahweh gives X into your hand'.[11] Even the final remark that Oswald shall return and 'reign happily' belongs in this context.

One must stress that these inciting encouragements are part of a holy war *covenant*. Thus, in Joshua 1:6: 'Take courage and be strong: for thou shalt divide by lot to this people the land, for which I swore to their fathers, that I would deliver it to them'. Or verse 7–8: 'Take courage therefore, and be very valiant: that thou mayest observe and do all the law, which Moses my servant hath commanded thee ... Let not the book of this law depart from thy mouth'. These

Constantine, and the Joshua reference to the tradition of Hiberno–Latin exegesis that links the names Jesus and Joshua. Hence, she maintains, Adomnán's allusion to Joshua 'does not simply evoke a familiar type of the warrior leader', but 'shows the saint to be involved in Christ's universal work of redemption'. For Adomnán, the real 'promised land' is eternal life, while Oswald's victory is 'part of the continuing fulfilment of this Old Testament prefiguring of the church' to be associated with Constantine's victory that 'led to the historical establishment of the Church throughout the peoples of the Roman Empire'. Although she rightly thinks in terms of covenant, she seeks to spiritualize Columba's war patronage so that she can move in the direction of the *New Testament* rather than the *Old*. J.-M. Picard pays less attention to scriptural interpretation but is closer to a clear interpretation of the British side of the evidence when he argues that the *VC* 'is Adomnán's answer to Northumbrian attacks on Columba': 'The purpose of Adomnán's *Vita Columbae*', 174. For Adomnán's 'realistic' attitude to warfare, see the convincing analysis of James E. Fraser, 'Adomnán and the morality of war' in Wooding et al. (eds), *Adomnán*, pp 95–112. Bede's version of events is unlikely to represent the actual seventh-century context. See Ian Wood, 'Constantinian crosses in Northumbria' in C.E. Karkov, K.L. Jolly and Sarah Larratt Keefer (eds), *The place of the cross in Anglo-Saxon England* (Woodbridge, 2006), pp 3–14. 11 Joshua 1:9: 'Behold I command thee, take courage, and be strong. Fear not and be not dismayed: because the Lord thy God is with thee ...': E.W. Conrad, *Fear not warrior: a study of the 'al tîrā' pericopes in the Hebrew Scriptures* (Chico, CA, 1985); R. Bach, *Die Aufforderungen zur Flucht und zum Kampf im alttestamentlichen Prophetenspruch* (Neukirchen, 1962), pp 51–112; P.-E. Dion, 'The "Fear Not" formula and holy war', *Catholic Biblical Quarterly*, 32 (1970), 565–70. This author notes seventeen examples of the *Übergabeformel* and four or five for 'fear not'.

refer back to Deuteronomy 31:23–24: 'And the Lord commanded Joshua the son of Nun, and said: Take courage, and be valiant: for thou shalt bring the children of Israel into the land which I have promised, and I will be with thee'. It is clear, therefore, that Adomnán has very carefully sought out and chosen his biblical texts. It is not just the exhortation that he wants the reader to ponder but the fact that Yahweh's words are part of a supernatural covenant treaty that is being created. In equating Oswald with Joshua, in the promises that are made to him and the conversion of his army that is referred to, Columba is acting as Yahweh does in the OT and establishing with Oswald a sacred agreement that includes his people. The biblical language and tone has been deliberately selected to indicate this formation. Northumbria is thus given to Oswald as *his* 'promised land'; indeed, all of Britain is to be *his* promised land, and Oswald has the right to subdue its peoples as Joshua ravaged the Canaanites. Oswald and the Northumbrians are to be as much Columba's people as Israel and the Hebrews belonged to Yahweh.

Because kings like Oswald are divinely protected under a Davidic style covenant, God will elevate and maintain them against all rivals. God's justice becomes their justice and God's enemy becomes their enemy. The 'hands' that David cursed because they turned against the Lord's anointed are blessed and transformed under these conditions with the vital skill of battle that is fought in the Lord's service: 'He teacheth my hands to war: and maketh my arms like a bow of brass' (2 Reges 22:35). As in David's psalm of thanksgiving:

> I will pursue after my enemies, and crush them: and will not return again till I consume them. I will consume them and break them in pieces, so that they shall not rise: they shall fall under my feet. Thou hast guided me with strength to battle: thou hast made them that resisted me to bow under me. My enemies thou hast made to turn their back to me: them that hated me, and I shall destroy them. They shall cry, and there shall be none to save: to the Lord and he shall not hear them. I shall beat them as small as the dust of the earth: I shall crush them and spread them abroad like the mire of the streets. (2 Reges 22:38–43)

Under this covenant, the king's enemies within his people will be thwarted and foreign peoples will be brought under his rule.

> Thou wilt save me from the contradictions of my people: thou wilt keep me to be the head of the Gentiles: the people which I know not, shall serve me. The sons of the stranger … will obey me … God who giveth me revenge, and bringeth down people under me … from the wicked man thou shalt deliver me. Therefore will I give thanks to thee … [who gives] great salvation to his king … to David his anointed, and to his seed for ever. (2 Reges 22:44–51)

Victory, wide rule and stability of tenure are part of God's promise. The covenanted king must then do his part. Because pagans are always God's enemies, for example, kings like Oswald must ensure that paganism is eradicated and replaced with true worship under church authorities possessing the power to advise and admonish the king. They must rule like Josiah (from 639BC), the most ideal of Hebrew kings after David and Solomon, who turned to the Lord 'with all his heart, and all his soul, and with all his strength, according to all the Law of Moses' (4 Reges 23:25). Following in his footsteps, they must correct the people, binding them to the covenant and to the law. Under Josiah, the 'book of the law' was famously rediscovered after long loss and the king 'with the priests and the prophets, and all the people' made a covenant with the Lord to 'perform the words of this covenant, which were written in that book'. Josiah then destroyed the 'high places' of syncretistic worship, slaughtered the Baalites and sooth-sayers, and filled their graves 'with the bones of dead men'. In this 'book of the law' that Josiah publicly read from, it was also written that the people must obey their priests and do according to the law whatever the presiding priests should say, declining 'neither to the right hand nor to the left hand' (Deut 17:9–12).

This rediscovery of the 'book of the law' under a model ruler who renewed the covenant and purified the state was a celebrated occasion in OT lore.[12] The 'Deuteronomistic reforms' that followed greatly strengthened priestly authority at the expense of kings and were supported by certain prophets, most notably Jeremiah.[13] The newfound book (which a consensus of modern scholars regards as a version of Deuteronomy) would have been familiar to Adomnán from his scriptural reading. He would have seen it as going back to Moses, who 'wrote the words' and placed it in the Ark of the Covenant as he passed leadership to Joshua (Deut 31:23–26). Likewise, Samuel after he had anointed Saul and supervised his election by lot 'told the people of the law of the kingdom, and wrote it in a book, and laid it up before the Lord' (1 Reges 10:25). Because of the (theoretically) perennial continuity of the law, Adomnán would probably have seen these books as identical, as a single sanctified volume touched by God and his prophets and miraculously preserved. The concept of the *passage* of a venerable book of the law would probably have been his inspiration for a narrative about a special holy book carried by an angel and brought from heaven who directed the anointing of Áedán mac Gabrain as king of Dál Riata (*VC* III 5). These directions created a covenant between prophet, king and people as in the OT. Adomnán's three uses of *ordinatio* for king creation, accompanied by a reference to 'the prerogative of the kingship of all Ireland' for Diarmait's son Áed Sláine, all contain the same implication of a covenant that is promised or brought to fruition, one that is demonstrated to exist by the victory and/or succession narratives that are tied to

12 See, for example, Rainer Albertz, *A history of Israelite religion in the Old Testament period* (Westminster, 1994), I, pp 198–206; von Rad, *Old Testament theology*, I, pp 71–7.   13 Albertz, *Israelite religion*, p. 200.

it. All are clauses from a Davidic covenant concept whose parts and applications in VC are becoming increasingly clear through an analysis of the sources that were used to create it.

Adomnán's starting point may have been the 'book of the covenant' that Moses read to the people after he had written 'all the words of the Lord' in Exodus 24:4–8. Only a short space before that, in Exodus 23:20–24, one finds that an angel will accompany and guide Moses on his journey after this writing. 'Behold', says Yahweh, 'I will send my angel, who shall go before thee, and keep thee in thy journey, and bring thee into the place that I have prepared'. Perhaps especially noteworthy is the command that Moses should 'take notice of him, and hear his voice, and do not think him one to be contemned: for he will not forgive when thou hast sinned, and my name is in him'. Here, one recalls that Adomnán did make Columba contemn God's angel during his commissioning in VC III 5. Neither did the angel forgive the sin but whipped him for it and left him with a scar. Yahweh goes on to declare that if Moses will hear the angel's voice and do what he is told, then 'I will be an enemy to thy enemies, and will afflict them that afflict thee'. A compact is thus being made and we are not far from the idea of a victory-bringer. Moreover, even within the narrative of a statement of support for a prophet, the concept of an angel whom the prophet may slight, and be unforgiven by the angel for that sin, is unusual, and thus seems to resonate with Columba's stubbornness in the Áedán episode. A variety of covenant and commission details are thus probably being meshed as Adomnán thinks about their usefulness and sign potential. Yahweh continues his statement by promising that his angel 'shall go before thee' as Moses enters foreign lands. This combination of book, angel and war-directing prophet is thus a connected identifiable theme.

Adomnán's choosing of an army camp for the site of Columba's appearance to Oswald is an even stronger indication of his overall intentions and also provides additional clues as to the precise effect that he is seeking to achieve. In Hebrew tradition, the army and its camp are *holy*. The former was consecrated to Yahweh (Josh 3:5), vows were made (Num 21:2; Judg 11:36; 1 Reges 14:24), and sexual purity was enforced (1 Reges 21:5; 2 Reges 11:11–12). Camp grounds had to be kept ritually clean. Because of this pattern, it is possible to identify precisely Adomnán's inspirational source: it derives from Deut 23:14, where all evil must be removed from the army camp site 'for the Lord thy God walketh in the midst of thy camp to deliver thee, and to give up thy enemies to thee: and let thy camp be holy'. It is not Constantine's camp that is referred to but the sacred site of the Hebrew people's army. Adomnán has thus designed Columba's miraculous appearance to imitate Yahweh's theophany. Columba thereby becomes like Yahweh the war god who now grants victory to Oswald and encourages him by the same fortifying exhortation that had earlier been vouchsafed Joshua. Here then is one important source for the concept of

Columba the victory-giver in VC I 1. His enduring gift derives from God's own earlier experience among the Hebrews and his prestige is enormously strengthened by showing that it is precisely God's own power that flows through him. He stands like Yahweh in the midst of an army camp. But is it holy? In fact, it becomes so since Columba sanctifies the camp by bestowing a blessed protection signified by his great shining robe that covered all 'except one far corner'. Apparently, only the few that sleep in this corner will die. The holy war pattern is thus clearly marked and so is Columba's imitation of Yahweh in its narrative. This assertion may well have been made earlier in the history of the Iona community, although probably still within Adomnán's own lifetime. One recalls the AU entry that portrays Columba praying against Diarmait mac Cerbaill at the Battle of Cúl Dreimne, and the tradition of Cathach Coluimb Chille as a battle standard (its presence in the field might well be linked to the holy war practice of the Ark of the Covenant carried in front of the army by priests).[14] These are probably authentic evidence of an early Columban connection with war that Adomnán turns in a biblical direction. To avoid any confusion, however, one should add that in Carolingian Europe the idea of the army camp as a holy place, the *castra Dei* whose commander was responsible to God, assumed some significance.[15] Ambrose, Augustine and Gregory the Great (who could define the church as God's *castra*) all commented on the idea that derives ultimately from Genesis 32:2, where Jacob met the angels of God's host and said of the site that 'these are the camps of God'. Adomnán did not follow this strain,[16] but rather focused on the materials of the conquest of Canaan and remained largely within its milieu.

Adomnán's application of holy war thematics appears further in his reference to Oswald's army going into battle 'with a modest force against many thousands'. Despite a huge disparity in manpower, the miraculous outcome is 'a happy and easy victory was given him [Oswald] by the Lord according to his promise'. Any actual conditions at the Battle of Denisesburn (near Hexham) in 634 are,[17] of course, irrelevant in this narrative. So are any hagiographic topoi by which a saint bestows victory on a small force even though that may be the way in which scholars have hitherto understood this famous episode. Adomnán, on the other

---

14 Mac Airt and Nac Niocaill, *Annals of Ulster*, pp 80–1, s.a. 560 *recte* 561: *per orationes Coluim Cille uicerunt*; Raghnall Ó Floinn, '*Insignia Columbae* I' in Bourke (ed.), *Cult of St Columba*, pp 136–61; Herbert, *Iona, Kells and Derry*, pp 27–8, 93. 15 Mary Alberi, '"Like the Army of God's Camps": political theology and apocalyptic warfare at Charlemagne's court', *Viator*, 41 (2010), 1–20. 16 Neither, as far as I can see, did Bede or the biographer of Wilfrid, who were more interested in relating Britons to Canaanites even though the former were Christian. See, most recently, Alan Thacker, 'Bede, the Britons and the Book of Samuel' in Stephen Baxter et al. (eds), *Early medieval studies in memory of Patrick Wormald* (London, 2009), pp 129–47; Judith McClure, 'Bede's Old Testament kings' in Patrick Wormald et al. (eds), *Ideal and reality in Frankish and Anglo-Saxon society: studies present to J.M. Wallace-Hadrill* (Oxford, 1983), pp 76–98. 17 Also often called Heavenfield: see Colgrave and Mynors, *Ecclesiastical history*, pp 214–17; Andrew Breeze, 'Bede's *Hefenfeld* and the campaign of 633', *Northern History*, 44 (2007), 193–7.

hand, is thinking of the holy war formula by which Yahweh's army must be a small and outnumbered one; in other words, 'a modest force against many thousands'. Indeed, if the Hebrew army be large or nearly equal in number to that of the enemy, it should be reduced to the most dedicated in order to demonstrate that victory is won by Yahweh himself and 'not with thy sword nor with thy bow'. This practice is enjoined in Deuteronomy's treatment of the army that goes off to war (Deut 20) and again illustrated in Judges 7, when Gideon takes to the field. The former text proclaims that if one goes to war against enemies, and the enemy army is greater, it should not be feared because the Lord will be in the midst of the Hebrew force to deliver it. Therefore, each captain should seek through the army for any man who has built a new house, has recently planted a vineyard, has taken a new wife or thinks himself to be faint-hearted. All these should return home, and when the army engages Canaanite people, none of them should be suffered to live. In the second case, the Lord declares to Gideon that the army massed against the Midianites is overlarge. He will not grant it victory lest the people believe that they win through their own strength. Twenty-two thousand men were thus encouraged to return home, and the remainder of the force, still perceived as too numerous, was weeded until only three hundred were left to win a triumph that could be attributed to the Lord alone. After several more victories, the kingship of Israel, hitherto governed by judges, was then offered to Gideon and his descendents in order that he form a dynasty. True to the strict principles of Yahweh, however, according to which Yahweh could be the only true king of his people, Gideon refused: 'I will not rule over you, neither shall my son rule over you, but the Lord shall rule over you' (Judg 8:23).

In time, a monarchy did develop, and out of one judge a prophet was made.[18] Samuel is the judge and prophet who unwillingly anoints Saul because of the people's desire for a king who would defend them. Yahweh very reluctantly agrees to allow this kingship (1 Reges 8:7–9; 12:12; 15:11), and thus Saul is anointed in order that he fight the Philistines, Ammonites and other enemies among the peoples of Canaan.[19] This connection of royal unction with warfare is a fundamental one.

Consider what is revealed by the motivational bundle that is now discernable. Adomnán is not at all averse to warfare. As per the OT, he views warfare as the necessary background to the prophet–king relationship in which the prophet

---

18 In general, see Lindblom, *Prophecy*, pp 105–97; R.W. Wilson, *Prophecy and society in ancient Israel* (Philadelphia, 1980), pp 135–297; Aune, *Prophecy in early Christianity and the ancient Mediterranean world.* 19 As discussed in chapter one. On Saul and Samuel, see now S.S. Brooks, *Saul and the monarchy: a new look* (Aldershot, 2005); F. Crüsemann, *Der Wiederstand gegen das Königtum* (Neukirchen-Vluyn, 1978); J.M. Miller, 'Saul's rise to power: some observations concerning I Sam 9:1–10; 10:26–11:14 and 13:2–14:26', *The Catholic Biblical Quarterly*, 36 (1974), 157–74. I include references to modern analyses because they are sometimes helpful in understanding the OT texts, but, in terms of *Adomnán's* understanding of these texts, they are

listens to Yahweh who inspires him, and the king, like Saul with Samuel, obeys the seer-like mediator (who acts to make him a king) by going to war according to Yahwist principles as revealed by the prophet.[20] These three items – inspired prophet, obedient king and warfare under Yahweh/prophet direction – are not separable motifs for Adomnán. He accurately reflects the OT combination when he links God directly to Columba, who acts as a battle director for Oswald at Denisesburn and then relates victory in battle to God's ordination of Oswald as emperor of the island. He acts according to the same essential pattern in other *VC* chapters on Áedán mac Gabrain, Eochaid Buide, Diarmait mac Cerbaill and Áed Slaine, among others. Although the Áedán comparison might seem weak on the assumption that his status was little more than that of a local ruler, Richard Sharpe has shown that Dál Riata controlled significant resources, and Barbara Yorke has noted that a survey of his full dossier reveals that Áedán campaigned throughout northern Britain and Ireland and, prior to his defeat by Aethelfrith *c.*603, was recognized as the dominant king in the north by Picts, British and Irish.[21] Columba, then acting in his own lifetime, prayed for him during an important battle while remaining in mystic contact with the battlefield, and he anointed him on Iona while prophesying the future of his dynasty.[22] In terms of comparison with overlordship, therefore, Adomnán remains in the right general sphere. Where he does seem a bit excessive, in going somewhat beyond the OT, is in his creation of the striking degree of Columba's identification with Yahweh in his patronage of warfare. Contrary to what one might assume (because of a remarkable lack of scholarly discussion in the area), Adomnán's emphasis on Columba the victory-bringer is not at all tangential to his thinking; it is a key to a mindset that interlocks with the prophet–king paradigm that he follows.

In regard to the latter point, it is notable that Adomnán also blurs the line between the actions of Samuel the prophet and Columba in his directions to Oswald. The crux lies in the background to a particular Samuel/Saul incident, whose dénouement is cited at the beginning of this chapter, and in which the prophet ends up by depriving Saul of his kingship because of disobedience to the prophet's command. Adomnán now takes these motifs, centring on disobedience and a time constraint, and reverses them in order to create a positive message for

frequently irrelevant. **20** On these forces at work in Hebrew society, see, for example, Bertil Albrektson, 'Prophecy and politics in the Old Testament' in Haralds Biezais (ed.), *The myth of the state* (Stockholm, 1972), pp 45–57; James Muilenburg, 'The "Office" of the prophet in Ancient Israel' in J.P. Hyatt (ed.), *The Bible in modern scholarship* (Nashville, TN, 1965), pp 74–98; W. McKane, 'Prophet and institution', *Zeitschrift für die alttestamentliche Wissenschaft*, 94 (1982), 251–66; Rex Mason, *Propaganda and subversion in the Old Testament* (London, 1997); R.P. Carroll, 'Prophecy and society' in Clements, *World*, pp 203–27; and, in the same volume, R. Davidson, 'Covenant ideology in ancient Israel', pp 323–49. The works of von Rad as in n. 6, above, should always be consulted. **21** Richard Sharpe, 'The thriving of Dalriada' in S. Taylor (ed.), *Kings, clerics and chronicles* (Dublin, 2000), pp 47–61; Barbara Yorke, 'The *Bretwaldas* and the origins of overlordship in Anglo-Saxon England' in Baxter et al. (eds), *Early medieval studies*, pp 81–95 at p. 89; Anderson, *Kings and kingship*, pp 145–50. **22** *VC* I 8 and III 5.

Oswald, and to show that he is the exact opposite of Saul, even though he too is the first rightfully ordained king of this land and people. His material is drawn from 1 Reges 7:3–10 and 13:5–14. In these verses, Samuel first speaks to the people and proclaims that the Lord will deliver them out of the hands of the Philistines if they reform their beliefs and put away their strange gods, Baalim and Astaroth. When they do so, Samuel offers a holocaust to the Lord and the Philistines are then defeated in battle. Here is a prime example of the prophet in his mode as victory-bringer. Nonetheless, in the chapters that follow, the people continue to clamour for their own king and, rather against his will, Yahweh directs Samuel to anoint Saul, 'who shall save my people out of the hand of the Philistines'. After his unction, Saul proves to be a successful general and the enemy raises a huge army with some thirty thousand chariots to fight against him. Samuel and Saul decide to face it together at Galgal and agree that Saul will wait there for Samuel for seven days so that Samuel can offer the necessary sacrifice before battle. The reason for delay is not explained. During this time, however, the Hebrew army begins to disintegrate as men fall away and desert out of fear. After waiting the appointed seven days under great pressure and with no sign of the prophet, Saul finally decides to offer the sacrifice himself. Samuel then suddenly appears to declare that Saul has been disobedient, has not kept the commandments of the Lord, and so the Lord has removed him from kingship and has sought another after his own heart.[23] The key motifs of this narrative are now applied to the Columba/Oswald episode in order to show that Oswald is obedient to the prophet, *does* keep to an arbitrary time schedule, and carries it out in the best holy war tradition, that is, despite the small size of his army and the great numbers of the enemy. Thus Columba issues the extraordinary order that Oswald should 'go out from your camp into battle' on 'this coming night' because 'at this time' your foes shall be put to flight. A third reference to the propitious interval is then made when Adomnán relates that on 'that same night, just as he had been told', Oswald marched into battle to win a happy and easy victory with only 'a modest force against many thousands'. A peculiar time span, obedience to the prophet, and a small force against a far larger are common motifs drawn from 1 Reges 13. The difference is that Oswald obeys, whereas Saul, lacking confidence in the prophet and hence in Yahweh, chooses to follow his own military judgment. Oswald is thus 'ordained by God as emperor of all Britain', whereas Saul has his kingdom removed by Samuel. Both small-force against large-force battles end in a statement by the prophet about kingship. Adomnán then takes this concept of victory plus ordination (already linked to victory plus unction in Saul's case) and joins it to the army's conversion from 'heathendom and ignorance' which is basically what Samuel does to achieve victory for the people over the Philistines in 1 Reges 7:3–5, 8–10, where his

23 Brooks, *Saul*, pp 100–20.

condition for Philistine defeat is that the children of Israel put away Baalim and Astaroth and serve the Lord only.

The Oswald episode is thus a retooled biblical holy war story from start to finish. It is designed to inspire confidence in the Yahweh-like and Samuel-like power of the prophet Columba and to show that obedience to this holy man is always necessary for princes who wish to become kings or for kings who wish to remain so or to flourish.[24] Warfare is the arena in which all forces come together for that is how conversion is most quickly achieved and royal power most convincingly won. In Adomnán's view, the major figures and religious mechanisms of the Hebrews constitute permanent verities that can and should be imitated. Oswald has become the loyal anti-Saul of the Northumbrians.

Some interesting implications follow. If Columba's identification with Yahweh and Samuel is so intimate, if his connection to God is so close, then precisely how should one interpret Adomnán's statement that Oswald was ordained emperor by God? This is not the same thing as Columba's ordination anointing of Áedán mac Gabráin on Iona, since that could only occur during his own lifetime. And yet, it is not God who is shown to be active in *VC* I 1, but the dynamic spirit of the former Iona abbot. It is Columba who takes the initiative, who decides to appear to Oswald in order to reveal to him his name, and to establish him in the triumph that creates imperial rule. True, God is the ultimate grantor of all this beneficence – but only at Columba's request. He is hardly a strong presence in the story and occupies only its background. The lesson of the text is not the simple one that God is responsible for all events or that God can mystically sanctify or prepare certain royal candidates; it is, rather, that Columba makes the effort to persuade him to do so and that God wishes it that way. God's principal significance in the Oswald episode is that he enables the holy man. For any attentive prince, this surely means that Columba is the indispensible figure to appeal to. Praying to God for victory, or to any other of his saints, can only be wasted effort, since, according to Adomnán, the triumph of conquest is securely in Columba's permanent gift. For military support, therefore, which necessarily requires the countergift of allegiance, one turns to Columba's community on Iona, who can indeed factually ordain in his name while also creating the physical results on the ground that give the act a palpable worldly meaning.

In OT terms, this transfer of allegiance is called 'covenant', an ordinary treaty in some cases but one that can bind directly to the supernatural in others.[25] It means that the king becomes Yahweh's king and the people Yahweh's people – Columba's people. Such was the pattern of Yahweh's relationship with the house

---

24 The difference between fact and propaganda in Iona's case is ably discussed by Immo Warntjes, 'The role of the church in early Irish regnal succession – the case of Iona' in *L'Irlanda e gli irlandesi nell'alto medioevo*, pp 155–213. 25 von Rad, *Theology*, *I*, pp 129–35, 308–54; Lindblom, *Prophecy*, pp 329–46; Dennis J. McCarthy, 'Covenant relationships' in *Institution and narrative: collected essays* (Rome, 1985), pp 54–67, and in the same volume, 'Compact and kingship: stimuli for Hebrew

of David and this is exactly what Adomnán has in mind. We know it because the model for his prophet's unction of Áedán was Samuel's anointing of Saul while his model for the selection of Áedán's son, Eochaid Buide in VC I 9 is drawn from Samuel's selection of David from among the sons of Jesse (1 Reges 16:5–13).[26] Of course, Adomnán is not the only writer of the time who can think in these terms. Bede, for example, can also use the holy war formula. Hence he writes of Aethelfrith of Northumbria (who defeats Áedán $c.603$) that he ravaged the Britons more extensively than any other English king, and, although a pagan, he might be compared to Saul, since no one had subjected more land to the English race or settled it 'having first either exterminated or conquered [*exterminatis vel subjugatis*] the natives'.[27] Bede represents the Britons as Canaanites, but the Saul reference also works because Bede is thinking about Aethelfrith's later defeat and replacement by Edwin, who will become the first Christian king of Northumbria, who will then act to make his people holy in the conversion that is like a royal Davidic covenant. Bede's historical propaganda is effective but the difference is that Adomnán (partly because he is writing in a different genre) is interested in applying a lesson of prophetic oversight to covenant. Thus he has Eochaid Buide of Dál Riata signal his loyalty to the covenant bond when he makes the small boy lean on the saint's bosom, a gesture that is reciprocated with a kiss followed by a prophecy of Eochaid's future rule. A covenant with the people of his kingdom would now also be renewed, one that had been created through the unction of his father, the representative of his people before God. Adomnán's pattern of holy war modelling has thus been devised in order to depict Oswald and his Northumbrians, *converted through Columba* (and not by his faith in Bede's 'standard of the holy cross'),[28] as one side

covenant thinking', pp 74–92. **26** Enright, *Iona, Tara and Soissons*, pp 15–17. **27** Colgrave and Mynors, *Ecclesiastical history*, pp 116–17; J. McClure and R. Collins (eds), *Bede: The ecclesiastical history of the English people* (Oxford, 1994), p. 374, n. 61; Alan Thacker, 'Bede, the Britons and the Book of Samuel' in Baxter et al. (eds), *Early medieval studies*, pp 129–47. **28** Although Bede made considerable use of Adomnán's *De Locis Sanctis* (which contains much holy cross material), there is no proof that he had read *VC*. Nor can it be shown that he was aware of Cumméne Find's mid-seventh-century collection of miracle stories about Columba, which likely alluded to Oswald and Northumbria. Oswald's cult may have developed fairly early after his death and may have included sacral kingship elements as well as Celtic elements relating to well cults and reverence for the severed head. See Alan Thacker, '*Membra Disjecta*: the division of the body and the diffusion of the cult' in Stancliffe and Cambridge (eds), *Oswald*, pp 97–128 at pp 97–105; Clive Tolley, 'Oswald's tree' in Tette Hofstra, L.A.J.R. Houwen and A.A. MacDonald (eds), *Pagans and Christians: the interplay between Christian Latin and traditional Germanic cultures in early medieval Europe* (Groningen, 1995), pp 149–75; David Rollason, *Saints and relics in Anglo-Saxon England* (Oxford, 1989). The Constantinian associations of the cult are learned ones, however, coming by way of Rufinus' translation of Eusebius, and reflecting sophisticated politico-ecclesiastical interest in connecting Oswald with a 'Romanist' past. This marks a point of departure from an existing tradition and should probably be connected with Wilfrid and his followers since, as Kirby points out ('Northumbria in the time of Wilfrid' in Kirby, *Wilfrid at Hexham*, pp 26–8), a central focus of the cult was at Wilfrid's institution at Hexham, where it was also supported by Wilfrid's intimate follower Acca. It almost certainly falsifies the origins of the cult, however. Given the facts that

of a biblically sanctioned covenant with Iona. He does this through referring to Oswald's baptism on Iona, by the victory bestowed and formulas cited in his narrative, by the conversion of the Northumbrian army, by Oswald's obedience to the saint, and by his reception of *imperium* through the holy man's efforts thereafter. This is a far more potent sequence than any simple victory miracle, however glorified. It is the sealing of a heavenly bond that establishes a permanent dialectic – between the Iona prophet and his successor, the Northumbrian king and his successor, and the Northumbrian people and their descendents who are thereby made into a holy nation (see also Ex 19:4–6).[29] It creates a sacramental compact whose breaking can only lead to tragedy and loss. It is one, moreover, in which, as per the camp and battle arrangements analysed above, Columba advises and guarantees victory, whereas the ruler obeys and follows his counsel. The biblical paradigm of the Yahweh-guided, king-anointing prophet who directs to victory is thereby recreated in hagiography in order that it later be created in fact.

From this covenant, Cadwallon and the Britons are excluded. Adomnán says that he was 'the most powerful king of the Britons'. He had defeated and killed Edwin at the Battle of Hatfield in 635 and aimed, wrote Bede, 'to wipe out the whole English nation from the land of Britain'.[30] In the following year, he killed the two kings who had succeeded Edwin and ruled himself as the king of Northumbria for a year until defeated by Oswald. The Britons are thus the victims of Columba's intervention, for Adomnán is willing to abet the Northumbrian fear/guilt complex that focuses on them. This is remarkable, since, unlike the Northumbrians, the Britons had been faithful Christians for

---

Oswald and his leading men were given refuge on Iona where they were converted and baptized, that they turned to Iona for alliance and missionaries thereafter and that Columba had a longstanding association with warfare, it is inherently probable that Oswald's Christian followers would have credited his victory to Columba whom, after all, they had recently accepted as their patron through baptism by an Iona abbot or bishop. The existence of the alliance itself appears to confirm this interpretation, as it supports the idea of reciprocity in both material and supernatural worlds. Despite Bede's respect for Iona, the Columba/Oswald covenant connection is one that he would earnestly have wished to conceal and replace with a Rome-based vision to accompany his invented dialogue for the Synod of Whitby. For various interpretations of the relevant Bedan chapters, see N.H. Higham, *(Re-)Reading Bede* (Abingdon, 2006); Walter Goffart, *The narrators of barbarian history (AD550–800)* (South Bend, IN, 2005); Henry Mayr-Harting, *The coming of Christianity to Anglo-Saxon England* (London, 1991); Marilyn Dunn, *The christianization of the Anglo-Saxons, c.596–700* (London, 2010). Because of Adomnán's journeys to Northumbria and his perhaps lengthy stay with Ceolfrith, it is likely that Bede had seen Adomnán if not met him as a boy. **29** 'You have seen what I have done to the Egyptians … If therefore you will hear my voice, and keep my covenant, you shall be my peculiar possession above all my people: for all the earth is mine. And you shall be to me a priestly kingdom, and a holy nation'. **30** Colgrave and Mynors, *Ecclesiastical history*, pp 202–5. David Rollason, *Northumbria, 500–1100: creation and destruction of a kingdom* (Cambridge, 2003), p. 100; L. Alcock, *Kings and warriors, craftsmen and priests in Northern Britain, AD550–850* (Edinburgh, 2003), pp 136–9. See further on Cadwallon, N.J. Higham, 'Medieval overkingship in Wales: the earliest evidence', *Welsh History Review*, 16 (1992), 145–59; Alex Woolf, 'Caedualla *Rex Brettonum* and the passing of the Old North', *Northern History*, 41 (2004), 5–24.

many generations.[31] Indeed, in 700, they were still Christians of the same 'anti-Romanist' posture as the Columban community in Britain. In VC I 1 then, written at a time when religious allegiances had changed in Northumbria and Adomnán (but not his Iona monks) had converted to the Roman Easter,[32] would not his emphasis on covenant through Columba's gift of Oswald's victory and ordination also have been a sign of his own new affiliation and hence of a plan to restore the successful combination that had once advanced both sides? The unfortunate results of the Synod of Whitby in 664[33] could thus be negated. Not all is clear, because the holdout of Adomnán's community until 716 created a distressing division, but Adomnán's emphatic statement about the value of Columba to Northumbria in defeating her enemies is both strongly emphasized and sharply defined in relation to overlordship over the entire island. Covenants are sacred joinings not meant to be broken and the historical reality of Iona's conversion of the Northumbrians was still a widespread living memory. The nature of Adomnán's covenantal description long after the fact of its rejection must have had some such resuscitatory purpose and its importance to him is signaled by the narrative's placement in his first chapter.[34]

Although the Oswald episode is not usually deemed relevant to VC II 46 entitled 'about the plague', the present interpretation, which reads it as describing and establishing a holy-war-type covenant, arguably changes that relationship. As with I 1, Adomnán numbers the events among Columba's 'miracles of power':

> This story … concerns the great plague which twice in one time has ravaged a large part of the world. Though I do not speak of the broader regions of Europe … yet the islands of the ocean, Ireland and Britain, have been twice ravaged by a terrible plague. Everywhere was affected except two peoples, the population of Pictland and the Irish who live in Britain, races separated by the mountains of Druim Alban. Although neither of these people is without great sin, by which the eternal Judge is moved to anger, none the less to this date he has been patient and has spared them both. Surely this grace from God can only be attributed to St Columba? For he founded among both peoples the monasteries where today he is still honoured on both sides.
>
> It is not without sorrow now that I say this, that there are in both nations many foolish people who ungratefully fail to recognize that they have been protected from the plague by the prayers of saints, and who abuse God's patience. But we often thank God that through the intercession of our holy patron he has preserved

---

31 Fergnae, the fourth abbot of Iona (605–23), was either British or part British: Sharpe, *Adomnán*, p. 370, n. 389, and see VC III 19.   32 For contrasting interpretations, see Clare Stancliffe, '"Charity with peace": Adomnán and the Easter question' in Wooding et al. (eds), *Adomnán*, pp 36–51, and in the same volume, David Woods, 'On the circumstances of Adomnán's composition of the *De Locis Sanctis*', pp 193–205.   33 This is another occasion on which Bede seeks to persuade to a particular view: see R. Ray, 'Bede and Cicero', *Anglo-Saxon England*, 16 (1987), 1–15 at 9.   34 See the works cited in n. 1, above.

us from the onslaughts of plague, not only at home among our islands, but also in England. For I visited my friend King Aldfrith while the plague was at its worst and many whole villages on all sides were stricken. But both on my first visit after Ecgfrith's battle and on my second two years later, though I walked in the midst of this danger of plague, the Lord delivered me, so that not even one of my companions died nor was any of them troubled with the disease.[35]

II 46 is often cited in studies about plague in the British Isles, but its main importance to Adomnán is as a vehicle for the message that Columba can protect his followers from it.[36] His shielding abilities are not divisible in categories, so that just as armed men could shelter under his robe in an army camp, so can all those who love him in the wider world. This is similar to the principles of *snádud* and *turtugud* in Irish law, by which a freeman could extend his protection to someone of equal or lesser status for a certain time. This safeguard also extends permanently to the freeman's home and its surroundings (known as *maigen dígona*) and fits neatly with the ecclesiastical concept of asylum within a protected area that links to OI *termonn* (from Latin *terminus*) around monastic lands.[37] Adomnán thus refers to monasteries founded by Columba among the Picts and the Irish of Dál Riata and he views these peoples as protected by the saint even though, as Adomnán laments, many foolish people of both nations fail to recognize the fact of intercession. Such protection also provides safe conduct on a journey like Adomnán has undertaken and, when necessary, immunity from legal prosecution for an allotted time. Thus, Adomnán and his party remain healthy within Northumbria, but not the natives who have forsaken the saint and lost his love. His protection only applies to those 'where today he is still honoured'. Adomnán is thus certainly thinking about the bond of friendship that

---

35 *Et hoc etiam ut aestimo non inter minora virtutum miracula connumerandum videtur, de mortalitate quae nostris temporibus terrarum orbem bis ex parte vastaverat majore. Nam ut de ceteris taceam latioribus Eoropae regionibus, hoc est Italia et ipsa romana civitate et cisalpinis Galliarum provinciis, hispanis quoque Pirinei montis interjectu disterminatis, ociani insulae per totum, videlicet Scotia et Brittannia, binis vicibus vastatae sunt dira pestilentia, exceptis duobus populis, hoc est Pictorum plebe et Scotorum Brittanniae inter quos utrosque dorsi montes brittannici disterminant. Et quamvis utrorumque populorum non desint grandia peccata, quibus plerumque ad iracondiam aeternus provocatur judex, utrisque tamen huc usque patienter ferens ipse pepercit. Cui alio itaque haec tribuitur gratia a deo conlata, nisi sancto Columbae, cujus monasteria intra utrorumque populorum terminos fundata ab utrisque ad praesens tempus valde sunt honorificata? Sed hoc quod nunc dicturi sumus ut arbitramur non sine gemitu audiendum est, quia sunt plerique in utrisque populis valde stolidi qui sé sanctorum orationibus a morbis defensos nescientes ingrati dei patientia male abutuntur. Nos vero deo agimus crebras grates qui nós et in his nostris insulis orante pro nobis venerabili patrono a mortalitatum invasionibus defendit, et in Saxonia regem Alfridum visitantes amicum adhuc non cessante pestilentia et multos hinc inde vicos devastante. Ita tamen nos dominus et in prima post bellum Ecfridi visitatione, et in secunda interjectis duobus annis, in tali mortalitatis medio deambulantes periculo liberavit, ut ne unus etiam de nostris comitibus moriretur, nec aliquis ex eis aliquo molestaretur morbo.* 36 J.R. Maddicott, 'Plague in seventh-century England', *Past and Present*, 156 (1997), 7–54; Ann Dooley, 'The plague and its consequences in Ireland' in L.L. Little (ed.), *Plague and the end of antiquity: the pandemic of 541–750* (Cambridge, 2007), pp 215–29. 37 Kelly, *A guide to early Irish law*, pp 140–1.

unites a patron saint and his followers; he is again thinking in covenantal terms. He is recalling that aspect of Yahweh's covenant with his people that protects them against plague. Hence, for example, the famous lamb's blood on the door posts of Egypt: 'And the plague shall not be upon you to destroy you, when I shall strike the land of Egypt' (Ex 12:13). In Adomnán's Christian frame of reference, an allusion to plague in a land is likewise an allusion to sin in a land, a sin in this case that flows from the breaking of a sacred bond.

Adomnán does not openly refer to that other consequence of a broken covenant: military defeat. He is, after all, visiting his 'friend', King Aldfrith, whom he may very well have helped to place on the throne. Subtly and indirectly, however, he does contrive an allusion. It is there in his reference to 'Ecgfrith's battle'. Ecgfrith (670–85), son of the powerful Oswiu (642–70), was that ruler who began the decline of Northumbrian *imperium* in the North. Although initially successful – Stephen of Ripon says that he continued to be so as long as he 'remained obedient to Bishop Wilfrid in all things'[38] – Ecgfrith suffered defeat against the Mercians in 679, which seems to have caused the loss of Lindsey, and a disastrous defeat against a Picto–Dál Riatan alliance in 685 at Nechtanesmere, where Northumbria lost control over southern Pictland and was driven south of the Firth of Forth. He also lost his life.[39] According to Bede, these afflictions occurred because he acted against the 'urgent advice' of St Cuthbert, and the 'holy father Egbert, who had urged him not to attack the Irish' [in Ireland]. And so

> from this time the hopes and strength of the English kingdom began to 'ebb and fall away'. For the Picts recovered their own land which the English had formerly held, while the Irish who lived in Britain and some part of the British nation recovered their independence, which they have now enjoyed for about forty-six years. Many of the English were either slain by the sword or enslaved.[40]

Bede, Stephen of Ripon and Adomnán all attribute success in war to following the advice of holy men, and loss to a failure to listen.[41] All of them display strong signs of an OT-type worldview. The difference is that Adomnán has developed an operational strategy of political influence based on its close ritual and

---

38 Bertram Colgrave (ed.), *The life of bishop Wilfrid by Eddius Stephanus* (Cambridge, 1985), pp 40–1. 39 James E. Fraser, *From Caledonia to Pictland: Scotland to 795* (Edinburgh, 2009), pp 215–16. 40 Colgrave and Mynors, *Ecclesiastical history*, pp 428–9. 41 It is thus worth noting that, according to the anonymous *Life of Ceolfrith*, Benedict Biscop was often away from his foundation because of giving advice to the king: C. Plummer (ed.), *Venerabilis Baedae opera historica* (Oxford, 1896), I, pp 395–8. For an overview of the politics of Northumbrian monasteries, see David Rollason, 'Hagiography and politics in early Northumbria' in P.E. Szarmach (ed.), *Holy men and holy women: old English prose saints' lives and the contexts* (Albany, NY, 1996), pp 95–115. King Aldfrith was the kind of man who listened to such advice also, at least according to Bede V 12: 'Brother Dryhthelm' told him of his visions – he 'listened to them gladly and attentively' – and 'whenever the king visited that region, he often went to listen to his story'. Writing of Gaul, Yitzhak

theological imitation. Ecgfrith's battle would have been an explosive topic in Adomnán's time and his simple allusion to it – when he could equally well have dated his journey by reference to Aldfrith's regnal year – is unlikely to be without purpose. He had, after all, made an extremely forceful statement about Columba as a bringer of victory in all warfare and he had done so in reference to a famed Northumbrian ruler. The chapter in which he mentions Ecgfrith's battle refers to Columba's power to protect his faithful followers within Northumbria, and elsewhere, in VC I 12, Adomnán indicates that rulers who neglect Columba suffer defeat and death. The plague chapter may thus be interpreted as a continuation of the theme of covenant between God/prophet, king and people, except that it now refers to a *broken* covenant.

Conceptually at least, the material from VC I 1 and II 46 belong on the same page. Once they are read together, it becomes clear that they fall within an even larger covenant pattern that Adomnán is appealing to, and it will be helpful to describe it. In the former case, Adomnán has written about the creation of a covenant by which conversion to *Columba's* faith goes hand-in-hand with victory in the promised land, kingship and empire, whereas in the latter, he comments on the illness and defeat that follows its breaking. This cosmic interpretation of contract is found also in Irish vernacular perception. The roughly contemporary legal text *Corus Béscnai* declares that in three periods 'the world is frenzied', during plague, war and the breaking of contracts; it is only the binding of each to his contract that prevents the dissolution of the world.[42] It is towards this reforging of contract that Adomnán aims. While he faintly praises the Picts and Irish of Dál Riata whom Columba protects in his mercy, he attacks by clear implication the Northumbrians (and the Irish of Ireland) for their falsity and impiety in violating the contract that Columba made with Oswald. Since Adomnán was writing over a generation after the Synod of Whitby, he was well aware of that outcome. But then, so too had been Columba, famous for his ability to prophesy. In this, Columba is again like the OT God (with his prophet Moses in this case) who foresees that his people will repeatedly stray from his service.[43]

Hen observes that 'for a king, it was an act of sacrilege to ignore his advisors, through whom, by biblical analogy, the prophets were given voice'. The term 'sacrilege' is a bit strong here, but the general point strikes me as apropos: see 'The uses of the Bible and the perception of kingship in Merovingian Gaul', *Early Medieval Europe*, 7 (1998), pp 277–89 at p. 285.   **42** On this 'Ordering of Discipline', see Kelly, *A guide to early Irish law*, p. 159; Liam Breatnach, *A companion to the Corpus iuris Hibernici* (Dublin 2005), pp 290–1; Ó Corrain, Breatnach, Breen, 'The laws of the Irish', *Peritia*, 3 (1984), 384.   **43** Among many examples: 'Why will you contend with me in judgment? You have all forsaken me, saith the Lord. In vain have I struck your children, they have not received correction: your sword hath devoured your prophets, your generation is like a ravaging lion' (Jer 2:29–30). 'And I appointed watchmen over you, saying: Hearken ye to the sound of the trumpet. And they said: We will not hearken' (Jer 6:17). 'For who shall have pity on thee, O Jerusalem? Or who shall bemoan thee? Or who shall go to pray for thy people? Thou hast forsaken me, saith the Lord, thou art gone backward: and I will stretch out my hand against thee, and I will destroy thee: I am weary of entreating thee'.

Adomnán works with this understanding, for it is the very frequency of rupture and repair of covenant in the OT that gives him hope for renewal. He refers to Joshua, not only because his victory is a key act in the making of covenant, but also because Joshua is aware that it will inevitably be broken. In such case, 'the Lord will judge his people', taking revenge on oath-breakers but having mercy on his servants (Deut 32:35–36). That is why VC II 46 refers to God as 'the eternal judge' who is moved to anger by great sin but can nonetheless spare the merely weak. Up 'to this date', the deity 'has been patient' because of Columba's intercession, but the foolish cannot long 'abuse God's patience'. Adomnán is probably again thinking of Deuteronomy 31 and 32, of those verses where Yahweh tells Joshua to 'take courage and be valiant ... and I will be with thee'. Moses, who is still present to advise Joshua at this point, knows that victory will come but is also aware of the backsliding and transgressions to follow. Therefore, he writes this law of covenant in a book that he has placed in the 'Ark of the Covenant'. It is there to testify to the people's future apostasy. As L.D. Hawk writes, 'Predictions of Israelite disobedience and divine anger overshadow the entire episode of Joshua's investiture' (Deut 31:1–29).[44] Waiting to die, Moses says of the people, 'I know thy obstinacy, and thy most stiff neck. While I am yet living ... you have always been rebellious against the Lord: how much more when I shall be dead?' He gathers the elders of the tribes and calls heaven and earth to witness against them: 'For I know that, after my death, you will do wickedly, and will quickly turn aside from the way that I have commanded you: And evils shall come upon you in the latter times, when you shall do evil in the sight of the Lord, to provoke him by the works of your hands'. It is this kind of knowledge that Columba the prophet had, must have had in Adomnán's view, and his references to plague, defeat and the 'eternal Judge's' punishment of the Northumbrians is in keeping with the citations above that follow the covenant with Joshua. These, along with the speech of Moses in chapter 32, echo a form of OT complaint that is sometimes called *Gerichtsrede* or 'covenant lawsuit'. In various forms of these, Yahweh can act as a plaintiff against his people, a prophet may act as his lawyer and the heavens and earth may act as witnesses.[45] Adomnán would almost certainly have been familiar with these fairly frequent OT episodes when the people acted against their pledged faith but, whether he was or not, his reference to Joshua and covenant contexts, followed by the 'eternal Judge' who punishes Northumbria but not those who have kept faith, indicates that this general framework is present even if only in the context of retributive justice. For Adomnán, of course, a contemplation of the entire working out of the scheme would have provided reason for hope. As Yahweh had chosen Israel despite her flaws, so had Columba behaved like Moses and committed to the Northumbrians

44 Hawk, *Joshua*, p. 12.   45 H.B. Huffman, 'The covenant lawsuit in the prophets', *Journal of Biblical Literature*, 78 (1959), 285–95.

even when aware of their coming apostasy. It looks as if Adomnán had pinned his faith in renewal of covenant on his friend and former student Aldfrith.[46] How that would have affected Iona's contemporary relations with the Picts and British is another question, as is its impact on politics within the *paruchia Columbae* itself.

Its possible relation to Adomnán's 'conversion' to an acceptance of the Dionysian Easter table, then used in Northumbria, over the Irish eighty-four-year table used in northern Ireland and Iona, is not an easy question to answer, but the suspicion of a connection cannot be dismissed out of hand. That acceptance certainly led to a serious and probably sorrow-filled division between the abbot and his monks.[47] Adomnán would not have taken this step lightly and the idea that he did so without being fully aware of the jarring consequences for his community is not credible. Adomnán had been the head of a great international paruchia since 679, he had achieved the release of Irish hostages in the year of Aldfrith's succession, and he was so skilled a political negotiator that he was able to gain the support of fifty-one secular rulers and forty churchmen from Britain and Ireland for his reform of the practices of warfare (called after him *Cáin Adomnáin*) at the Synod of Birr in 697.[48] Controversy over the date of Easter had been a festering wound ever since 664 at least, and Adomnán would not have turned against the Columban tradition during a visit to the king of Northumbria when he was apart from his monks if he had not viewed it as essential to the wellbeing of the *familia Iae*. On the assumption, therefore, that his act was one of deliberate policy by the governing head of a monastic federation, he was probably seeking to renew the Iona–Northumbrian alliance under his own royal former student and/or seeking to undermine the influence of the anti-Iona party at court whose principle figure for all that we know may still have been the formidable Bishop Wilfrid or else one of his supporters.[49] It was Wilfrid who had claimed at Rome in 679 to speak 'for all the northern part of Britain and Ireland and the islands, which are inhabited by the races of Angles and Britons as well as Scots and Picts'.[50] Either of Adomnán's goals might have served the other. We know too little about Northumbrian politics of the time – except that they were complicated and life-threatening – to precisely define how Adomnán's move influenced the game, but we can be sure that it produced a

---

46 On Aldfrith (whose fellow student on Iona may have been Aldhelm), see Colin Ireland, 'Aldfrith of Northumbria and the learning of a *sapiens*' in K.A. Klar, Eve Sweester and Claire Thomas (eds), *A Celtic florilegium: studies in memory of Brendon O'Hehir* (Lawrence, MA, 1996), pp 63–77; Barbara Yorke, 'Adomnán at the court of king Aldfrith' in Wooding et al. (eds), *Adomnán*, pp 36–51; eadem, Rex Doctissimus: *Bede and King Aldfrith of Northumbria* (Jarrow, 2009); Michael Lapidge, 'The career of Aldhelm', *Anglo-Saxon England*, 36 (2007), 15–69 at 22–7.   47 Recently stressed by Woods, 'Circumstances', pp 195–6.   48 Máirín Ní Dhonnchadha, 'The guarantor list of *Cáin Adomnáin* 697', *Peritia*, 1 (1982), 178–215.   49 Still the most helpful study is Kirby, *Wilfrid at Hexham*; Charles-Edwards, *Early Christian Ireland*, pp 429–38.   50 Colgrave, *Bishop Wilfrid*, pp 114–15; Fraser, *Caledonia*, pp 192–9, 208–28.

strong impact in that it would have markedly reinforced a party of compromise while also weakening opponents of Iona's independence or of Aldfrith the 'friend'. It is within these parameters that Adomnán's move should be assessed since, although the parties involved certainly perceived it as a grave issue, the dating of Easter comes close to being a theologically meaningless conflict. Adomnán may have come to see it this way in his old age, but whether he did or not, he was willing to accept potential abbatial destabilization on Iona in order to achieve his aim in Northumbria.[51] For all one can tell, his action at the time may have been politically crucial.

The Oswald episode is thus an exquisitely constructed propagandistic narrative that reflects the biblical themes of holy war leadership, supernatural covenant and prophetic direction. It invites Aldfrith (and any subsequent Northumbrian ruler) into the kind of alliance that Joshua and David had with Yahweh and probably signals, in keeping with Adomnán's own turn to the Roman Easter, a break with the Britons, whom he is now (if he had not been earlier) willing to view, apparently, as rightly defeated. It does not seem likely that Adomnán could have celebrated this British defeat in such a charged context unless, at the time of writing, he too had abandoned the Columban tradition of reckoning Easter.

The paragraph that follows the Oswald episode in the VC is outwardly different in kind in that kingship is not an issue and there is no reference to a giant saint. Armed men do clash, however, and the theme of a Yahwistic patron of war in action continues. In this case, most of a group of guilty and bloodstained men are able to escape death from flames, swords and spears by calling Columba's name and singing Irish songs in his praise. The few who do not are the ones who perish. The emphasis on supernatural protection is thus maintained and the basic narrative construction is parallel to what went before. The house full of armed men is not that different from the camp containing an army and neither is the relation of only a small number out of a larger group suffering death. The second incident casts light on the first, however, because the fact that the only ones who die in this case are those who do not call on Columba suggests that the small proportion destined to die in the preceding case of the camp are not just the unavoidable casualties of a coming battle, but rather those whom the saint can judge to be unworthy, and so his robe does not shelter them. It is, apparently, the offering of an expression of loyalty – or a judgment about it – that is the pivotal circumstance. It is exactly that loyalty that Oswald suggests by his obedience to Columba and that Saul failed to show when he refused to wait for the prophet Samuel. Sharpe's translation makes it appear that the men in the burning house are outlaws, however, marauders being justly

---

51 Miko Tanaka, 'Iona and the kingship of Dál Riata in Adomnán's *Vita Columbae*', *Peritia*, 17–18 (2003–4), 199–214 at 210–14; Warntjes, 'Role of the church', pp 171–85.

punished for a life of heartless murder. Hence, he refers to them as 'brigands'. That may be unduly constricting. *Scelerati laicae conversationis homines et sanguinarii* will certainly bear that interpretation if one reads it in terms of OI *díbergach* and Hiberno-Latin *laicus*, Irish *láech*, which Sharpe has elsewhere insightfully explained.[52] As he points out of the *VC* text, however, this linkage is already a matter of interpretation since the sentence literally refers to certain men 'guilty of a lay way of life and bloodstained'.[53] That is essentially the way in which the Andersons understood it. I tend to favour the non-outlaw interpretation of laymen in military service, since this paragraph shares with the preceding one the theme of armed men involved in warfare, all of them living the most extreme form of lay life and thus all perceivable as bearing the guilt of shedding blood. Adomnán would then have been thinking more of soldiers or military followers and not just of brigands. This might seem to better accommodate the full scope of Adomnán's remarks about the ubiquity of the kind of event described: 'for the same occurrence did not just happen at one place or time but it can be clearly shown to have happened at different places and times in Ireland and Britain and in the same way with the same reason for the deliverance'.

Adomnán is thus making a further argument on behalf of Columba's patronage of warfare and the armed men who engage in it. His statement now is designed to expand that of the Oswald anecdote to stress that the saving shelter of Columba's robe that preserved the king and his army on one occasion is available to all armed men on all occasions once they call to the holy man in heaven. They then become *his* men, ultimately in *his* service, and the expected return for his good offices, as both anecdotes suggest, is loyalty and obedience. A further significant point to stress is the universalist nature of the claim. Columba's interventions were common and 'happened at different places and times in Ireland and Britain'. There is, as Adomnán insists, 'no room for doubt' since 'informed people in each area' can testify to the miracles. Excepting the emphasis that he places on Columba's prophetic power, this underscoring is about as forcefully uncompromising a statement about veracity as Adomnán makes. His reference to Columba's unfettered control over armed men on the two islands interlocks with his allusions to Oswald as ordained emperor of 'all Britain' and, in Ireland, with his description of Diarmait as 'ordained by God's will as king of all Ireland'.[54] Their advancement is owed to Iona. Patronage of international warfare thus goes hand-in-hand with an ordained international *imperium* over other potentates. Columba is the true and final arbiter of kingship regardless of other saints, other kings, or other ecclesiastical jurisdictions in the entire British Isles. The relation of the burning house event to his OT model of thought is suggested again by Adomnán's legitimating declaration that 'it would

52 Richard Sharpe, 'Hiberno-Latin *Laicus*, Irish *Láech* and the devil's men', *Ériu*, 30 (1979), 75–92.   53 Sharpe, *Adomnán*, p. 253, n. 45.   54 F.J. Byrne, *The rise of the Uí Néill and the high kingship of Ireland* (Dublin, 1969).

be possible to produce not just two or three witnesses of this event, enough to satisfy the law, but a hundred or more'. The 'law' he refers to is not Irish law but that of Deuteronomy 19:15: 'One witness shall not rise up against any man, whatsoever the sin or wickedness be: but in the mouth of two or three witnesses every word shall stand'. A continued reading is instructive. The following chapter (20) of Deuteronomy tells us that the Lord fights in the midst of the army (v. 3–4), gives an example of deliberately reducing the size of the Hebrew army, and includes a reference to killing all Canaanite enemies, while chapter 21 gives an example of removing blood guilt for a killing.[55] Chapter 23 cites the statement that the Lord walks in the midst of the army's camp and chapter 31 takes up the issue of a future breech of covenant. The law that Adomnán lives by, and the principles of alliance and governance that he seeks to inculcate in VC I 1, are thus demonstrably linked to the practices and events of the OT.

The story of the burning house is intended to expand the message of the Oswald episode and both have been crafted for related reasons. First, to demonstrate the fact of the prophet's ability to grant victory in warfare. Second is to show that his favour must be sought by any prince who seeks to overcome his enemies, enlarge his kingdom or win territorial lordship. No other power can guarantee to do this effectively or continually because it is God's will to honour Columba uniquely with that gift. Third is to show that all armed men who simply call on Columba can presume to benefit from his friendship. Although the special sponsor of rulers whom he chooses and anoints (and whose death he revenges), he looks kindly on ordinary warriors and is intent on saving the lives of all who belong to him, even when they are unworthy in all else except their faith in him. Adomnán's primary targets are thus princes, aristocrats and free men bearing arms. It is not that he lacks a desire to aid the weak and vulnerable in society, indeed he is famous for doing so at Birr,[56] but even that is in the context of warfare – the field, next to prophecy, of Columba's most notable expertise. Fourth is to demonstrate that Columba's power is dominant throughout the islands of Ireland and Britain, the two sites of his paruchia. Adomnán insists on this. Whereas he legitimates his Oswald anecdote by reference to the testimony of Abbot Failbe, who had heard it from Oswald himself, the saving of followers in Britain and Ireland is backed by reference to 'a hundred or more' witnesses and a proclamation of 'no room for doubt'. The rhetoric is now especially strong to mark a point of special interest.

Even taking a variety of factors into account, however, Adomnán's motivation for creating his prophet–king–covenant warfare triad warrants a larger elucidation, for hitherto we have been analysing the nature of tactics rather than strategy, and one may also wonder as to why Adomnán has seemingly forgotten

---

55 This may be related to but it is not quite the same thing as Adomnán is referring to in VC I 1. Hence, I do not discuss it, but, given the pattern of citation, I do regard it as likely to have been a prompt.   56 Ní Dhonnchadha, 'Birr and the Law of the Innocents'.

that other bit of biblical wisdom about not putting one's trust in princes. The fact is, perhaps contrary to appearances, that he has not! Close analysis indicates that princes are only to be trusted insofar as they obediently defer to Columba's wishes. On the other hand, and I think this to be a determinative reason, Adomnán's own life experience had taught him that, as dubious as a prince's character might be, it might well be more dependable that than of a bishop.[57] It was not really a king who had sought a way to injure the *familia Iae* at the Synod of Whitby in 664 when Adomnán was about thirty-six years of age (however much that king may wrongly have assented), and a generation after that trauma, it was still bishops like Wilfrid who were advancing claims to jurisdiction over Iona and the rest of the north, while equally ambitious bishops of Armagh were loudly rattling the same sabre in Ireland.[58] But none of them could hope for success without consistent royal backing and enforcement! The logical strategy for a monastic leader, therefore, is to drive a wedge between rulers and acquisitive bishops. A turn to the OT provides ammunition for exactly that, since it offers a model that inherently undercuts episcopal prestige by favouring prophets over prelates – the antagonism between shrine/temple leaders and prophets is no small theme in a number of areas of scripture[59] – and then by providing a divinely approved approach to prophetic guidance in warfare, to the ordination of kings and to covenant agreement. In the nature of things, warfare or its threat will never be absent and so a prophet of war who can guarantee a ruler or his dynasty always has a good chance of coming out ahead if belief in his control over battle is convinced. With care, why should it not be? As Amos 3:7 proclaims, 'The Lord God doth nothing without revealing his secret to his servants the prophets'.

Despite its size and proven ability to defend itself, however, Adomnán's community is unusually vulnerable because it straddles two islands and must thus contend with a disproportionate excess of rulers and jockeying interest groups. Adomnán can never rest easy because no matter how solid his position seems at any single moment, the death, bribery or changing convictions of a few key individuals can always create a worrying imbalance in the next. No matter how historians assess the position of Iona in the decades on either side of 700, Adomnán was certainly worried about it since he would not otherwise have decided to refer to Dál Riata and Pictland as the only two territories being protected by Columba from the plague.

57 A condition perhaps also recognized by Wilfrid who, as he was expecting death, ordered that one third of his wealth be given to the monasteries of Hexham and Ripon in order that 'they may be able to purchase the friendship of kings and bishops': Colgrave, *Wilfrid*, pp 136–7.   58 Ludwig Bieler, 'Liber Angeli' in *Patrician texts*, pp 184–92; Doherty, 'Politics of Armagh' in Picard (ed.), *Ireland and northern France*, pp 53–94.   59 Jeremiah is a famous example, but one might also point to the antagonism between Amasias the priest of Bethel and Amos: 'And Amasias said to Amos: Thou, seer, go, flee away into the land of Juda: and eat bread there, and prophesy there. But prophesy not again any more in Bethel: because it is the king's sanctuary, and it is the house of the kingdom'

Iona also confronts politico-theological threats from rising powers with increasingly large lordships and bishoprics. Iona's self-interest, therefore, calls for her to ally with the most powerful secular lords, and to assist them in advancing their territorial ambitions through a broadcast spiritual effort, and acts of legitimation taken from the same biblical recipe. A few great powers are easier for an international paruchia to deal with than a hundred lesser governors. Given the constraints of her geography, Iona is safer with overkings than kings. The tyranny of these conditions means that Adomnán's work must reflect an umbrella strategy of promoting imperial power, elite appeal and the condition of Columba's sovereign competence to work military miracles on each island. Here, too, he can find biblical support, although less with a Hebrew overkingship than with the model of the Persian Empire. There are signs in the VC that his thinking about *imperium* was influenced by OT reference to Cyrus the Great, who, despite being a non-Hebrew pagan king of kings, is nonetheless recognized as Yahweh's own chosen instrument whom he has anointed to rule.[60] This governance theme (in Isaiah) accompanies the new universalizing argument that Yahweh is not just the god of the Jews but of all who inhabit the earth.

Adomnán's outstanding originality – his politico-theological inventions of a war prophet who anoints kings and promotes the concept of island-ruling emperors – derives from three conditions, all of which could only develop after a thorough immersion in biblical study. First is his vision of Columba as God's chosen prophet 'called' and 'sent' to reform his age as OT prophets had done so often before him. Second is the stimulus of belligerent rhetoric by imperially minded bishops of the later seventh century who made claim to govern foundations that they had not built, and to define a faith that they had not instilled. Third is Iona's geography that required her to stitch islands together with cow-hide boats, and then to invent a *common* appeal and a *common* rite that could join cultures through a benign wonder-worker competent to advise an order-maintaining overlord. It is only when these heterogeneous elements impinge together upon an experienced agile mind that a sufficient condition for such surprising theoretical innovations can be envisioned.

(Amos 7:12–13). **60** See chapter one. This modelling on a pagan Persian emperor (who is nonetheless anointed by God) is especially important for understanding how a pagan ruler like Diarmait mac Cerbaill could still be considered by Adomnán as 'ordained' by God as 'king of all Ireland'. The OT text makes the connection both possible and legitimate. It removes a longstanding source of confusion from the historiography. As Columba's basis for the cursing of Diarmait's killer is the *nolite tangere christos meos* theme from the *First Book of Kings*, the linkage between *ordinatio* and *unctio* in the actual inauguration of Áedán is also considerably strengthened. Like Oswald, Diarmait receives a patronage miracle, an ordination and a statement of imperial territorial rule. These items are thus part of a Columban package. Ireland's exclusion from the lands protected by Columba from plague, however (and note also the attribution of serious crime to Diarmait's son that prevents his all-Ireland rule in I 14), suggests that Irish politics are not running in Iona's favour no matter how one might otherwise interpret the available evidence.

Conclusion

The preceding chapters do not fully analyse the contents of the *VC*; such an undertaking would require a much larger book. Rather, they seek to provide evidence for a new reading of those parts of the text that focus on kingship and prophetic status and awareness, while exploring the questions as to why and how Adomnán constructed and assembled them. Because each chapter offers its own conclusions, sometimes at the cost of a certain amount of repetition, it seems unnecessary to repeat a list of particulars here, but it may be worthwhile to comment on a few highlights of the larger themes that have emerged.

The impact of the OT on Irish sensibilities is extraordinary. If the NT offered the means to save one's soul and to reach heaven through the sacraments of the church, the OT was perceived to retain a living force that had not been superseded. Because the Lord had frequently spoken in his own voice to the Hebrews, had demanded certain behaviours of them, had provided kings to rule and prophets to guide them over a long millennium, that accumulated experience of the divine could not easily be set aside. Indeed, much of that experience seemed exceptionally well suited to contemporary societies in Ireland and Britain. Even after a new covenant according to which Hebrew law and custom no longer needed to be followed, that people's interactions with the deity remained valuable in themselves and should be modified only to the extent necessary to remain in accord with Christian revelation. That reminds one of the response of many communities of Jewish Christians during the first four centuries of the church, but the fact is that something like it appears to have been Adomnán's view as well. That is why he wished to replicate the OT king/prophet paradigm in the Iro-British sphere that, in his opinion, included a Northumbria that had, temporarily, gone astray. Columba had been a divinely commissioned prophet in the true 'monastic' tradition of Elijah and Elisha, and the desert 'sons' of those prophets prefigured his own communities of Iona and elsewhere. On the same biblical and typological basis, the operative Irish concept of prophecy included an ability both to know the future and to perceive contemporary happenings in other places; its ultimate source lay in the same prophetic/'monastic' model that informed the stories of Elijah, Elisha and Samuel. This attitude towards the OT impelled Adomnán to turn to Hebrew inauguration ritual. The divinely inspired narratives surrounding it could legitimate both the details of a reform plan as well as a certain narrow measure of retention of native tradition in the case of the threefold death.

This readiness to respect the wisdom of both ancient and modern scriptures can certainly be found on the Continent, but it is there in considerably lesser degree. While the trend of such response can be found in both areas, that of the Irish is radical in its intensity and in its desire for socio-political replication. Although scholars have not typically viewed it in this light, it is hard to separate this response from the existence of learned native orders among the Irish and the gradual compromise with the pagan past that was reached in the seventh century, which allowed the traditional learning of poets and jurists to survive as the ancient craft learning of culturally honoured groups. Both reactions bespeak a profound reverence for tradition and are found again in a great deal of vernacular literature that insists on knowing the *origins* of ideas and practices. It is the archetypical that counts most. Irish culture asserts that it is only through such linkage to origins that later developments can be justified. Certain features of this pivotal consensus have been discussed in a number of well-known studies, but a full-scale exploration of what we can know about it remains a desideratum.

As with certain revered figures of the OT, Adomnán's Columba functions as the assayer of kings and royal candidates. He carries on the task of the OT prophet who oversees armies and commanders, the spokesman for Yahweh who arranges the troops and decides their fate. He is 'a mighty and triumphant champion' of battles who retained his power 'after he quit this flesh'. Although modern scholars sometimes shy from discussing it, peoples of the early Middle Ages exulted in personal prowess and closely linked the successful perpetration of violence with successful kingship. So did the continental church, which provided many prayers and masses for kings. Perhaps especially relevant in the present discussion is the *Missa pro principe* inserted into the Bobbio Missal.[1] It is made distinct from other such masses by its liberal use of OT exempla. In it, Moses appears as a victor instead of a law-giver; Joshua is a warrior rather than Moses' helper; David is the boy who defeats Goliath rather than a ruler or singer, and Abraham, who, with 318 servants, wins victory over five kings and booty for his followers, appears more as a conqueror than as a father for his people. Nonetheless, the prayers uttered are mainly for 'our ruler', although it is victory that is emphasized and not royal virtues. As Mary Garrison observes, it is God's power to create victory against mighty odds that is magnified and it is placed against the ruler's dire need for divine assistance.[2] One thus encounters a situation in which the ruler is depicted as necessary for the sake of justice and discipline, but, as all but one of the instances cited refer to an Israel before kingship had been established, the outwardly almost paradoxical message is that

---

1 Yitzhak Hen and Rob Meens (eds), *The Bobbio Missal: liturgy and religious culture in Merovingian Gaul* (Cambridge, 2009). 2 Mary Garrison, 'The *Missa pro principe* in the Bobbio Missal' in Hen and Meens (eds), *Bobbio Missal*, pp 187–205. Helpful also is her discussion of 'The Franks as the new Israel? Education for an identity from Pippin to Charlemagne' in Yitzhak Hen and Matthew Innes (eds), *The uses of the past in the early Middle Ages* (Cambridge, 2000), pp 114–61.

the significance of kings as the winners of victories is less important than the power of the holy and prophetic figures who preceded them or, by implication, those who would later create and counsel them. This is exactly the intellectual stance that one finds in *VC* and, had Garrison been aware of Columba's status as prophet or of the full background to the Oswald episode that she cites in her epigraph, it would have considerably strengthened her persuasive argument that the Bobbio *Missa pro principe* reflects the influence of insular missionaries. Seeking for greater exactitude, it may now seem more likely that they had been followers of Columba, but, as we have seen with Muirchú, the attitude in question was widespread in Ireland. This Missa example is thus analogous to the case of the hand-anointing ritual, which also appears to have an insular background.

A final word about the royal anointing allusions in *VC*. While it is now established that Adomnán included both an unction and the idea of protection that it conferred when he wrote of royal ordinations, it is still not wholly clear how he distinguished between Columba's unction of Aedán and God's unction of Diarmait and Oswald. It is thus interesting to note how the Bible manages a similar phenomenon that is an important aspect of the Hebrew concept of kingship. In ancient Israel, the king ruled not in his own right but as Yahweh's man, his vassal. It was held that Yahweh himself was the actual anointer of this vassal, even when the visually obvious physical act was carried out by his representative. There are many examples. In the very first case of Saul in I Reges 10:1, it is Samuel who pours the oil on his head but it is Yahweh who is credited with the deed:

> Behold, the Lord hath anointed thee to be prince over his inheritance, and thou shalt deliver his people out of the hands of their enemies that are round about them. And this shall be a sign unto thee, that God hath anointed thee to be prince.

In I Reges 15:17, Samuel spoke to Saul, recalling that he had originally seemed little in his own eyes but that God had made him leader of the tribes of Israel: 'and the Lord anointed thee to be king over Israel'. Or in 2 Reges 12:7, where Nathan speaks to David: 'Thou art the man. Thus saith the Lord the God of Israel: I anointed thee king over Israel, and I delivered thee from the hand of Saul'. Prophets are thus seen as the active servants of Yahweh in the anointing ritual, but it is not they but the Lord working in them who guides their hands and moves their tongues. If Adomnán had indeed adopted this approach from his sources, then regardless of the historical difficulties involved, he probably wished his readers to think that Columba had anointed both Dearmait and Oswald. If not, he may simply have applied the biblical formula that God is always the anointer and left it at that. In either case, although nuances will always escape us, the duality of Adomnán's references is now something that might be seen as deriving from the OT itself. In all instances Adomnán makes sure that Columba acts in the presiding role of reigning prophet.

Bibliography

Alberi, Mary, '"Like the army of God's camp": political theology and apocalyptic warfare at Charlemagne's court', *Viator*, 41 (2010), 1–20.

Albertz, Reiner, *A history of Israelite religion in the Old Testament period*, I (Westminster, 1994).

Albrektson, Bertil, 'Prophecy and politics in the Old Testament' in Haralds Biezais (ed.), *The myth of the state* (Stockholm, 1972), pp 45–57.

Alcock, L., *Kings and warriors, craftsmen and priests in Northern Britain, AD550–850* (Edinburgh, 2003).

Anderson, Bernhard W. (ed.), *Israel's prophetic heritage: essays in honor of James Muilenburg* (New York, 1962).

Anderson, M.O., *Kings and kingship in early Scotland* (Edinburgh, 1980).

Anderson, Alan O., and Marjorie O. Anderson (eds), *Adomnán's Life of Columba* (London, 1961).

Angenendt, Arnold, 'Pippins Königserhebung und Salbung' in Becher and Jarnut (eds), *Dynastiewechsel*, pp 179–211.

Angenendt, Arnold, '"Mit reinen Händen": Das Motiv der kultischen Reinheit in der abendländischen Askese' in Jenal (ed.), *Herrschaft, Kirche, Kultur*, pp 297–317.

Angenendt, Arnold, *Kaiserherrschaft und Königstaufe* (Berlin, 1984).

Angenendt, Arnold, 'Bonifatius und das Sacrementum initiationis', *Römische Quartalschrift für christliche Altertumskunde und Kirchengeschichte* (1977), 133–83.

Auerbach, Erich, 'Figura' in Auerbach, *Scenes from the drama of European literature* (New York, 1959), pp 11–79.

Auerbach, Erich, *Mimesis: the representation of reality in western literature* (Princeton, NJ, 2003).

Aune, David E., *Prophecy in early Christianity and the ancient Mediterranean world* (Grand Rapids, MI, 1983).

Bach, R., *Die Aufforderungen zur Flucht und zum Kampf im alttestamentlichen Prophetenspruch* (Neukirchen, 1962).

Baltzer, Klaus, 'Considerations regarding the office and calling of the prophet', *Harvard Theological Review*, 61 (1968), 567–81.

Barr, James, *History and ideology in the Old Testament: biblical studies at the end of a millennium* (Oxford, 2000).

Baxter, S., C.E. Karkov, J.L. Nelson and David Pelteret (eds), *Early medieval studies in memory of Patrick Wormald* (London, 2009).

Becher, Matthias, and Jörg Jarnut (eds), *Der Dynastiewechsel von 751: Vorgeschichte, Legitimationsstrategien und Erinnerung* (Münster, 2004).

Berman, Joshua A., *Created equal: how the Bible broke with ancient political thought* (Oxford, 2008).

Bieler, Ludwig (ed.), *The Patrician texts in the Book of Armagh* (Dublin, 1979).

Bieler, Ludwig (ed. and trans.), *The Irish penitentials* (Dublin, 1963).

Binchy, D.A. (ed.), *Crith Gablach* (Dublin, 1979).

Binchy, D.A., 'Patrick and his biographers, ancient and modern', *Studia Hibernica*, 2 (1962), 7–173.

Binchy, D.A., 'The Fair of Tailtiu and the Feast of Tara', *Ériu*, 18 (1958), 113–38.

Bisagni, Jacopo, 'The language and date of Amrae Coluimb Cille' in Stefan Zimmer (ed.), *Kelten am Rhein. Akten des dreizehnten Internationalen Keltologiekongress* (Bonn, 2010), II, pp 1–11.

Bitel, Lisa M., *Isle of the saints: monastic settlement and Christian community in early Ireland* (Ithaca, NY, 1990).

Bhreathnach, Edel (ed.), *The kingship and landscape of Tara* (Dublin, 2005).

Bhreathnach, Edel, *'Níell cáich úa Néill nasctar géill*: the political context of *Baile Chuinn Chétchathaig'* in Bhreathnach (ed.), *Kingship and landscape*, pp 49–65.

Blenkinsopp, Joseph, *A history of prophecy in Israel* (Louisville, KY, 1996).

Böcher, Otto, 'Wölfe in Schafspelzen: zum religionsgeschichtlichen Hintergrund von Matth. 7, 15', *Theologische Zeitschrift*, 24 (1968), 405–26.

Bourke, Cormac (ed.), *Studies in the cult of Saint Columba* (Dublin, 1997).

Breatnach, Liam, *A companion to the* Corpus iuris Hibernici (Dublin, 2005).

Breatnach, Liam (ed.), *Uraicecht na Ríar: the poetic grades in early Irish law* (Dublin, 1987).

Breatnach, Liam, 'The caldron of poesy', *Ériu*, 32 (1981), 45–93.

Breeze, Andrew, 'Bede's Hefenfeld and the campaign of 633', *Northern History*, 44 (2007), 193–7.

Brooks, S.S., *Saul and the monarchy: a new look* (Aldershot, 2005).

Broun, Dauvit, and Thomas Owen Clancy (eds), *Spes Scotorum: hope of Scots. Saint Columba, Iona and Scotland* (Edinburgh, 1999).

Bruce, James, *Prophecy, miracles, angels and heavenly light?* (Eugene, OR, 2004).

Byrne, Francis John, *Irish kings and high-kings* (2nd ed. Dublin, 2001).

Byrne, Francis John, *The rise of the Uí Néill and the high-kingship of Ireland* (Dublin, 1969).

Byrne, Francis John, 'The Ireland of St Columba', *Historical Studies*, 5 (1965), 37–58.

Byrnes, Michael, 'The Ard Ciannachta in Adomnán's *Vita Columbae*: a reflection of Iona's attitude to the *Síl nÁeda Sláine* in the late seventh century' in Smyth (ed.), *Seanchas*, pp 127–37.

Cannadine, David, and Simon Price (eds), *Rituals of royalty: power and ceremonial in traditional societies* (Cambridge, 1987).

Carey, John (ed.), *King of mysteries: early Irish religious writings* (Dublin, 1998).

Carey, John, 'An edition of the pseudo-historical prologue to the Senchas Már', *Ériu*, 45 (1994), 1–32.

Carey, John, 'The two laws in Dubthacht's judgment', *Cambridge Medieval Celtic Studies*, 19 (1990), 1–18.

Carney, James, 'Patrick and the kings' in James Carney (ed.), *Studies in Irish literature and history* (Dublin, 1979), pp 324–74.

Carroll, Robert P., 'Prophecy and society' in Clements (ed.), *The world of ancient Israel*, pp 203–27.

Carroll, Robert P., 'The Elijah–Elisha sagas: some remarks on prophetic succession in ancient Israel', *Vestus Testamentum*, 19 (1969), 400–15.

Casiday, A.M.C., *Tradition and theology in St John Cassian* (Oxford, 2007).

Cassian, John, 'Institutes' in Philip Schaff and Henry Wace (eds), *A select library of Nicene and Post-Nicene fathers of the Christian church* (Grand Rapids, MI, 1998 repr.).

Chadwick, Nora, 'Imbas Forosnai', *Scottish Gaelic Studies*, 4 (1934), 98–135.

Chadwick, Owen, *John Cassian* (Cambridge, 1968).

Charity, A.C., *Events and their afterlife: the dialectics of Christian typology in the Bible and Dante* (Cambridge, 1987).

Charles-Edwards, T.M., 'The structure and purpose of Adomnán's *Vita Columbae*' in Wooding et al. (eds), *Adomnán of Iona*, pp 205–19.

Charles-Edwards, T.M., 'Early Irish Law' in Ó Cróinín (ed.), *A new history*, pp 334–7.

Charles-Edwards, T.M., 'Saints' cults and the early Irish church', *Clogher Record*, 19 (2008), 173–84.

Charles-Edwards, T.M., *Early Christian Ireland* (Cambridge, 2000).

Charles-Edwards, T.M., 'A contract between king and people in early medieval Ireland? *Críth Gablach* on kingship', *Peritia*, 8 (1994), 107–19.

Charles-Edwards, T.M., *Early Irish and Welsh kinship* (Oxford, 1993).

Clancy, Thomas Owen, 'King-making and images of kingship in medieval Gaelic literature' in Richard Welander, David J. Breeze and Thomas Owen Clancy (eds), *The stone of destiny* (Edinburgh 2003), pp 85–107.

Clancy, Thomas Owen, 'Personal, political, pastoral: the multiple agenda of Adomnán's *Life of St Columba*' in E.J. Cowan and D. Gifford (eds), *The polar twins: Scottish history and Scottish literature* (Edinburgh, 1999), pp 38–60.

Clancy, Thomas Owen, and Gilbert Márkus, *Iona: the earliest poetry of a Celtic monastery* (Edinburgh, 1995).

Clements, R.E. (ed.), *The world of ancient Israel: sociological, anthropological and political perspectives* (Cambridge, 1989).

Colgrave, Bertram (ed.), *The Life of Bishop Wilfrid by Eddius Stephanus* (Cambridge, 1985).

Colgrave, B., and R.A.B. Mynors (eds), *Bede's Ecclesiastical history of the English people* (Oxford, 1969).

Conrad, E.W., *Fear not warrior: a study of the 'al tîrā' pericopes in the Hebrew scriptures* (Chico, CA, 1985).

Cowles, C.S., Eugene H. Merrill, Daniel L. Gard and Tremper Longman III, *Show them no mercy: four views on God and Canaanite genocide* (Grand Rapids, MI, 2003).

Crüsemann, F., *Der Wiederstand gegen das Königtum* (Neukirchen-Vluyn, 1978).

Daniélou, J., *From shadows to reality: studies in the biblical typology of the fathers* (London, 1960).

Davidson, R., 'Covenant ideology in ancient Israel' in Clements, *The world of ancient Israel*, pp 323–49.

De Gregorio, Scott (ed.), *Bede: on Ezra and Nehemiah* (Liverpool, 2006).

de Lubac, Henri, *Exégèse médiéval: les quatre sens de l'ecriture I, II* (Paris, 1959).

de Paor, Liam, 'The aggrandisement of Armagh' in T. Desmond Williams (ed.), *Historical Studies*, 8 (Dublin, 1986), pp 95–110.

Dietrich, W., 'The "Ban" in the age of the early kings' in V. Fritz and P.R. Davies (ed.), *The origins of the ancient Israelite state* (Sheffield, 1996), pp 195–211.

Dillon, Myles, 'The story of the finding of Cashel', *Ériu*, 16 (1952), 61–73.

Di Lella, Alexander A., 'Wisdom of Ben-Sira' in Gary A. Herion et al. (eds), *Anchor Bible dictionary* (New York, 1992), VI, pp 931–45.

Dion, P.-E., 'The "Fear Not" formula and holy war', *Catholic Biblical Quarterly*, 32 (1970), 565–70.

Doherty, Charles, 'The cult of St Patrick and the politics of Armagh in the seventh century' in J.-M. Picard (ed.), *Ireland and northern France, AD600–850* (Dublin, 1991), pp 53–94.

Doherty, Charles, 'Kingship in early Ireland' in Bhreathnach (ed.), *Kingship and Landscape*, pp 3–31.

Dooley, Ann, 'The plague and its consequences in Ireland' in L.L. Little (ed.), *Plague and the end of antiquity: the pandemic of 541–750* (Cambridge, 2007).

Dudley, Martin and Geoffrey Rowell (eds), *The oil of gladness: anointing in the Christian tradition* (London, 1993).

Dumville, David, *Saint Patrick, AD493–1993* (Woodbridge, 1993).

Dumville, David, 'The Armagh list of "coarbs of St Patrick"' in Dumville, *Saint Patrick*, pp 273–8.

Dumville, David, 'Auxilius, Iserninus, Secundinus and Benignus' in Dumville, *Saint Patrick*, pp 89–105.

Dunn, M., *The Christianization of the Anglo-Saxons, c.596–700* (London, 2010).

Enright, Michael, 'Prophets and princes on isles of ocean: a "call" for an Old Testament-style regime in *Vita Columbae*', *Peritia*, 21 (2010), 56–135.

Enright, Michael, *The Sutton Hoo sceptre and the roots of Celtic kingship theory* (Dublin, 2006).

Enright, Michael, 'Further reflection on royal ordinations in the *Vita Columbae*' in Michael Richter and Jean-Michel Picard (eds), *Ogma* (Dublin 2002), pp 20–36.

Enright, Michael, *Iona, Tara and Soissons: the origin of the royal anointing ritual* (Berlin, 1985).

Enright, Michael, 'Royal succession and abbatial prerogative in Adomnán's *Vita Columbae*', *Peritia*, 4 (1985), 83–103.

Erkens, Franz-Reiner, *Herrschersakralität im Mittelalter: Von den Anfängen bis zum Investiturstreit* (Stuttgart, 2006).

Fischer, B., I. Gribomont, H.F.D. Sparks, W. Thiele, Robert Weber, H.I. Frede and Roger Gryson (eds), *Biblia sacra iuxta vulgatem versionem* (Stuttgart, 1994).

Fraser, James E., 'Adomnán and the morality of war' in Wooding et al. (eds), *Adomnán of Iona*, pp 95–112.

Fraser, James E., *From Caledonia to Pictland: Scotland to 795* (Edinburgh, 2009).

Fraser, James E., 'Ádomnán, Cumméne Ailbe and the Picts', *Peritia*, 17–18 (2003–4), 183–98.

Fritz, Volkmar, *1 & 2 Kings: a Continental commentary* (Minneapolis, MN, 2003).

Frye, Northrup, *The great code: the Bible and literature* (New York, 1982).

Garrison, Mary, 'The *Missa pro principe* in the Bobbio Missal' in Hen and Meens (eds), *Bobbio Missal*, pp 187–205.

Garrison, Mary, 'The Franks as the new Israel? Education for an identity from Pippin to Charlemagne' in Yitzhak Hen and Matthew Innes (eds), *The uses of the past in the early Middle Ages* (Cambridge, 2000), pp 114–61.

Gaster, Theodore, *Myth, legend and custom in the Old Testament* (New York, 1969).

Goffart, Walter, *The narrators of barbarian history (AD550–800)* (South Bend, IN, 2005).

Goldingay, John, *Isaiah* (Peabody, MA, 2001).

Guy, Jean-Claude (ed. and trans.), *Jean Cassian: institutions cénobitiques* (Paris, 1965).

Gwynn, Lucius (ed. and trans.), 'De Shíl Chonairi Móir', *Ériu*, 6 (1912), 130–43.

Habel, Norman C., 'The form and significance of the call narrative', *Zeitschrift für die Alttestamentliche Wissenschaft*, 77 (1965), 297–323.

Hanson, R.P.C., *Saint Patrick: his origins and his career* (Oxford, 1968).

Hawk, L.D., *Joshua* (Collegeville, MN, 2000).

Henry, P.L. 'The caldron of poesy', *Studia Celtica*, 14/15 (1979/80), 114–28.

Hen, Yitzhak, 'The uses of the Bible and the perception of kingship in Merovingian Gaul', *Early Medieval Europe*, 7 (1998), 277–89.

Hen, Yitzhak, *The royal patronage of liturgy in Frankish Gaul: to the death of Charles the Bald (877)* (London, 2001).

Hen, Yitzhak, *Culture and religion in Merovingian Gaul, AD481–751* (London, 1995).

Hen, Yitzhak, and Rob Meens (eds), *The Bobbio Missal: liturgy and religious culture in Merovingian Gaul* (Cambridge, 2009).

Herbert, Máire, *Iona, Kells and Derry: the history and hagiography of the monastic familia of Columba* (Oxford, 1988).

Herbert, Máire, 'Latin and vernacular hagiography in Ireland from the origins to the sixteenth century', *Histoire international de la literature hagiographique latine et vernaculaire en Occident des origins a' 1550*, 3 (2001), pp 329–60.

Herbert, Máire, and Pádraig Ó Riain (eds), *Betha Adamnain: the Irish Life of Adamnán* (London, 1988).

Higham, N.J., *(Re-)reading Bede* (Abingdon, 2006).

Higham, N.J., 'Medieval overkingship in Wales: the earliest evidence', *Welsh History Review*, 16 (1992), 145–59.

Hobbs, T.R., *A time for war: a study of warfare in the Old Testament* (Wilmington, DE, 1989).

Hood, A.B.E. (ed.), *St Patrick: his writings and Muirchú's life* (Totowa, NJ, 1978).

Howlett, David (ed.), *Muirchú moccu Macthéni's 'Vita sancti Patricii': Life of Saint Patrick* (Dublin, 2006).

Huffman, H.B., 'The covenant lawsuit in the prophets', *Journal of Biblical Literature*, 78 (1959), 285–95.

Hughes, Kathleen, *The church in early Irish society* (Ithaca, NY, 1966).

Hurst, D. (ed.), *In Ezram et Neemiam* (Turnhout, 1969).

Hvidt, Niels Christian, *Christian prophecy: the post-biblical tradition* (Oxford, 2007).

Ireland, Colin, *Old Irish wisdom attributed to Aldfrith of Northumbria: an edition of Bríathra Flainn Fhina maic Ossu* (Tempe, AZ, 1999).

Ireland, Colin, 'Aldfrith of Northumbria and the learning of a sapiens' in K.A. Klar, Eve Sweester and Claire Thomas (eds), *A Celtic Florilegium: studies in memory of Brendon O'Hehir* (Lawrence, MA, 1996), pp 63–77.

Jenal, Georg (ed.), *Herrschaft, Kirche, Kultur: Beiträge zur Geschicht des Mittelalters. Festschrift fur Friedrich Prinz zu seiner 65 Geburtstag* (Stuttgart, 1993).

John, Jeffrey, 'Anointing in the New Testament' in Dudley and Rowell (eds), *Oil of gladness*, pp 46–77.

Jones, G.H., 'The concept of holy war' in Clements (ed.), *The world of ancient Israel* (1989), pp 299–323.

Joynt, Maud, '*Echtra mac Echdach Mugmedóin*', *Ériu*, 4 (1908), 91–111.

Kelly, Fergus, *A guide to early Irish law* (Dublin, 1988).

Kelly, Fergus (ed. and trans.), *Audacht Morainn* (Dublin, 1976).

Kirby, D.P., *Saint Wilfrid at Hexham* (Newcastle, 1974).

Kleinheyer, Bruno, *Die Priesterweihe im römischen Ritus: Eine liturgiehistorische Studie* (Trier, 1962).

Knierim, Rolf, 'The vocation of Isaiah', *Vetus Testamentum*, 18 (1968), 47–68.

Kottje, Raymund, *Studien zum Einfluss des Alten Testaments auf Recht und Liturgie des frühen Mittelalters (6–8. Jahrhundert)* (Bonn, 1970).

Lacey, Brian, *Cenél Conaill and the Donegal kingdoms, AD500–800* (Dublin, 2006).

Lacey, Brian, 'Adomnán and Donegal' in Wooding et al. (eds), *Adomnán*, pp 20–36.

Lambkin, Brian, '"Emigrants" and "exiles": migration in the Irish and Scottish church', *Innes Review*, 58 (2007), 133–55.

Lapidge, Michael, 'The career of Aldhelm', *Anglo-Saxon England*, 36 (2007), 15–69.

Lattimore, Richard (trans.), *Hesiod* (Ann Arbor, MI, 1959).

Lindblom, J., *Prophecy in ancient Israel* (Philadelphia, 1962).

Lind, M.C., *Yahweh is a warrior: the theology of warfare in ancient Israel* (Scottsdale, PA, 1980).

Longman, Tremper, 'The case for spiritual continuity' in Cowles et al., *Show them no mercy*, pp 161–87.

Mac Airt, S., and G. Mac Niocaill (eds), *The annals of Ulster (to AD1131)* (Dublin, 1983).

Mac Cana, Proinseas, 'Aspects of the theme of king and goddess in Irish literature', *Études Celtiques*, 7 (1955), 76–144, 356–413, and 8 (1958–9), 59–65.

MacShamhráin, Ailbhe, '*Nebulae discutiuntur?* The emergence of Clann Cholmáin, sixth–eighth centuries' in Smyth (ed.), *Seanchas*, pp 83–98.

MacShamhráin, Ailbhe, and Paul Byrne, 'Prosopography I: kings named in Baile Chuinn Chétchathaig and The Airgíalla charter poem' in Bhreathnach (ed.), *Kingship and landscape*, pp 159–225.

Maddicott, J.R., 'Plague in seventh-century England', *Past and Present*, 156 (1997), 7–45.

Mason, Rex, *Propaganda and subversion in the Old Testament* (London, 1997).

Mayr-Harting, H., *The coming of Christianity to Anglo-Saxon England* (London, 1991).

McClure, Judith, 'Bede's Old Testament kings' in Patrick Wormald with Donald Bullough and Roger Collins (eds), *Ideal and reality in Frankish and Anglo-Saxon society: studies presented to J.M. Wallace-Hadrill* (Oxford, 1983), pp 76–98.

McClure, Judith, and R. Collins (eds), *Bede. The ecclesiastical history of the English people* (Oxford, 1994).

McCone, Kim, 'A tale of two ditties: poet and satirist in Cath Maige Tuired' in Donnchadh Ó Corráin, Liam Breatnach and Kim McCone (eds), *Sages, saints and storytellers: Celtic studies in honour of Professor James Carney* (Maynooth, 1989), pp 122–43.

McCone, Kim, 'Dubthacht maccu Lugair and a matter of life and death in the pseudo-historical prologue to the *Senchas Már*', *Peritia*, 5 (1986), 1–35.

McCone, Kim, 'An introduction to early Irish saint's lives', *Maynooth Review*, 11 (1984), 26–59.

McCone, Kim, *Pagan past and Christian present in early Irish literature* (Naas, 1980).

McGowan, Megan, 'Royal succession in earlier medieval Ireland: the fiction of tanistry', *Peritia*, 17–18 (2003–4), 357–81.

McKane, W., 'Prophet and institution', *Zeitschrift für die alttestamentliche Wissenschaft*, 94 (1982), 251–66.

Meckler, Michael, 'The assassination of Diarmait mac Cerbaill', *CSANA Yearbook*, 7 (Dublin, 2010).

Meehan, Denis (ed.), *Adamnan's* De Locis Sanctis (Dublin, 1958).

Meyer, Kuno (ed.), *Cáin Adomnáin: an Old Irish treatise on the Law of Adomnán* (Oxford, 1905).

Meyer, Kuno, 'The Laud genealogies and tribal histories', *Zeitschrift für celtische Philologie*, 8 (1911), 291–338.

Miller, J. Maxwell, 'Saul's rise to power: some observations concerning I Sam 9:1–10; 10:26–11:14 and 13:2–14:26', *Catholic Biblical Quarterly*, 36 (1974), 157–74.

Miller, J. Maxwell, 'The Elisha cycle and the accounts of the Omride wars', *Journal of Biblical Literature*, 85 (1966), 441–54.

Miller, J. Maxwell, and John H. Hayes, *A history of ancient Israel and Judah* (Philadelphia, 1986).

Miller, P.D., *The divine warrior in early Israel* (Cambridge, MA, 1973).

Mohlberg, Leo Cunibert (ed.), *Missale Francorm* (Rome, 1957).

Moisl, H., 'The Bernician royal dynasty and the Irish in the seventh century', *Peritia*, 2 (1983), 103–26.

Moricco, Umberto (ed.), *Gregorii Magni Dialogi libri IV* (Rome, 1924).

Myers, Jacob M., *I and II Esdras: introduction, translation and commentary* (Garden City, NY, 1980).

Muilenburg, James, 'The "Office" of the prophet in ancient Israel' in J.P. Hyatt (ed.), *The Bible in modern scholarship* (Nashville, TN, 1965), pp 74–98.

Mowinckel, Sigmund, *The spirit and the word: prophecy and tradition in ancient Israel* (Minneapolis, MN, 2002).

Mouw, Richard J., *When the kings come marching in: Isaiah and the New Jerusalem* (Grand Rapids, MI, 2002).

Murphy, Gerard, *Saga and myth in ancient Ireland* (Cork, 1955).

Murphy, Gerard, 'On the dates of two sources used in Thurneysen's Heldensage', *Ériu*, 16 (1952).

Newman, Murray, 'The prophetic call of Samuel' in Anderson (ed.), *Israel's prophetic heritage* (1962).

Nelson, Janet, 'The Lord's anointed and the people's choice: Carolingian royal ritual' in Cannadine and Price (eds), *Rituals of royalty*, pp 137–81.

Ní Chatháin, Próinseás, and Michael Richter (eds), *Irland und Europa: die Kirche im Frühmittelalter* (Stuttgart, 1984), pp 58–73.

Ní Dhonnchadha, Máirín, 'Birr and the Law of the Innocents' in Thomas O'Loughlin (ed.), *Adomnán at Birr, AD697: essay in commemoration of the Law of the Innocents* (Dublin, 2001), pp 13–32.

Ní Dhonnchadha, Máirín, 'The *Lex Innocentium*: Adomnán's law for women, clerics and youths, 697AD' in Mary O'Dowd and Sabine Wichert (eds), *Chattel, servant or citizen: woman's status in church, state and society* (Belfast, 1995), pp 58–69.

Ni Dhonnchadha, Máirín, 'The guarantor list of Cáin Adomnáin, 697', *Peritia*, 1 (1982), 178–215.

Ó Corráin, Donnchadh, 'The Irish church and secular institutions' in *L'irlanda e gli Irlandesi nell'Alto Medioevo: Settimane di Studio della Fondazione Centro Italiano di Studi sull'Alto Medioevo*, 57 (Spoleto, 2010), pp 261–323.

Ó Corráin, Donnchadh, 'Irish regnal succession: a reappraisal', *Studia Hibernica*, 11 (1971), 7–39.

Ó Corráin, Donnchadh, Liam Breatnach and Aidan Breen, 'The laws of the Irish', *Peritia*, 3 (1984), 382–438.

Ó Cróinín, Dáibhí, 'Ireland, 400–800' in Ó Cróinín, *A new history*, pp 206–9.

Ó Cróinín, Dáibhí (ed.), *A new history of Ireland: prehistoric and early Ireland* (Oxford, 2008).

Ó Cróinín, Dáibhí, *Early medieval Ireland* (London, 1995).

Ó Cuív, Brian, 'The motif of the threefold death', *Éigse*, 15–16 (1973–6), 145–50.

Odell, Margaret S., 'You are what you eat: Ezekiel and the scroll', *Journal of Biblical Literature*, 117 (1998), 229–48.

O'Donovan, John, *Miscellany of the Celtic Society* (Dublin, 1849).

Ó Floinn, Raghnall, '*Insignia Columbae* I' in Bourke (ed.), *Studies in the cult of Saint Columba*, pp 136–61.

Ó hÓgain, Dáithí, *The sacred isle: belief and religion in pre-Christian Ireland* (Cork, 1999).

O'Leary, Aideen, 'An Irish apocryphal apostle: Muirchú's portrayal of St Patrick', *Harvard Theological Review*, 89 (1996), 287–301.

O'Loughlin, Thomas, 'Muirchú's poisoned cup: a note on its sources', *Ériu*, 56 (2006), 157–62.

O'Loughlin, Thomas, *Discovering Saint Patrick* (London, 2005).

O'Loughlin, Thomas, 'Map and text: a mid-ninth-century map for the Book of Joshua', *Imago Mundi*, 57 (2005), 7–22.

O'Loughlin, Thomas, 'Reading Muirchú's Tara-event within its background as a biblical "trial of divinities"' in Jane Cartwright (ed.), *Celtic hagiography and saints' cults* (Cardiff, 2003), pp 123–35.

O'Loughlin, Thomas, 'The tombs of the saints: their significance for Adomnán' in John Carey, Máire Herbert and Pádraig Ó Riain (eds), *Studies in Irish hagiography: saints and scholars* (Dublin, 2001), pp 1–14.

O'Loughlin, Thomas, 'Living in the ocean' in Bourke (ed.), *Studies in the cult of Saint Columba*, pp 11–23.

O'Reilly, Jennifer, 'Adomnán and the art of teaching spiritual sons' in Wooding et al. (eds), *Adomnán of Iona*, pp 69–95.

O'Reilly, Jennifer, 'The wisdom of the scribe and the fear of the Lord in the Life of Columba' in Broun and Clancy (eds), *Spes Scotorum* (1999), pp 159–211.

O'Reilly, Jennifer, 'Reading the scriptures in the Life of Columba' in Bourke (ed.), *Studies in the cult of St Columba*, pp 80–106.

Ó Riain, Pádraig, 'St Finnbarr: a study in a cult', *Journal of the Cork Historical and Archaeological Society*, 82 (1977), 63–82.

Ó Riain, Pádraig, *A dictionary of Irish saints* (Dublin, 2011).

Petchenig, M. (ed.), Corpus Scriptorum Ecclesiasticorum Latinorum, 17 (Vienna, 1888).

Peckham, B., *History and prophecy: the development of late Judean literary traditions* (New York, 1993).

Picard, J.-M., 'The purpose of Adomnán's *Vita Columbae*', *Peritia*, 1 (1982), 160–77.

Plummer, C. (ed.), Venerabilis Baedae opera historica (Oxford, 1896).

Porter, J. Roy, 'Oil in the Old Testament' in Dudley and Rowell (ed.), *Oil of gladness*, pp 35–46.

Quinn-Miscall, Peter D., *Reading Isaiah: poetry and vision* (Louisville, KY, 2001).

Radner, Joan N., 'The significance of the threefold death in the Celtic tradition' in Patrick K. Ford (ed.), *Celtic folklore and Christianity: essays for W.W. Heist* (Santa Barbara, CA, 1983), pp 180–99.

Ray, R., 'Bede and Cicero', *Anglo Saxon England*, 16 (1987), 1–15.

Richter, Michael, 'Die frühmittelalterliche Herrschersalbung und die *Collectio canonum hibernensis*' in Becher and Jarnut (eds), *Dynastiewechsel* (Münster, 2004), pp 211–20.

Rollason, David, *Northumbria, 500–1100: creation and destruction of a kingdom* (Cambridge, 2003).

Rollason, David, 'Hagiography and politics in early Northumbria' in P.E. Szarmach (ed.), *Holy men and holy women: Old English prose saints' lives and their contexts* (Albany, NY, 1996), pp 95–115.

Rollason, David, *Saints and relics in Anglo-Saxon England* (Oxford, 1989).

Ross, James F., 'The prophet as Yahweh's messenger' in Anderson (ed.), *Israel's prophetic heritage* (1962), pp 98–107.

Sawyer, John F. A., *Prophecy and the prophets of the Old Testament* (Oxford, 1987).

Sayers, William, '*Guin* & *crochad* & *gólad*: the earliest Irish threefold death' in Cyril Byrne, Margaret Harry and Pádraig Ó Siadhail (eds), *Celtic languages and Celtic peoples* (Halifax, NS, 1992), pp 65–82.

Semmler, Josef, *Der Dynastiewechsel von 751 und die fränkische Königssalbung, Studia Homaniora* 6, Series Minor (Düsseldorf, 2003).

Sharman, Stephen, 'Visions of divine light in the writings of Adomnán and Bede' in Wooding et al. (eds), *Adomnán*, pp 289–303.

Sharpe, Richard, 'The thriving of Dalriada' in S. Taylor (ed.), *Kings, clerics and chronicles* (Dublin, 2000), pp 47–61.

Sharpe, Richard (trans.), *Adomnán of Iona: Life of St Columba* (London, 1995).

Sharpe, Richard, 'Saint Mauchteus, discipulus Patricii' in A. Bammesberger and A. Wollmann (eds), *Britain, 400–600: language and history* (Heidelberg, 1990), pp 85–93.

Sharpe, Richard, 'Armagh and Rome in the seventh century' in Próinseás Ní Chatháin and Michael Richter (eds), *Irland und Europa* (Stuttgart, 1984), pp 58–73.

Sharpe, Richard, 'St Patrick and the see of Armagh', *Cambridge Medieval Celtic Studies*, 4 (1982), 33–59.

Sharpe, Richard, 'Hiberno-Latin *Laicus*, Irish *Láech* and the Devil's Man', *Ériu*, 30 (1979), 75–92.

Smyth, Alfred P. (ed.), *Seanchas: studies in early and medieval Irish archaeology, history and literature in honour of Francis J. Bryne* (Dublin, 2000).

Smyth, Alfred P., *Warlords and holy men: Scotland, AD80–1000* (London, 1984).

Stalmans, Nathalie, *Saints d'Irlande: analyse critique des sources hagiographique (VIIᵉ–IXᵉ siècles)* (Rennes, 2003).

Stancliffe, Clare, '"Charity with peace": Adomnán and the Easter question' in Wooding et al. (eds), *Adomnán of Iona*, pp 51–68.

Stancliffe, Clare, *Bede, Wilfrid and the Irish* (Jarrow, 2003).

Stancliffe, Clare, 'Oswald, "most holy and most victorious king of the Northumbrians"' in Stancliffe and Cambridge (eds), *Oswald*, pp 33–84.

Stancliffe, Clare, and Eric Cambridge (eds), *Oswald: Northumbrian king to European saint* (Stamford, 1995).

Stansbury, M., 'The composition of Adomnán's *Vita Columbae*', *Peritia*, 17–18 (2003–4), 154–82.

Stokes, Whitley, 'The death of Crimthann son of Fidach and the adventures of the son of Eochaid Muigmedón', *Revue Celtique*, 24 (1903), 172–207.

Stokes, Whitley, 'The Bodleian *Amra Choluimb Chille*', *Revue Celtique*, 20 (1899), 31–5, 132–83, 248–89, 400–37.

Stolz, F., *Jahwes und Israels Kriege: Kriegstheorien und Kriegserfahrungen im Glauben des alten Israel* (Zurich, 1972).

Soggin, J. Alberto, *A history of ancient Israel* (Philadelphia, 1984).

Swift, Catherine, 'St Patrick, Skerries and the earliest evidence for local church organization in Ireland' in Ailbhe MacShamhráin (ed.), *The island of St Patrick: church and ruling dynasties in Fingal and Meath, 400–1148* (Dublin, 2004), pp 61–79.

Swift, Catherine, 'Pagan monuments and Christian legal centres in early Meath', *Ríocht na Midhe*, 9 (1996), 1–26.

Swift, Catherine, 'Tirechán's motives in compiling the Collectanea: an alternative explanation', *Ériu*, 45 (1994), 53–82.

Tanaka, Miko, 'Iona and the kingship of Dál Riata in Adomnán's *Vita Columbae*', *Peritia*, 17–18 (2003–4), 199–214.

Thacker, A., 'Bede, the Britons and the Book of Samuel' in Baxter et al. (eds), *Early medieval studies*, pp 129–47.

Thacker, A., 'Membra Disjecta: the division of the body and the diffusion of the cult' in Stancliffe and Cambridge (eds), *Oswald*, pp 97–128.

Thompson, E.A., *Who was Saint Patrick?* (Woodbridge, 1999).

Tolley, C., 'Oswald's tree' in Tette Hofstra, L.A.J.R. Houwen and A.A. MacDonald (eds), *Pagans and Christians: the interplay between Christian Latin and traditional Germanic cultures in early medieval Europe* (Groningen, 1995), pp 149–75.

von Rad, Gerhard, *Old Testament theology: the theology of Israel's prophetic traditions*, trans. D.M.G. Stalker (2 vols, New York, 1965).

von Rad, Gerhard, *Die heilige Krieg im alten Israel* (Zurich, 1958).

Wallace-Hadrill, J.M., *Bede's Ecclesiastical history of the English people: a historical commentary* (Oxford, 1993).

Walker, G.S.M. (ed. and trans.), *Sancti Columbani Opera* (Dublin, 1957).

Walsh, Maura, and Dáibhí Ó Cróinín (eds), *Cummian's Letter* De Controversia Paschali *together with a related Irish computational tract* De Ratione Computandi (Toronto, 1988).

Warntjes, Immo, 'The role of the church in early Irish regnal succession: the case of Iona' in *L'irlanda e gli Irlandese nell'Alto Medioevo* (Spoleto, 2010), pp 155–214.

Wasserschleben, Herrmann (ed.), *Die irische Kanonensammlung* (2nd ed. Leipzig, 1885).

Weisweiler, Josef, *Heimat und Herrschaft: Wirkung und Ursprung eines irischen Mythos* (Halle, 1943).

Williams, James G., 'The prophetic "Father": a brief explanation of the term "Sons of the Prophets"', *Journal of Biblical Literature*, 85 (1966), 344–8.

Wilson, R.R., *Prophecy and society in ancient Israel* (Philadelphia, 1980).

Wilson, R.R., 'Prophecy and ecstasy', *Journal of Biblical Literature*, 98 (1979), 321–37.

Witherington, Ben, *Jesus the seer: the progress of prophecy* (Peabody, MA, 1999).

Wood, Ian, 'Constantinian crosses in Northumbria' in C.E. Karkov, K.L. Jolly and Sarah Larratt Keefer (eds), *The place of the cross in Anglo-Saxon England* (Woobridge, 2006), pp 3–14.

Woods, David, 'On the circumstances of Adomnán's composition of the *De Locis Sanctis*' in Wooding et al. (eds), *Adomnán*, pp 193–205.

Woods, David, 'Four notes on Adomnán's *Vita Columbae*', *Peritia*, 16 (2002), 40–67.

Wooding, Jonathan M., with Rodney Aist, Thomas Clancy and Thomas O'Loughlin (eds), *Adomnán of Iona: theologian, lawmaker, peacemaker* (Dublin, 2010).

Woolf, Alex, '*Caedwalla Rex Brettonum* and the passing of the Old North', *Northern History*, 41 (2004), 5–24.

Yorke, Barbara, 'Adomnán at the court of King Aldfrith' in Wooding et al. (eds), *Adomnán*, pp 36–50.

Yorke, Barbara, 'The Bretwaldas and the origins of overlordship in Anglo-Saxon England' in Baxter et al. (eds), *Early medieval studies*, pp 81–95.

Yorke, Barbara, *Rex Doctissimus: Bede and King Aldfrith of Northumbria* (Jarrow, 2009).

Yorke, Barbara, *The conversion of Britain: religion, politics and society in Britain, 600–800* (Harlow, 2006).

Young, Frances M., *Biblical exegesis and the formation of Christian culture* (Cambridge, 1997).

Zimmerli, Walter, *Ezekiel I: a commentary on the book of the prophet Ezekiel* (Philadelphia, 1979).

Zimmerman, Odo John (trans.), *Saint Gregory the Great: dialogues* (New York, 1959).

Index